THE REFORMATION
OF UNION STATE
SOVEREIGNTY

THE REFORMATION OF UNION STATE SOVEREIGNTY

The Path Back to the Political
System Our Founding Fathers
Intended–
A Sovereign Life, Liberty,
And a Free Market

M. Kenneth Creamer

iUniverse, Inc.
Bloomington

THE REFORMATION OF UNION STATE SOVEREIGNTY
The Path Back to the Political System Our Founding Fathers Intended–A Sovereign Life, Liberty, And a Free Market

iUniverse books may be ordered through booksellers or by contacting:

iUniverse
1663 Liberty Drive
Bloomington, IN 47403
www.iuniverse.com
1-800-Authors (1-800-288-4677)

Because of the dynamic nature of the Internet, any web addresses or links contained in this book may have changed since publication and may no longer be valid. The views expressed in this work are solely those of the author and do not necessarily reflect the views of the publisher, and the publisher hereby disclaims any responsibility for them.

Any people depicted in stock imagery provided by Thinkstock are models, and such images are being used for illustrative purposes only.
Certain stock imagery © Thinkstock.

ISBN: 978-1-4759-8335-7 (sc)
ISBN: 978-1-4759-8337-1 (hc)
ISBN: 978-1-4759-8336-4 (ebk)

Printed in the United States of America

iUniverse rev. date: 04/01/2013

Table of Contents

Appendices

Dedication

This book is being dedicated to my Grandchildren, their parents and to my wife who had to endure my life-interrupting stubborn dedication to this cause and to all my friends and family who stuck it out over the last 50 years. May it prove to be a helpful aid in the Pursuit of Happiness for them, their friends & families, and ALL our fellow Union State People. I would also like to dedicate this work to my now deceased parents, Malcom and Alice, in appreciation for their giving me the tenacity to dig through the labyrinth of Constitutional mischief to bring this work to fruition.

Pop Pop, Dad, & Ken

Acknowledgements

I would like to express my gratitude and sincere appreciation to the following persons for their excellent work and dedicated effort, without which this book would never have happened:

Dr. Bambi Lobdell, SUNY Oneonta, for her fantastic editing and assistance in many places to improve the grammar and linguistic construction of the book. Thanks so much Bambi!

My Son, for his creative ideas and graphic construction of the Cover together with his neat and appropriate text inserted on the front and back covers. "Thanks for doing it son."

The Author

Preface

It is my sincerest belief that Union State Sovereignty is the single most important political problem facing us today. In this era in our history where education has become a euphemism for indoctrination, we've come to accept the day to day propaganda that our unique Constitutional Republic has degenerated into a federal takeover where the Federal Government is, in reality, pursuing a path to become just another Central Government nefariously mislabeled as a Democracy. This is, in whole, due to the fact that the Union States have forfeited their Sovereignty and have unconstitutionally become instrumentalities to the Constitutionally out of control Federal Government, violating the very intent of our founders who created our unique political system in the first place. While the title of this book refers to the loss of Union State Sovereignty, it could well have been given the title of "The Loss of Human Liberty for the Want of Knowledge." Consequently, I see it necessary to set the record straight and lay out the true and intended power hierarchy and the first principle concepts stemming from the events (steps) taken by the political geniuses that guided us through the inception and creation of our Constitutional Republics, which were for the sole purpose of establishing an environment of individual Liberty with a political structure to protect and preserve it. While this isn't political rocket science, few of us understand the rights and powers encompassed by the real and intended power structure. To paraphrase Vince Lombardi "Liberty isn't everything, it's the ONLY thing and it takes Union States Sovereignty to preserve and protect it."

The Power Hierarchy

First and foremost, we declared ourselves to be Sovereign by and through the Declaration of Independence. This established the fact that all political power devolved to the Citizenry, i.e., we were the Sovereigns, Sovereigns without subjects[1]. With this power established and defended by the Revolution, We the People of each Colony (later to be termed States) delegated certain of our powers to the individual State governments by and through our State Constitutions. By and large, each State recognizes to this day the "Ultimate Political Power resides in and with We the People." Examples of this can be explicitly found in the Constitutions of Pennsylvania[2] and New Jersey[3]. We the People then created a political structure by and through a Continental Congress to act as our agent to protect the endowment of our rights and powers declared by said Declaration of Independence. In turn, each Colony/State was recognized by each of the other Colonies/States to be a Sovereign among Sovereigns by and through the Articles of Confederation, but each of the State Constitutions also recognized that the ultimate political power remained within the citizenry/people of the States.

While the States were united together in a Continental Congress as a designated agent for whatever foreign intercourse may be needed from time to time, the Continental Congress as a body had no territorial powers and thus no political authority to perform any specific local duties due to the fact that no Delegation of Authority existed by and through a Constitution. In order to remedy this, the two newly created Sovereigns, the new States and their Citizenry, We the People, joined together to create a new agent by and through a Constitution for the sole purpose of creating a new entity with specific powers and duties to stand in as the intermediary for the Union of New States and given the moniker of *The United States* by Constitutional

---

[1]   See Appendix A which elaborates on this in greater detail.

[2]   All power is inherent in the people, and all free governments are founded on their authority and instituted for their peace, safety, and happiness. Article 1, Section 2 of the Constitution of the Commonwealth of Pennsylvania

[3]   All political power is inherent in the people. Article 1, Section 2 of the New Jersey State Constitution.

decree. This new agency, *The United States*, would replace the Continental Congress and the new Constitution for[4] the United States would now also replace the Articles of Confederation. Unlike the original Continental Congress, the new Congress was given territorial powers and the new Congress was given the power to manage and legislate for this newly assigned territory. While the Federal Constitution carries with it its own power harness, there can be no argument that today the federal horsepower has escaped from the harness.

This means that while the newly created United States is an international Sovereign among the other international Sovereigns, it was designed to be low man on the Totem Pole of Power with respect to the other two Sovereigns that created it here in our "homeland." It was intended to be governed by a House of Sovereigns (Congress) comprised of representative agents representing the two Sovereigns responsible for its creation, namely the Union Colonies/States (in the Senate) and their respective Citizens possessing the Ultimate Political Power in the House of Representatives.

However, that balance of power structure comprising a bottom up power hierarchy is now in jeopardy of being supplanted with a traditional central power scheme to be controlled and ruled by a worldwide central power orchestrated by internationalist mole implants within the elected agents taking office in our House of Sovereigns (Congress).

Unfortunately this is all crumbling before our very eyes because one of the Sovereigns, the Union States, represented in the House of Sovereigns has, whether by ignorance or espionage, given up its appointed Sovereignty. This forfeiture of Sovereignty is allowing the Power it helped to create by Constitutional decree, the United States, to politically invade the Union States

---

[4]   I use the word "for" here, because the Constitution was created to assign duties and establish control <u>for</u> the newly created entity, the United States.

with unconstitutional powers of aggression. Such an invasion is robbing the citizens of their own political power, their Liberty, and the right to full ownership of their body and property. Since the purpose of creating the Union States (Colonies), in the first place, was to have them protect and preserve their Citizen's Liberty, declared rights, and power. That purpose has disappeared because Union States have, by forfeiture of their appointed Sovereignty, politically and factually reneged on their Constitutional purpose leaving We the People high and dry to fend for ourselves; that is to say leaving us without political or physical protection from the loss of our Lives, Liberty, and Property. This treatise is an analysis of how the Union States lost their Sovereignty, the divulging of the facts proving it, and what needs to happen for them to regain their Sovereignty and perform the duties attached to their Constitutional mandates, i.e., the preservation and protection of the Life, Liberty, and property of the Union State People.

There is a medical information TV program hosted by Doug Kaufman titled "Know the Cause." Such a directive is indeed as important in politics/law as it is in medicine. Just treating the symptom is as useful as a snake dance in the desert. The problem we are facing today in the political/law arena in these difficult times is that many of the people in this great Constitutional Republic and their elected representatives want to return to our primary root philosophies, i.e., Liberty for We the People and the restoration of sovereignty for the 50 Union States, the latter being a requirement for the former. However, wanting to fix something is not enough. Those concerned must, as a matter of intellectual fact, "Know the Cause" before any meaningful steps can be taken to implement the cure. Unfortunately, there exists a very large segment of our society across our great Republic barking at the symptom without one scintilla of knowledge about what either the cause might be or how to achieve a cure. This work divulges the cause for those possessing the necessary patience and desire to completely read this discourse and thus gain the knowledge to correspondingly know the cure, which believe it or not, doesn't require any more legislation by Congress. The solution lies within the Union States themselves! To quote Pogo, the cartoon character, "We have met the Enemy, and the He is us!" Remember from Black's Commentary:

Sublata causa tollitur effectus.

Remove the cause and the effect will cease. 2 Bl. Com. 203.

The First Principle of Sovereignty is that he who claims to be Sovereign must first act like a Sovereign; otherwise, by his own hand he makes a false claim. That is what lies herein.

It seems that less than ten in a million of the population of this Great Republic has the faintest idea or understanding of the basic differences between our own Constitutional Republic and other forms of governments throughout the world. Most, if not all, other governments in the world are structured as a central top down national government where the citizens are subjects and thus under complete and absolute control of said central governments which are simply large bureaucracies run by bureaucrats. No such structure attains here. Here the people are the sovereigns and the government is the agent thereto. To fully understand this difference, the reader is again encouraged to read Appendix A for comprehension. This will help serve the reader with a beginning view of the unique bottom up Power Structure this Constitutional Republic has wherein the People are the Sovereigns and thus the ruling class making the agents of government the ruled as compared to the other way around for most other governments which have a central and top down power structure, leaving the citizens as mere subjects of the ruling class.

With respect to the 50 Union States, one of the defining principles we inherited from our founders was this unique structure of a Dual Sovereignty between the Union States and the federation of Union States (given the moniker of United

States). The fundamental objective of this Dual sovereignty was to maintain the balance of specific delegated powers which We the People surrendered to each of them to achieve an orderly society in the face of individual sovereignty.[5] The federation, like each Union State, was created via a Constitution depicting its limited powers with absolute declarations that those powers not relinquished to the new federation, named the United States, because these powers were reserved for the (Union) States and the people respectively.[6] However, the Union States have not kept up their end of the bargain to maintain the balance of power and have unconstitutionally permitted themselves to become Federal States, thus forfeiting their Union State Sovereign status, making them each subordinate to the entity they helped create, namely the United States. At the same time as a result of this subordinating of the Union States, the concept of a Dual Sovereignty was also destroyed, eradicating the political architecture our founders so painstakingly structured as a balancing mechanism for the various delegated Constitutional powers between the Federal Government and each of the Union States. The Supreme Court has referred to this notion of Dual Sovereignty "as the defining feature of our Nation's Constitutional blueprint." This work, hopefully, will reveal the necessary law and facts which properly demonstrate why our structure has been broken and what needs to happen in order to put it back together.

This work is based on Supreme Court opinions, federal Law, and the basic founding principles of the founders which have been coupled with the research and facts learned by the author over the past 35 odd years of his life as they apply to the political/Constitutional structure of this unique Constitutional Republic. The unique structure being that of Dual, but mutually exclusive, Sovereignties encompassing the United States and the 50 Union States as the primary peer sovereigns/agents of

---

5   See Appendixes A &B.
6   U.S. Constitution, 10th Amendment

government created to preserve and protect the Liberties of the sovereign individuals.

A quip I once read may hopefully be applicable here: "Ye shall know the Truth and the Truth shall make you mad." That certainly explains the goal of the author for writing this discourse. For it is not until We the People become sufficiently motivated and educate enough to inform ourselves of the truth as to just how we, our parents, and our parents' parents have been duped through the 20th century by the very agents we elected to take office under oaths to abide by and protect our Constitutions and thus our Liberties, will we support the necessary steps required to restore our liberties and the rule of law as set forth by our Constitutions, State and Federal.

A great number of us blame the Federal Government for the ills of our not so free life and loss of Liberties such as, heavy income taxes, fiat money, the underground creeping roots of socialism, a foreign policy not unlike that of King Richard the Lion Hearted, and a second (self-appointed) King George[7] who mimics many of the very acts of the first King George from which we gained our independence in this country of sovereign citizens. However, we will find herein that the major fault which allows the Federal Government to meddle in our lives is much closer to home than Washington, DC. Even though it appears that the Federal Government is busy sowing the seeds of socialism, communism, and fascism throughout our Republic, this work will bring to the fore that our state agents are the ones primarily at fault for removing the Constitutional harnesses strapped upon the Federal Government by our founders.

Since the term "State" carries a different definition in federal law[8] than what we are accustomed to in our everyday speech

---

[7]   See the Declaration of Independence for the list of transgression of the First King George.

[8]   There are nearly one thousand, if not more, redefinitions of the term "State" in the body (50 Titles) of Federal law.

that is being reviewed herein, we will use the term "Union State" when referring to any one of the 50 States of the Union of States and "Federal State" when referring to States within federal territory in order to keep the discussion precise by delineating between the two. The reader will observe on his or her own that this is very consistent with federal law except that federal law uses the term "State" in either reference which may be for the purposes of confusion or simply to keep the reader of the law "accidently" distracted. To suggest that it is confusing is a gross understatement.

We mention in several places the notion that our elected Union State agents take oaths of offices to obey and protect both the Union State and federal (United States) Constitutions. Since an oath is an oath, we must take cognizance of the disparity of consequences between violating the oath of a witness to tell the truth and an elected official's oath of office to protect the various Constitutions. Noting that a witness takes oaths that they will "tell the truth, the whole truth, and nothing but the truth" or suffer the penalties of perjury. Then, how much different is an Oath of Office to perform from an Oath to tell the truth? Both are promises to perform. When a public official fails to perform his or her duties such as are required or presumed in his or her oath, why then are we not taking these agents to task for dereliction of duty in violation to their oath of office just like perjury for a witness? It is pointed out later that an Oath of Office must contain the word **obey** proceeding the word Constitution, both federal and state.

The main objective of this work is to impress upon the reader the fact that our Union States, 50 in number, have forfeited their Constitutional Sovereignty, thus taking on the posture of a federal state, subject to all the whims and controls of Washington, D.C. We will examine how that has come to pass, what the ramifications are to us, and some suggestions that may be pursued to correct such a Constitutional travesty.

Democracy

But first, we mentioned above that our Constitutional Republics as a country has been nefariously mislabeled as a Democracy. The following is to establish, at the very beginning, that this depiction is a treasonous myth. You will first observe that the great majority of those guilty of such a constitutional infraction are high ranking officials in both federal and state governments and includes such officials as the President, Senators, Congressmen, governors, state legislatures, and officials of local governments. Now there are only 2 reasons for anyone doing this: ignorance and/or a conscious desire to destroy our Civil Liberties and thus this Constitutional Republic. While anyone can observe the existence of the term Republic in our Constitution for the United States and in our Pledge of Allegiance to the Flag of the United States, no one will be able to find the term "Democracy" anywhere in any of our founding documents or find any positive opinion about Democracies in the founder's discussions.

I've been told that the genesis of the word "democracy" as the label for the designation of the political structure for this country came about during the Woodrow Wilson campaign for president, because he was a Democrat and saw fit to denigrate the country he was about to become President of. Woodrow Wilson is the President who also ushered in the private banking system titled the Federal Reserve, which began to eat out the substance of the Citizens of our Constitutional Republic in 1913 and did so for the next 100 years.

Words are used to convey concepts and when one uses the wrong word to express the concept of our Country political structure such as "democracy," "communist," or whatever, they are not telling the truth or they lack the necessary intellect to use the correct word. Our Founders created a Constitutional Republic which they professed was created to protect the Sovereignty of the individual People from encroachments upon their Liberties.

The following is a series of quotes from our founders on what they thought of "democracies."

"Democracies have ever been spectacles of turbulence and contention; have ever been found incompatible with personal security or the rights of property; and have, in general, been as short in their lives as they have been violent in their deaths."—**James Madison**

"Remember, democracy never lasts long. It soon wastes, exhausts, and murders itself. There never was a democracy yet that did not commit suicide."—**John Adams**

"*A democracy is a volcano which conceals the fiery materials of its own destruction. These will produce an eruption and carry desolation in their way. The known propensity of a democracy is to licentiousness which the ambitious call, and ignorant believe to be liberty.*" Further, he stated that, "*Liberty has never lasted long in a democracy, nor has it ever ended in anything better than despotism.*" In fact he believed that it was "*democracy that pollutes the morals of the people before it swallows up their freedoms.*"—**Fisher Ames**[9]

"We have seen the tumult of democracy terminate . . . as [it has] everywhere terminated, in despotism . . . ."—**Gouverneur Morris**

"*[T]he experience of all former ages had shown that of all human governments, democracy was the most*

---

[9]   Since Woodrow Wilson instigated the Federal Reserve, it may have been his wish or the instrument of the Federal Reserve to "pollute the morals of the people before it swallowed up their Liberties."

unstable, fluctuating and short-lived."—**John Quincy Adams**

"A simple democracy . . . is one of the greatest of evils."—**Benjamin Rush**

"In democracy . . . there are commonly tumults and disorders . . . . Therefore a pure democracy is generally a very bad government. It is often the most tyrannical government on earth."—**Noah Webster**

"Pure democracy cannot subsist long nor be carried far into the departments of state; it is very subject to caprice and the madness of popular rage."—**John Witherspoon**

"Democracy is two wolves and a lamb voting on what to have for lunch. Liberty is a well-armed lamb contesting the vote."—**Benjamin Franklin**

To understand why they had such a negative opinion of democracies, we need only to look into some of the facts behind the makeup of democracies.

So technically, what is a Democracy? Webster says it is "1. Government in which people hold the ruling power either directly or through elected representatives; rule by the ruled. . . . 3. Majority rule. 4. Principle of equal rights, opportunity, and treatment . . ." At first blush, this sounds a lot like what the Supreme Court articulated as pertaining to our Republic, but further analysis will demonstrate the gross differences.

First, in a Democracy the "people hold the ruling power," "rule by the ruled." In our Republic, the people are the "sovereigns without subjects and have none to govern [(rule)] but themselves,"[10] so as sovereigns we have only the power to rule ourselves but not our neighbor.

Second, in a Democracy the "majority rule" which is to say the majority through its representatives determines what the law is, what prohibitive acts and what specific performance the majority wishes to impose on the masses, i.e. you and your neighbor. In our Republic no such concept exists. Remember, "in our system, while sovereign powers are delegated to agencies of government, sovereignty itself remains with the people, by whom and for whom all government exists and acts. For, the very idea that one man may be compelled to hold his life, or the means of living, or any material right essential to the enjoyment of life, at the mere will of another, [including ones neighbor or the masses] seems intolerable *in* any country where freedom prevails." (Restated from Yick Wo, *Yick Wo v. Hopkins, Sheriff,* 118 US. 356 (1886)) Consequently, the fact that "no man [can] be compelled to hold his life or the means of living, or any material right to the enjoyment of life, at the mere will of another" means that even the majority cannot dictate their wishes on any individual to compel him to behave contrary to his wishes, save he violate the rights of another.

Third, a Democracy operates under the "principle of equal rights, opportunity, and treatment." So, if all individuals have the right to work but not the right to own gold or guns or allodial property, and if all individuals have the opportunity to start a "sanctioned" business but no opportunity to establish a "non-sanctioned" business, and if all individuals are treated as subject citizens, serfs on the land required to obey all instructions and procedures from all agencies of government instead of going about their daily business as they see fit, then the principles of Democracy are fully intact. That is, all have equal rights, but not all unalienable rights (rights endowed by his or her creator), all have equal opportunity but not all opportunity, and all receive equal treatment as subject class Citizens, serfs,

---

but are not recognized as sovereigns. In our Constitutional Republic, all <u>rights</u> are endowed by (come from) our Creator, are unalienable, and are not enumerated. See the <u>Declaration of Independence</u> and the 9th and 10th Amendments to the Constitution. One individual's <u>rights</u> stop at the deprivation of another individual's <u>rights</u>. Consequently, in our Constitutional Republic, <u>rights</u> are therefore equal and unlimited.

In our Constitutional Republic, <u>opportunities</u> are unlimited. However, are all individuals subject to the same <u>opportunities</u>? In an abstract sense, yes, but in a real sense, no. In the abstract sense every individual draws on his own personal human capabilities to provide himself with his own <u>opportunities</u> and on that basis every individual has an <u>opportunity</u> to capitalize on his own personal capabilities. However, in the real sense, not everyone's human capabilities are equal and therefore every individual will create <u>opportunities</u> for himself which will ultimately not have the same or equal result as all others. Herein lays the strength of our Republic. While Henry Ford established a much larger <u>opportunity</u> for himself with his creative contributions to the automobile and its manufacturing than did the family farmer or laborer toiling in the hot sun baked fields, the family farmer and the laborer benefited from Mr. Ford's <u>opportunity</u> far more than if Mr. Ford had chosen to work beside them in their sun baked fields. Henry Ford's cars and trucks improved the farmer's own <u>opportunity</u> to participate in the market. Such an improvement in the farmer's <u>opportunity</u> also filtered down to his workers and the large amount of merchants who also benefited from the free market activity of Mr. Ford's automobiles. By capitalizing on his own human capabilities to maximize his own <u>opportunity</u>, Mr. Ford's cars and trucks raised the standard of living of all inhabitants in our Republic. It should not go unnoticed here that maximized <u>opportunity</u>, like the automobile example, begets additional opportunity throughout the Republic.

As for <u>treatment</u>, in our Republic the agencies of government have no access to individuals except those who have contracted with said agency or who have been the subject of a complaint from another individual initiating a cause of action in the courts for some controversy or common law crime, trespass, fraud, murder, etc. However, whenever a cause of action is properly established, equal and just <u>treatment</u> is required as demanded by the 4th, 5th 6th, 7th, and 8th Amendments to the Constitution.

Consequently, in Our Constitutional Republic as defined, one can say that every individual has a right to act in any manner he sees fit according to his own moral values so long as he doesn't interfere or otherwise influence another individual's life without his consent.[11] In a Democracy, every individual is compelled to act in whatever manner the government dictates as sanctioned (commanded) by the majority. In short, a Democracy is based on the principle of an Ochlocracy (mob rule) while our own Constitutional Republic is based on the unique concept of individual sovereignty. In our Republic, the majority has no influence whatsoever on the minority, not even the smallest minority, the individual. One will not find another example of this anywhere in the world. So why do we want to dilute our system of governance by flirting with the concept of mob rule (Ochlocracy) by referring to it as a democracy?

So what took us from ungoverned sovereign individuals to governed subjects, serfs on the land governed by the will of the majority?[12] It didn't happen overnight. It happened over a span

---

[11]   This brings about two doctrines which cover the total gambit of all human behavior. The *Doctrine of Non-Existing Rights* states that "no one has the right to interfere with or influence the life of another without his consent." The corollary, *The Doctrine of Rights* states that "everyone has a right to do or act or conduct his affairs in any manner he chose so long as he does not interfere with the life of another without the other's consent." Together, these stated doctrines represent the "Doctrines of liberty."

[12]   It is interesting to note that one of our modern religions has its roots in mob rule, ala Pontius Pilate. Remember? Our founders did.

of forty (40) plus years and fifty (50) years later, the majority of the people are still completely unaware of its occurrence, mainly because they have not a clue of what our Constitutional Republic really encompasses.

Franklin D. Roosevelt once said that nothing in politics happens by accident, so let's touch on some of the his key "non-accidents" that enslaved us on the road from our a Republic to a Democracy. While other federal legislation expanding the power of the federal government occurred prior to 1913, such legislation is paled by what took place in 1913. The first, and probably the most damaging blow to our Republic in the long term, was the passing of the Federal Reserve Act creating the **privately** owned Federal Reserve central banking system. One of the members of the Rothschild's international banking family candidly stated around the turn of the 19th century that "if I can control a country's banking system, I care not who makes its laws." This may have been the real reason for the creation of the central banking system, the privately owned Federal Reserve System, but it was sold to the people as a "monetary stabilization" mechanism. However, aside from the fact that "monetary stabilization of fiat money" is an oxymoron, the newly created Federal Reserve System was anything but a mechanism associated in any way with "monetary stabilization." In sixteen (16) short years later, 1929, it brought the United States free market to its knees by first dolling out cheap un-backed paper debt, (we were on a gold standard at the time) and then abruptly recalling the debt, the interest of which had to be paid in gold to this newly created central bank, causing a collapse of the market wiping out most of our family fortunes and savings.

The second 1913 debacle was the ratification of the 16th Amendment, the "Income Tax" Amendment. However, in 1916 the Supreme Court ruled that the 16th Amendment **created no new form of taxation**. It said that the federal income tax was merely an indirect excise (or privilege) tax where taxable income (net profit) was the measure of the benefit from the exercise of the privilege and therefore the measure of the tax.[13] Notice that the concept of a privilege tax,[14] rights are still not taxable, but scarcely anyone today understands this distinction.

Third, and probably the cornerstone of advancing the concepts of a Democracy, was the passing of the 17th Amendment changing how Senators were seated in Congress. The original Constitution specified that Senators as representatives of the interests of the individual states would consequently be appointed by the state legislatures. The 17th Amendment, while it didn't substantively change anything else, it provided that the Senators would be elected by the popular vote of the People. The Senate was designed by the architects of the Constitution to give the sovereign Union states equal representation in federal legislation alongside the sovereign People. Each, the Union states and the People, were sovereigns with respect to the federal legislature (Congress) in the eyes of the Framers of the Constitution. While nothing in the 17th Amendment actually changed the responsibility of the Senators to represent their Union state as an entity represented in the Senate, the Senators themselves now look to the people to maintain their appointed jobs and therefore have loyalty to none but the majority of the People. Consequently, the Union states themselves now have no voice in the federal government making the 17th Amendment the key spring board or the first shoe to drop in the effort to the establishment of a Democracy. It is a simple fact that a sovereign with no voice is not recognized and is therefore, by definition, not a sovereign[15].

---

[13]   This is also verified in the 1943 Congressional record.
[14]   Corporations, for example, are artificial entities which exist by privilege.
[15]   The cause and cure of this concept is examined in much greater detail later on in this work.

The next "non-accidental blow to our Republic was the 1929-30 Great Depression triggered by the private Federal Reserve banking system, as earlier mentioned. As an aside, this writer authored a paper titled the "Power Trinity," which exposes the three (3) components required to take absolute control over the People, which are <u>dependence</u>, <u>obedience</u>, and <u>monitoring</u>. The Great Depression established the first component of the Power Trinity, <u>dependence</u>, by making a huge segment of the total population dependent on the federal government when it created massive work programs funded by newly printed fiat money funneled through the Federal Reserve private banking system (legislated counterfeiting). Work camps and federally funded projects sprang up all over the country replacing what was once a prospering productive free market. This monopolistic use of fiat money coupled with wage and price supports prevented the free market from establishing its own natural equalization and reconstruction remedies. Consequently, a large percentage of the population now owed its very existence to the whims of the federal government. The dependence leg of the "Power Trinity" was now firmly in place.

While the <u>obedience</u> leg of the Power Trinity wasn't established overnight. The first "notch in the handle" occurred in 1933 when Congress declared that it was "against public policy for the people of the United States to own gold," and the people <u>obediently</u> turned in their gold in exchange for paper. It is a little known fact among the citizens of this country that the Constitution gives the federal government, Congress, "exclusive legislative jurisdiction" <u>only</u> over Washington, D.C. and other federally owned lands where such jurisdiction has been transferred to it from the Union state in which the land was originally situated (See Constitution, Article I, Section 8, Clause 17 and Article IV, Section 3, Clause 2). However, Congress has no delegated power to govern the People of or in any one of the various Union states that are party to the Constitution. When the people of the states <u>obediently</u> turned in their gold in exchange for private paper notes they sent a huge message of ignorant obedience to Washington, D.C. While we all know that ignorance of the law is no excuse; one must be ever mindful of the fact that it is actually preferred in matters of <u>obedient</u> performance. But even worse, where did the people go to turn in their gold for paper? Why they went to the private central Federal Reserve Bank, of course. NOW, who owns the gold?[16]

Two years later: Congress passed the Federal Insurance Contribution Act, a.k.a. the Social Security Act. This "non-accidental" legislation was arguably the most nefarious and fraudulent assault on the sovereignty of the People and therefore the foundation of our Constitutional Republic. The people thought they were (or are) participating in a "federal old age insurance plan" but a simple reading of the statutes reveals the fact that it is nothing less than a deviously levied income tax measured by the wages of federal employees. (See Section 3101 of the Internal Revenue) When one contributes to Social Security, he not only pays an income tax measured by his wages, he makes a declaration that his wages are taxable income and therefore establishes prima facie that he is a federal taxpayer subject to all the provisions of the Internal Revenue Code including the Chapter One income taxes. Getting the people to participate in this camouflaged taxing scheme was another "notch in the handle" of the <u>obedience</u> leg of the Power Trinity. Keep in mind that the Constitution forbids the federal government from taxing the people directly. But since the Supreme Court ruled that the income tax was a benefit tax and Social Security is a "benefit," the payment of the Social Security deduction was presumed to be a voluntary participation in a federal benefit program for which a benefit tax (income tax) could be levied in exchange for the benefit. It only took us fifty (50) years to figure this out and most people, including many tax researchers, to this day fail to recognize this devious tax scheme.

---

[16] Interestingly, Hitler called in the gold in Germany at about the same time and the Jewish population refused to comply—what followed has been well documented but misrepresented, as a religious issue.

In 1939 Congress passed the "non-accidental" legislation called the "Public Salary Tax Act" taxing its employees for the privilege of working for the federal government, but few people cared.[17] One, not that many people worked for the federal government in 1939 and two, those that did didn't mind the one or two percent tax on their salaries; after all they had many benefits working for the federal government worth more than this new tax, like full retirement, paid vacations, etc. The full impact of this "non-accidental" legislation would not be felt for another 15-20 years. Then the tax rate would be much higher, nearly 20 percent, and the number of federal government employees would be a significant percentage of the total labor force. Now what do we have? We now have a huge jealous federal bureaucracy assisting in the collection of an income tax mistakenly publicized to be imposed on the general population with the attitude that "if I have to pay, you have to pay,"

To help soften the general population to the acceptance of a general income tax, Congress in 1943 passed the "non-accidental" Victory Tax Act capitalizing on the people's patriotism to help finance the Second World War." It was to be a temporary "voluntary tax" which was to be refunded at the cessation of hostilities. But what it really accomplished was to get the general population accustomed to filing 1040 forms for those obedient enough to volunteer. However, one had to apply for the refund to realize the "promise" of the Act. At the cessation of hostilities everyone was so preoccupied with trying to put their lives and their families back together that no one remembered (and the federal government didn't remind them) to apply for their Victory Tax Act refund. Instead: the federal government simply proceeded as if the Victory Tax Act was still in force and the general population obediently continued to file form 1040's as if the income tax was here to stay. Aided

---

[17] Some research points to the fact that the actual legislation didn't actually tax federal employees; it just "permitted or allowed them to be taxed." However, such a postulation could only come from the linguistically illiterate.

by the "hype" of the Cold War, the Korean "police action", and the propaganda mechanisms of the press and the big business establishment (i. e. international corporations and international banking establishments) the final "notch in the handle" of <u>obedience</u> was now established.

This final concession of <u>obedience</u> where the individual citizens were obediently filing annual 1040 forms also carries with it the final leg of the Power Trinity—<u>monitoring</u>. Coupled with the mountain of morality legislation' (i.e. gun laws, drug laws, & terrorist laws, & etc.) and the enforcement thereof together with another mountain of specific performance legislation (i.e. the required use of a Social Security number for a drivers license, etc., the inferred requirement to file tax returns, etc.) to <u>monitor </u>the general population individually, the People have lost all semblance of sovereignty. They have become <u>dependent</u>, <u>obedient</u>, and <u>monitored</u> serfs on the land under full control of a self-appointed aristocracy. Sovereigns to serfs in forty (40) short years! We the People became Sovereigns in a Republic to serfs (subjects) in a Democracy.

While the people have equal <u>rights</u> as provided by statute, they do not have unalienable rights as provide by Nature and Nature's God in the Declaration of Independence: while they have equal <u>opportunity</u> as provided by statute, they do not have unlimited <u>opportunity</u> limited only by their own personal capabilities and desires as declared by the Declaration of Independence; and while they get equal <u>treatment</u> as provided by statute, they are not <u>treated</u> as sovereigns who are, by definition, permitted to go about their daily business as they see fit. As subjects under a Democracy the people are obligated to specific performance as defined by statute, as sovereigns under a Republic there is no concept of specific performance by statute, only such performance as mutually agreed to by contract with fellow sovereigns.

The road from a Republic to a Democracy can be symbolized by the allegory of a Frog. If you put a frog in a pan of very hot water he will immediately jump out. However, if you put a frog in a pan of cool water and gradually apply heat to it, he will not only not jump out, he will sit there in the pan as the water is gradually heated to boiling, thereby tolerating being thoroughly "cooked to perfection."

If the sovereign citizens of our Republic had been "forced marched" down the road to Democracy in one quick journey, there would have been one mass revolt. However, as it was, the journey was a slow stroll spanning multiple generations and the people never became aware of the gradual erosion of their sovereign status. They became <u>dependent</u>, <u>obedient</u>, and <u>monitored</u> subject class citizens thoroughly "controlled to perfection."

And finally, reread above on page xix what our founders had to say about "democracies:"

Article IV of the Constitution mandate's that "The United States shall guarantee every State in this Union a Republican Form of Government and shall protect them against Invasion;." But what happens when the protector assumes the role of the invader. The Constitution says that "Treason against the United States shall consist only in levying War against them, or adhering to their Enemies, giving them Aid and Comfort. No Person shall be convicted of Treason unless on the Testimony of two Witnesses to the same Act, or on Confession in open Court." Any attempt to covertly alter a nation's political structure is an Act of War because it is an attempt to replace the power structure in office prior to the attempt and thus occupy the nation with an alien or foreign power. Thus, any attempt to alter the political structure of this Constitutional Republic to that of a Democracy is attempting to replace the Sovereign People and the Sovereign Union States with Peon Serfs for the purpose of Occupation. Occupation is an Act of War, Consequently, any person who openly declares the this Constitutional Republic is a Democracy is openly admitting that they are aiding and abetting an Alien construct to destroy the very essence of this Country which was created to protect and preserve the Liberty of the sovereign People. To say this Country is a Democracy is an attempt to give aid and comfort for an Alien occupation. Since occupation is an Act of War any such reference to this Country as a Democracy is an Act of Treason, particularly if it is made by an elected official or a person running for public office. It should be easy enough to find two Witnesses.

Two Counter Opposing Basic Principles

In 1913, two events with contrary principles took place that precipitated the exact opposite effects on the people of this Constitutional Republic. The one was enacted when Henry Ford doubled his hired worker's pay and the other was the Federal Reserve Act which took almost 100 years to come out of the closet to demonstrate its profound effects on the people of this Constitutional Republic. We are just beginning to discover the true character of the Federal Reserve as a glorified ponzi scheme by the demonstration of its nefarious effects on our civilization in the early stages of the 21st Century.

Henry Ford is credited with creating the first assembly line to assemble automobiles (Model T's) using interchangeable parts. Henry, being the "hands on" business man that he was, noticed that his workers couldn't afford to purchase his cars with the current wages he was paying them. This observation caused Henry to double his workers' pay over one weekend. As a result his worker's disposable compensation, i.e., money spendable in the local community after necessities, was effectively increased by an order of magnitude. Since the average worker was living hand to mouth, so to speak, that is to say that between he and his family they were consuming all that he made just to house, feed, and cloth his family (necessary essentials), he had very little, if any, disposable compensation left over to participate in the local market for purpose of improving his standard of living. Consequently, except for the grocery and clothing businesses, very little money was circulating within the local community as a result of Henry Ford's automobile assembly line plant prior to his doubling of their pay. Following the huge expansion of the Ford worker's disposable compensation, not only could the workers now buy Model T Fords, but the local economy and the wellbeing of all the local residents' sky rocketed from the added disposable compensation of the Ford workers and now the local business owners and workers could also afford to buy Henry Ford cars. This could be labeled as a prime example of the **Free Market.**

Unfortunately, as afore said, that same year, 1913, Congress passed the Federal Reserve Act, which unconstitutionally transferred Congress' own fiduciary duty to coin money and regulate the value thereof to a consortium of wealthy private bank owners. Because the Federal Reserve Act, which allowed money and debt to be created out of thin air by means of the printing press[18] through a mechanism called Fractional Reserve Banking, this Republic was to learn nearly a hundred years later that between the income tax, Fractional Reserve Banking and the nefarious shenanigans between Congress and the owners of the Federal Reserve, the country would be saddled with trillions upon trillions of dollars in debt created by the printing press and various mortgage contracts void of any consideration whatsoever. In contradistinction to Henry Ford's doubling of his worker's pay, the outcome of the Federal Reserve (and Congress) has been to nearly eliminate all disposable revenue for the middle class by the income tax and debt obligations, thereby crippling commerce and the ability for productive individuals to support themselves and their families. In the case of Henry Ford's management decision, the results occurred almost immediately. However, in the case of the Federal Reserve through its Ponzi scheme of Fractional

---

[18]   Absent consideration. Consideration represents the element of bargaining to indicate that each party agrees to surrender something of value for in return for what is to be received. It is consideration that distinguishes a contract from a mere **gift**. (emphasis in original) *Barron's Law Dictionary, 1996*

Reserve Banking[19] and the income tax, it took nearly a hundred years to siphon off most of the property of the populous before they woke up to discover that something was wrong—almost too late to establish a workable cure. Somewhere along the way to this humongous debt, the Union States on their own, whether by accident or by design, forfeited their Constitutionally secured sovereignty. This work shows what took place to cause such forfeiture to occur, what some of the Constitutional/ political ramifications exist as a result of said forfeiture, who may be culpable for civil damages, some possible solutions for the Union States to assert their sovereignty, and what cause and effect unfinished business may still be necessary once the Union States have restored asserted their Sovereignty. This could be labeled as a prime example of the private monopolization of money and credit by a very wealthy private consortium.

---

[19]   Fractional Reserve Banking is a façade scheme where it fools the public into believing that each Federal bank holds back the amount of the reserve requirement to cover bad loans and save the financial integrity of the bank in question. So if the Reserve Requirement is 10%, one might conclude that on a 1000 dollar deposit, 100 dollars would be put up as the reserve to be deposited with the FDIC as the reserve allowing the bank to loan out 900 dollars. However, the bank deposits the total 1000 dollars with the FDIC permitting it to loan out 10,000 dollars, the amount of the 1000 dollars deposit plus 9000 dollars of money created out of thin air. Consequently, for 18% annual interest, the amount of money collected in interest is 1,800 dollars for a customer deposit of 1000 dollars. That's how you turn 18% loans (like credit cards) into 180%. While that may not be usury in the revised sense of the word because none of the borrowers pays the 180%, it certainly must be a violation of the common law statute against unjust enrichment.

PART 1

Introduction

At the outset, those wishing to acquire a homeschooled doctorate in Liberty and the political philosophy associated thereto should read and study the Quotes of our Founders, particularly Thomas Jefferson, found in Appendix F. It will be a mind expanding experience, I guarantee it.

In 1984 the author was convicted of willful failure to file income tax returns. It was a four day trial and during the testimony of the author's employer's payroll accounting clerk, the clerk was asked two questions by the judge. The first question was, "Is there a Social Security number on Defendant's pay stub?" And the second question was "Are there any Social Security deductions shown to have been taken out of Defendant's pay?" The payroll clerk answered "yes" to both of the Judge's questions. The judge sought no other information throughout the trial. However, during the jury instructions the judge told the jury that "if you find the Defendant had wages, I am instructing, you that those wages were income as a matter of law." To his or her dismay, the reader will soon know why the judge gave such an instruction and it will be "The Truth that makes you mad." Was the judge hinting that Social Security is the root cause of ALL income taxes or was he telling us outright? In Part 2, this issue will be dissected and analyzed in detail in order to better understand the significance of the Judges Jury instruction.

Also, because the following analysis is steeped in legal theory and prior court decisions, this treatise includes Appendixes, A-F. It is hoped that this additionally included material will be helpful in improving the reader's comprehension by providing added proof for the points and conclusions expressed in the following discussions.

Thus, in order to properly set the stage before we undertake the discussion below, the reader might well want to review the 6 appendixes in an effort to lay some groundwork, using first principal legal concepts found therein which are generally not well understood by the average Person.

PART 2

The Misapplication
of Federal Law

There exists in many of the Union States a desire by some of its legislators to rid their Union State of the shackles of much of the recent federal legislation and, in effect, return their Union State to its rightful Constitutional Sovereign Statehood status. However, to do so requires an extremely necessary and bold move on the part of the State legislators, and quite possibly the Union State governor, to pull it off. Anyone concerned with the history of this Republic should be aware of the first principle fact that each of the 50 Union States are Sovereign in their powers and duties for the single purpose to protect the people's sovereignty from all aggressors, foreign and domestic. If you have had the occasion to read Appendix B you learned that the following quote from the United States Supreme Court[20] in Federal Marine Commission (FMC) v. South Carolina State Ports Authority, 535 U.S. 743 (2002), wherein Justice Thomas, writing the opinion for the Court, expresses in abstract the long chain of legal opinions regarding Union State sovereignty:

> Dual sovereignty is a defining feature of our Nation's Constitutional Blueprint. See Gregory v. Ashcroft, 501 U.S. 452, 457 (1991). **States, upon ratification of the Constitution, did not consent to become mere appendages of the Federal Government. Rather, they entered the Union "with their sovereignty intact."** Blatchford v. Native Village of Noatak, 501 U.S. 775, 779 (1991). [Emphasis added] An integral component of that "residuary

---

[20] Together with the analysis on jurisdictions within our Republic found in Appendix B.

and inviolable sovereignty," The Federalist No. 39, p. 245 (C. Rossiter ed. 1961) (J. Madison), retained by the States is their immunity from private suits. Reflecting the widespread understanding at the time the Constitution was drafted, Alexander Hamilton explained:

States, in ratifying the Constitution, **did surrender a portion of their inherent immunity by consenting to suits brought by sister States or by the Federal Government.** See *Alden* v. *Maine*, 527 U.S. 706, 755 (1999). Nevertheless, the Convention did not disturb States' immunity from private suits, thus firmly enshrining this principle in our constitutional framework. **"The leading advocates of the Constitution assured the people in no uncertain terms that the Constitution would not strip the States of sovereign immunity."** *Id.*, at 716. (Emphasis added)

While a sovereign, such as any one of the 50 Union States, has the option to consent to being a defendant in private suites, it does not have the Constitutional option to volunteer to pay a tax imposed by another sovereign. I bring this point up here because it is a little known fact that each and **every one of the 50 Union States is paying an excise tax to the Federal Government**, and that excise tax is the so-called employer's share of FICA and Medicare taxes. The people of New York, for example, will find the line item expense for the FICA and Medicare Employer Excise Taxes listed as an expense item under the account number 9030.8 in the New York State budget which is also true for each of its instrumentality's budgets. As we will soon learn, it is this tax that causes the Union States to forfeit their Sovereignty because the paying of a tax is an absolute admission of subject status and in the case of paying and collecting Chapter 21 taxes, the Union States in question are emulating a federal State[21] thus creating an inference that the Union States are mere appendages to the Federal Government. This then creates an additional inference that the Union State territory is now federal territory under the jurisdiction of Congress power to exclusively legislate with the entirety of federal territory. Paying a tax is different from consenting to suite. The people of said Union State(s) in their Constitution never gave said Union State(s) the option to **pay** taxes to any other sovereign, let alone the Federal Government (the United States) which is a creature created by both the Sovereign Citizens and their respective Sovereign States. The notion that a creation can turn around and tax its Creator is a logical, linguistic, and constitutional absurdity. If that were not true, such a notion would contradict the above set out Supreme Court opinion due to the fact that a taxable sovereign is an oxymoron and a semantic contradiction of terms. Sovereigns act like sovereigns and subjects act like subjects and never the twain will meet within the same entity. In other words, no entity can be both.

To begin with, there is a very naïve misunderstanding of jurisdiction among the general public and also, unfortunately, among the agents they elect as their representatives to enforce and protect their respective Constitutions. A white paper has been included in Appendix B which shows that Union State territory such as the territory of New York, Oklahoma, etc., is, in general, not within the territory over which Congress has been given the power to legislate. The federal legislation reviewed herein requires a healthy understanding of the limits of its jurisdiction. Such understanding is necessary to fully comprehend the shift in the semantics of the common words being redefined within federal statutes to new meanings as we will be discussing. Also, please take note that in the general arrangement of the statutes being discussed herein, Congress chose to redefine many of the terms after they would have been read assuming the reading occurred in the same sequence as

---

[21]   As in the case of § 3121(e) below.

they are catalogued in the published law code. Consequently, during the first reading they would seem to contain the concepts conveyed by the common use of the term, not the concepts conveyed by Congress' redefinition. It is doubtful that the average reader of the originally read statute would go back and reread a statute containing a redefined term and be able to adequately comprehend the true meaning of the law now in the redefined sense.

Think of it this way. In our Constitutional Republic there are a total of 51 unique sovereign territories, the 50 Union States and federal territory with the moniker of the United States. In the Union States the laws applicable and enforceable therein are enacted by a Union State Legislature. In the case of Federal territory, the laws applicable and enforceable therein are enacted by the Congress of the United States. Consequently, the simple concept here with respect to the Union States' association with the federal territory is simply that the federal territory is a separate and independent sovereign State possessing the same scope of authority over its sovereign territory as does any one of the Union States exercises over its sovereign territory. In other words, Congress exercises the same legislative authority over federal territory as does a Union State Legislature likewise exercise over the sovereign territory of a Union State. So whenever one thinks of jurisdiction, think of the 50 Union States and one Federal State which together represents all the unique territory of our Constitutional Republic, none of which overlaps in the least.

To cast this into a political bed of concrete, the Supreme Court stated further that the sovereignty of the United States was established through Article I, Section 8, Clause 17, which Lopez [United States v. Lopez, 514 U.S. 549, 131 LEd. 2d 626, 115 S.Ct. 1624] characterized as the "Constitutionally mandated division of authority." This "division of authority" uniquely created, in fact, a dual but mutually exclusive sovereignty in the United States of America; one being that of the United States and the other (albeit 50 in number) being that of each of the States of the Union.

Since each governmental sovereign organs have constitutionally delegated powers, the fundamental first principle question is what is the scope and sphere of said delegated powers? The answer is that each is sovereign within the boundary(s) of its assigned and/or acquired territory(s); the United States being sovereign over all territory ceded to it by the States and the States remaining sovereign over their own territory "as to all powers reserved."

> "Each State in the Union is <u>sovereign</u> as to all powers reserved. It <u>must necessarily be so</u>, because the United States have no claim to any authority but such as the States have surrendered to them." <u>Chisholm v. Georgia</u>, 2 Da11 (U.S.) 419, 435, 1 LEd. 440 (1793) Iredell, J. (Emphasis added)

The conduit through which all constitutionally delegated powers flow is jurisdiction. As to what jurisdiction remained with the States, the Supreme Court asked and answered the question:

> "What then, is the extent of jurisdiction which a state possesses? We answer, without hesitation; the jurisdiction is co-extensive with its territory; co-extensive with its legislative [sovereign] power." <u>United States v. Baevans</u>, 16 U.S. (3 Wheat) 336, 386, 387.

Since the sphere and scope of the delegated powers for each is co-extensive with the jurisdiction of its legislature, coextensive with its territory, it remains to be shown just what basis one uses to determine such jurisdiction as a first principle issue of Constitutional law. The whole concept of dual but mutually exclusive jurisdictions between the United States and the States of the Union was further ratified by an <u>Interdepartmental</u>

Committee for the Study of Jurisdiction over Federal Areas within the States, convened in 1957, and chaired by the then Assistant Attorney General, Mansfield D. Sprague during the Eisenhower administration. The Committee published the text of their findings and recommendations in two volumes, the first designated as Part I, The Facts and Committee Recommendations and the second as Part II, A Text of the Law of Legislative Jurisdiction. It is in Part II that the Committee ratifies the concept of dual but separate sovereignties," to wit:

> **"The Constitution gives express recognition to but one means of Federal acquisition of legislative jurisdiction—by State consent under Article I, section 8, Clause 17 . . . . Justice McLean suggested that the Constitution provided the sole mode of jurisdiction and that if this mode is not pursued, no transfer of jurisdiction can take place. Id @ 41**

> "It scarcely needs to be said that unless there has been a transfer of jurisdiction (1) pursuant to clause 17 by Federal acquisition of land with State consent, or (2) by cession from the State to the Federal Government, or unless the Federal Government has reserved jurisdiction upon the admission of the State, the Federal Government possesses no Legislative jurisdiction over any area within the State, such jurisdiction being for the exercise by the State, subject to non-interference by the State with (lawful) Federal functions and subject to the free exercise by the Federal Government of rights with respect to the use, protection, and disposition of its property. Id @45(emphasis added)

> "The Federal Government cannot, by unilateral action on its part, acquire legislative jurisdiction over any area within the exterior boundaries of a State. Id @46 (emphasis added)

"On the other hand, while the Federal Government has power under various provisions of the Constitution to define, and prohibit as criminal, certain acts or omissions occurring anywhere in the United States [of America], it has no power to punish for various crimes [such as drugs and firearms], jurisdiction over which is retained by the States under our Federal-State system of government, unless such crime occurs in areas as to which legislative jurisdiction has been vested in the Federal Government.' Id @ 107. (Insertions added by the author)

The last paragraph of the Committee's findings parallels exactly what Thomas Jefferson had to say opposing the "Sedition Act" when he wrote The Kentucky Resolutions addressing Congress' authority to punish such crimes, to wit:

"2. Resolved, That the Constitution of the United States, having delegated to Congress a power to punish treason, counterfeiting the securities and current coin of the United States, piracies, and felonies committed on the high seas, and offenses against the law of nations, and no other crimes whatsoever . . . ." (emphasis added)

In the context of the Dual Sovereignty what then is the Constitutional jurisdictional relationship between a Union State and the Federal Government, known as the United States, in federal legislation.

"The United States Government is a Foreign Corporation with respect to a State." 19 Corpus Jurus Secundum §883, In re: Marriam's Estate, 36 N.Y. 505, 141 N.Y. 479, Affirmed in United States v. Perkins, 163 U.S. 625.

Consequently, if the United States Government is a Foreign Corporation with respect to a State, it follows, conversely, that a State is foreign with respect to the United States Government. Since the United States Government's legislation has no authority in a foreign land, it therefore has no authority in a State which is foreign to the United States Government. This is a very important concept to keep in mind.

The title of this Part hints that the problem herein being addressed is the misapplication of Federal Law as it pertains to the excise tax being paid by each of the Union States and that is, in fact, exactly the base cause of the loss of Sovereignty among the Union States. The tax law we are concerned about is, as aforesaid, the FICA/Medicare excise tax on employees and employers found in the Internal Revenue Code (IRC) at Chapter 21. § 3101[22] It is firstly an income tax on employees engaged in the act of "employment" where the income is measured by the employee's wages and secondly it is an "excise,[23]" tax legislated in § 3111, on the employers also engaged in the act of "employment" and also measured by the amount of wages paid to the employee.

OK, so hold your nose and let's dive into the abyss of some federal law, but the author must initially warn the reader that the following analysis could be termed as the unraveling of transmogrified semantics. When a term has been redefined in or for statutes, it loses its commonly understood meaning or concept, but rather takes on the meaning of the redefinition as specified at the exclusion of all other possible previously known meanings.

First, to be encountered is what is termed commonly termed the "employee's share" of the FICA tax.

---

[22]   The character "§" is shorthand for the term "Section."

[23]   An excise tax is also known as a privilege tax, i.e., a tax on a privilege granted by government.

§ 3101. Rate of tax for the Employee's share of the FICA tax

(a) Old-age, survivors, and disability insurance

> In addition to other taxes, there is hereby imposed on the **income**[24] of every individual a tax equal to the following percentages of the **wages**[25] (as defined in section 3121(a)) received by him with respect to **employment**[26] (as defined in section 3121(b))—(Emphasis added)

Here's where we learn the truth about why the above mentioned Judge gave his jury instruction, and why we seemingly volunteered to the income tax. § 3101 says that if a individual had wages as defined and was engaged in the act of employment as defined, he or she had taxable income as measured by a certain percentage of the wages received while engaged in the act of "employment." Now the Judge found from sworn testimony that my pay stub indicated that I had FICA wages of a certain amount. Since I never disputed that fact as stated on my pay stub, my cashing of the check provided prima facie evidence that my wages were taxable income by that one listed item in and of itself and I (presumably) knew it. However, the statute further qualifies the receipt of the "wages" as stemming from being involved in the act of employment. OK, so now what does the act of Employment entail? Of course, it certainly could be supposed by most people that the act of employment was simply working for someone, but if that were true, why would Congress think it necessary to provide a definition of the term? The answer to this question lies in the linguistic dissection of the term "employment," as defined.

§ 3121 Definitions

---

[24] Highlighted for emphasis because its definition or redefinition is critical to the understanding of the points herein being made.

[25] Same

[26] Same

(b) Employment

For purposes of this chapter, the term "**employment**" means any service, of whatever nature, performed,[27]

    (A) by an employee for the person employing him, irrespective of the citizenship or residence of either,

        (i)[28] within the **United States**[29], or

        (ii)[30] on or in connection with an American vessel or American aircraft under a contract of service which is entered into within the **United States** or during the performance of which and while the employee is employed on the vessel or aircraft it touches at a port in the **United States**, if the employee is employed on and in connection with such vessel or aircraft when outside the United States, or

    (B)[31] outside the **United States** by a citizen or resident of the **United States** as an employee for an **American employer** (as defined in **subsection (h)**), or

    (C) . . .

So, if one works "for the person employing him **within**" United **States**, or in connection with an American vessel or American aircraft under a contract of service entered into within the United States, or **outside the United States** as an **employee** for an **American Employer** (as defined), one is deemed to be involved in the **act of employment** and is thus subject to the above listed FICA tax.

---

[27] Seems simple enough, but wait, there's more.
[28] Oops, there's conditions.
[29] The United States has yet to be defined so the reader must wait to read **§ 3121(e)** before he or she has any idea of what the term United States actually means.
[30] And more conditions.
[31] And more conditions.

Now, it's no secret that the average citizen of the 50 Union States and federal territory has been led to believe, by one means or another, that the term "United States" includes all the 50 States and federal territory. Since the meaning of the term "United States" is critical to the application of Chapter 21, we need to verify that the pervasive premise of the last sentence is correct. So before we dissect the required pre-condition of being an employee of an **American Employer** it might prove prudent for us to first understand the exact meanings of the terms "**State**," and "**United States**."

To understand the meaning of **within the United States** and **outside the United States** we need to discover how Congress defines the **United States**

§ 3121(e) State, United States, and citizen

For purposes of this chapter—(i.e., Chapter 21 of the IRC)

(1) State

> The term "**State**" includes the District of Columbia, the Commonwealth of Puerto Rico, the Virgin Islands, Guam, and American Samoa[32].

Here, we see that Congress has defined federal territories as "States," a semantic error to obviously buttress a false implication or inference that the territories are really Union States.

---

[32] This definition of the term "State" will hereinafter be referred to as a "**Federal State**" thus differentiating it from a "**Union State**."

(2) United States

> The term "**United States**" when used in a geographical sense[33] includes the Commonwealth of Puerto Rico, the Virgin Islands, Guam, and American Samoa.

So we now know that the term "United States" includes only those areas or territories listed in the definition and the term "State" includes only each separate territory so listed within the definition of the United States.

Should the reader believe that the term "includes" is a term of expansion rather than a term of confinement, he or she is strongly encouraged to review Appendix C. Additionally, the term "**United States**" as defined is <u>consistent</u> with the territory over which Congress was given exclusive legislation jurisdiction as set out in the Constitution for United States at Article I, Section 8, Clause 17 and Article IV, Section 3, clause 2 and subsequently the area over which federal law is Constitutionally applicable and enforceable.

Likewise when one considers the definition of the term "**State**," one observes that the term "**State**" does not include any one of the 50 Union States. Consequently, the term "**State**" is confined and defined to be better known as a "federal state," i.e. a state within the **United States** or federal territory. The term "**State**" as defined (federal State in this case) could also be accurately designated as a "**State of the United States**." In addition, a "**State**" as defined, i.e., a "federal State," can also appropriately be designated as an "**instrumentality of the United States**". It is therefore imperative to understand from this that Union States are Constitutional Sovereign States and are NOT and never can be **instrumentalities** of the United States. And also, by the discipline of linguistics as discussed further below, a Union State, as Sovereign, can

---

[33]   Which is to say a territorial sense and thus a Jurisdictional sense.

never conceptually be an **instrumentality** or the subject of any other sovereign. However, since old habits are hard to break, it takes a conscious effort and concentration to realize that while, in this case, the definition of the term "State" is a federal state, as used in Chapter 21, and is likewise consistent with the Constitutional application and enforcement of federal law, it is, nonetheless, **inconsistent** with the term "State" as used in the federal Constitution. In other words, the term "State" means a Sovereign Union State in the Federal Constitution while in the definition for Chapter 21 it means a federal State, i.e., an **instrumentality of and a subservient political body to the United States**, at the exclusion of all Union States.

The question at this point stemming from the above discussion is, as a matter of law "are the 50 Union States **instrumentalities** of the United States?" Aside from the analysis of federal law, the Supreme Court as quoted above states that:

> Dual sovereignty is a defining feature of our Nation's constitutional Blueprint. See *Gregory* v. *Ashcroft*, <u>501 U.S. 452, 457</u> (1991). **States, upon ratification of the Constitution, did not consent to become mere <u>appendages</u> of the Federal Government. Rather, they entered the Union "with their sovereignty intact."** *Blatchford* v. *Native Village of Noatak*, <u>501 U.S. 775, 779</u> (1991). [Emphasis added]

Two things are apparent here. One, a Sovereign entity is not an appendage and therefore not an instrumentality of another Sovereign, and two, the notion of "Dual Sovereignty" negates that both of the sovereigns involved, the 50 Union States and the Federal Government, from being an instrumentality of the other.

Now let's finish the definition of "**Employment**" by dissecting the term "**American Employer**"

§ 3121(h) American employer

For purposes of this chapter, the term "**American employer**" means an employer which is—

    (1)   The **United States** or **any instrumentality** thereof,

    (2)   An individual who is a resident of the **United States**,

    (3)   a partnership, if two-thirds or more of the partners are residents of the **United States**,

    (4)   A trust, if all of the trustees are residents of the **United States**, or

    (5)   A corporation organized under the laws of the **United States** or of any **State**[34].

So, from §3121(h)(1**) if a person is employed by the United States** or **an instrumentality thereof,** he is engaged in the act of **employment** as defined. Likewise, according to §3121(h)(2) if a person is employed by an individual who is a resident of the United State he too is engaged in the act of **employment**. The same for a person working for a partnership, if two-thirds or more of the partners are residents of the **United States** (§ 3121(h)(3)), or a trust, if all of the trustees are residents of the **United States** (§ 3121(h)(4)), or a corporation organized under the laws of the **United States** or of any **State** (§ 3121(h)(5)). There has already been some confusion as to whether a Union State is, in fact and law, **an instrumentality of the United States.** The answer, of course, is that it is not. **Instrumentalities of the United States** are **federal states** as they are defined in the definition of "**State**" at 3212(e)(1) and the "**United States**" at 3121(e)(2). One more possibly obvious bit of clarification; Union States are Constitutionally Sovereign States, while federal states (Territories) are not

---

[34]   Now, remember that "any State" herein means any "Federal State." Those not included in the list of the definition for the term "State" are by law excluded. This also applies to Union State chartered corporations, as they are not organized under the Laws of the United States.

Here we hit another bump in the road by coming to grips with "a corporation organized under the laws of the United States or any State." Here's where it might help to review the whole posture of federal law. Since the federal Constitution gives Congress the power and duty to exclusively legislate within federal territory, Congress is basically providing the same legislative function in federal territory as a Union State legislature provides within the territory of any one of its respective 50 Union States. In other words, federal law is functionally the same as Union State law except that the former applies primarily in federal territory the same as Union State law which only applies within the territorial boundaries of the Union State in question. So could a corporation organized under the laws of the Union State of Delaware also be a corporation organized under the laws of the United States? It should be obvious by now that the answer is "NO." So if you worked for a corporation organized under the laws of any Union State, you could NOT be engaged in the act of **employment** as defined for Chapter 21 as a matter of law. Sorry 'bout that.

There are seven subtleties that one must take particular note of at this point. First is that § 3101 transforms the individual's **wages** into taxable income due to the fact that the tax is an income tax and his wages are the measurement of the tax imposed, if and only if, the individual is involved in the **act of employment (**is working within federal territory or hs is working for an **American Employer outside of the territory of the United States)**. Second is that the tax isn't levied <u>on</u> the employee's wages but is levied on his or her participation in **the act of employment**. So while **the act of employment** is the benefit or privilege provided by the Federal Government to be compensated for, **the wages** derived therefrom are simply the measure or magnitude, if you will, of the benefit or privilege from which the tax is computed. Third, since the fact that the redefinition of the terms, **employee** and **employer** are convoluted definitions within the definition of the term "**employment**" which comes after the law reader has encountered these terms, he or she has no knowledge of the new lawful concept conveyed by the definitions at the time he or she has first encounters them in the reading. Fourth is that the Chapter 21 taxes are the roots from which the individual citizen's income tax obligation springs; pay the Chapter 21 tax and you are now, as a matter of fact and law an income taxpayer which makes you also liable for the Chapter 1 income tax in toto as well. Fifth, the definition for "**State**" is a federal state; the definition for the "**United States**" is only that territory over which Congress was given the power to exclusively legislate by and through Article I, Section 8, Clause 17 and Article 4, Section 3, Clause 2. Sixth, the definition of an "**American Employer**" is only those Employers directly connected to the United States (Federal Government) as defined. And Seventh, hidden in all this is the fact that by paying the afore mentioned FICA tax also makes one prima facie a federal employee (subject) thus prima facie making one also subject to ALL federal legislation.

By way of review, there are essentially 7 different required preexisting conditions, any one of which is a necessary fact element for anyone to be involved in the act of "Employment" as defined:

1.   If the service being rendered for the person employing him or her occurred within the **United States** as defined;

2.   If an Employee provided service in connection with an **American vessel** or **American aircraft** under certain other conditions;

3.   If the employer is the **United States** or an **instrumentality**[35] thereof;

4.   If the Employer is resident of the **United States**;

5.   If the Employer is a Partnership and two-thirds or more of the partners are residents of the **United States**,

6.   If the Employer is a trust and all of the trustees are residents of the **United States**, or

---

[35]   i.e., one of the Federal States as defined.

7.   If the Employer is a corporation organized under the laws of the **United States** federal **State**.

If none of the seven above listed required conditions exist in fact, one is not engaged in the act of **employment** as defined for purposes of federal employment taxation, whether one be tagged as an employee or an employer.

Now for the MAIN issue of the transmogrified status of Union States. Starting with the statute at § 3111 we see the following:

§ 3111. Rate of tax (Commonly referred to as the Employer's share of FICA)

(a) **Old-age, survivors, and disability insurance**

> In addition to other taxes, there is hereby imposed on every **employer** an **excise** tax, with respect to having individuals in his employ, equal to the following percentages of the **wages** (as defined in section 3121(a)) paid by him with respect to **employment** (as defined in section 3121 (b))—

> First, let's investigate what an excise tax is.

> "The terms "**excise tax**" and "**privilege tax**" are synonymous. The two are often used interchangeably." *American Airways v. Wallace 57 F.2d 877, 880*

> "Excises are taxes laid upon the manufacture, sale or consumption of commodities within the country, upon licenses to pursue certain occupations and upon corporate **privileges**; the requirement to pay such taxes involves the exercise of the privilege." *Flint vs. Stone Tracy Co. 220 U.S. 107 (1911).*

Since "**excise taxes**" are synonymous with "**privilege taxes**" and since § **3111** imposes an excise tax on employers engaged in the act of **employment,** as mutually **exclusive sovereigns,** what possible privilege could have been bestowed upon a Sovereign Union State from the United States (Federal Government) for which an excise tax could be extracted? So, notwithstanding the absence of all seven of the above listed conditional elements in which at least one must be present in order to ascertain the factual existence of the act of employment, there must also be a preexisting privilege bestowed upon the Union States by the United States (Federal Government) for which an excise tax may be levied; and the normal (common law) act of "employment" transpiring anywhere within a Sovereign Union State does not, by any stretch of the imagination, qualify as federally granted privilege. It is semantically and logistically impossible for Mutually two exclusive Sovereigns to bestow a privilege upon the other.

Since we discovered above that only federally connected employers can lawfully be involved in the act of employment, the Dual Sovereignty companion to the United States, each of the Union States, being themselves sovereigns, are beyond the reach of Congress and therefore not subject to the employer's share of FICA. As we've learned from the above discussion, a Union State cannot, by definition or by any other means, be a federally connected employer involved in the act of "employment" as defined. A Union State is not one of the Employers listed as an **American Employer** and it is not involved in being provided a service by an employee within the **United States** and therefore cannot be engaged in the act of Employment as a matter of fact and law. As an additional matter of fact and law, as we will soon also learn, the Union States are **not at liberty to pay a tax to any other sovereign by virtue of their sovereignty and/or through their own Constitutions.**

But, why all this concern associated with the Union States paying the Employer's share of the FICA tax? Because, it is fundamentally a devious and constitutionally destructive fact that when a Union States pays the "Employer's Share" of FICA taxes, it loses its constitutionally intended Sovereignty. It's as if the Union State officials, most particularly the governors, were mesmerized into believing their Union State was an **instrumentality of the United States** by the convoluted linguistics of Chapter 21 because the only "Employer" similar to a Union State that the Union State could be erroneously posing as being under the definition of **"employment"** is an **"Instrumentality of the United States"** as set forth at § **3121(h)**; to wit: for purposes of this chapter, the term "**American employer**" means an employer which is—(1) the "**United States or any instrumentality** thereof." Certainly a Union State could not possibly believe it was (2) an individual who is a resident of the **United States**, or (3) a partnership, if two-thirds or more of the partners are residents of the **United States**, or (4) a trust, if all of the trustees are residents of the **United States**, or (5) a corporation organized under the laws of the **United States** or of any **State**[36]. Consequently, by the process of elimination we're left with the fact that the Union States must be politically acting as if they are instrumentalities of the Federal Government either by ignorance or engaged in espionage as enemy combatant, but it is certainly an unconstitutional relationship that was never intended to be. In fact, the Founders took every precaution to guarantee that would never happen. The bottom line is that if a Union State cannot be defined as an employer, (as redefined) and it cannot, it is constitutionally immune to the Chapter 21 excise tax, or any tax for that matter. It would certainly be a constitutional contradiction for the Union States as Sovereigns to become, at the same time, subservient taxpayers. Becoming subservient tax-payers causes the Union States to lose their

---

[36]   Now, remember that "any State" herein means any "Federal State." Those not included in the list of the definition for the term "State" are by law excluded. This also applies to Union State chartered corporations, as they are not organized under the Laws of the United States either.

constitutionally intended sovereignty, thereby destroying the defining feature of our Nation's Constitutional blueprint[37].

Sovereigns Taxing Sovereigns

So far we've discovered five (5) show stopper reasons as to why the Union States have unlawfully and unconstitutionally forfeited their sovereignty by paying the employer's Share of FICA; **1**) A Union State is not a "State" as defined in Chapter 21; **2**) A Union State missing all seven (7) of at least one necessary conditional element required to be an "Employer" as defined; **3**) A Union State is Constitutionally prohibited from becoming an instrumentality (appendage) of the United States (Federal Government); **4**) The United States (Federal Government) has no Constitutional power to bestow a privilege upon a Union State for which an excise tax could be imposed; and **5**) The defining feature of our Nation's Constitutional Blueprint of dual sovereignty has been destroyed. However, the coup de grace as to why Union State Sovereignty evaporates by the paying of the Chapter 21 FICA Employer excise tax is found in the analysis of the validity of the concept suggested by the phrase "a Sovereign Taxing a Sovereign."

Some may be of the opinion that the sovereign Federal Government has the power to tax the Sovereign Union States. The following is incorporated here using logic and Constitutional Law to debunk that opinion.

But before we jump into the analysis of the viability of having a Sovereign tax another Sovereign, we need to understand the Sovereignty issue as it pertains to this country. Basically, this Constitutional Republic is made up of a triad of Sovereigns; 1) We the People who declared our Sovereignty via the Declaration of Independence (See Appendix A); 2) The Colonies later to become known as the Union States, each

---

[37]   See Supreme quote on page 27

of which was created by their Constitutional decrees by We the People, with specific Sovereign Powers of State (See the constitution of Your Union State and Appendix B); and 3) the United States (Federal Government) created by the now two existing Sovereigns, namely We the People and the Colonies/ Union States, with explicit powers and limited functions in order to provide a single voice with other national sovereigns on an international basis (See the Constitution for the United States). Appendix A is a treatise based on an opinion by the first Chief Justice of the Supreme Court, Justice John Jay, declaring why and how **We the People** are Sovereign and the genesis of the concept of sovereignty among the people(1st Sovereign). Appendix B is a Treatise on the subject of the defining feature of our Republic's Constitutional blueprint of *Dual Sovereignty* and describes in detail the constitutional role of each in that *Dual Sovereignty* between each of the **Union States** (2nd Sovereign) and the **United States** (Federal Government) (3rd Sovereign). One very important element to be cognizant of here is that **We the People** were the genesis and therefore the Mother of it all making them high man on the power Totem Pole.

In this analysis we need to keep in mind that Justice John Marshal's decision in *McCulloch v. Maryland*, 17 U.S. 316 (1819) which has become axiomatic, at least in this republic, that "[A]n unlimited power to tax involves, necessarily, a power to destroy."

The concept of **Sovereigns Taxing Sovereigns** is an oxymoron and a Political and Linguistic Absurdity. And here's why. First the concept evaporates on its own simply by recognizing Justice Marshall's axiom that the power to tax begets the power to destroy. Additionally, the evaporation of the concept also lies in the definition of the term sovereign. In addition to the Appendixes A and B discussions on Sovereignty we also find the pertinent definitions in the following listed Dictionaries.

Sovereign defined:

> *Black's Law Dictionary 4*[th] *Edition* defines **Sovereign** as; "A person, body, or State in which independent and supreme authority is vested; a chief ruler with supreme power . . ."

> The word which by itself comes nearest to being the definition of 'sovereignty' is will or volition as applied to political affairs. *City of Bisbee v. Cochise County, 52 Ariz. 1, 78 p.2d 982, 986. Black's Law Dictionary, 4*[th] *Revised Edition*

From *Bouvier's 1914 Edition* we find the following.

> ***Sovereign***. A chief ruler with supreme power; one possessing sovereignty. (q.v.)

> ***Sovereign State***. One which governs itself independently of any foreign power.

> ***Sovereignty***. 1. The union and exercise of all human power possessed in a state; it is a combination of all power; it is the power to do everything in a state without accountability; to make laws, to execute and to apply them: to impose and collect taxes, and, levy, contributions; to make war or peace; to form treaties of alliance or of commerce with foreign nations, and the like. *Story on the Const. Sec. 207.*

> 2. Abstractedly, sovereignty resides in the body of the nation and belongs to the people. But these powers are generally exercised by delegation.

> 3. When analyzed, sovereignty is naturally divided into three great powers; namely, the legislative, the executive, and the judiciary; the first is the power to make new laws, and to correct and repeal the old;

the second is the power to execute the laws both at home and abroad; and the last is the power to apply the laws to particular facts; to judge the disputes which arise among the citizens, and to punish crimes.

4. Strictly speaking, in our republican forms of government, the absolute sovereignty of the nation is in the people of the nation; (q.v.) and the residuary sovereignty of each state, not granted to any of its public functionaries, is in the people of the state. (q.v.) *2 Dall. 471;* and vide, generally, *2 Dall. 433, 455; 3 Dall. 93; 1 Story, Const. Sec. 208; 1 Toull. n. 20 Merl. Repert. h.t.*

So the key attributes I gather from reading the above definitions is **independence from any foreign or outside power** and **supreme power over designated areas or territory**. The question is can a circumstance such as a Sovereign Taxing a Sovereign really, in fact, exists? The maybe not so obvious answer is NO. The taxed Sovereign is no longer sovereign because it loses the main two attributes of sovereignty, namely independence and supreme authority over the designated territory and furthermore becomes a subservient body, or better, an inferior body compared to the taxing sovereign. Further, there is a distinction between constitutionally separate "sovereigns." For one sovereign entity (the United States) to tax another (i.e., any one of the Union states) leaves the taxed one (the Union State) subservient to that authority (of the United States) and by definition a subservient entity cannot be Sovereign. This is true because the once sovereign entity[38] is now stripped of its independence and superior authority simply by paying the tax, and therefore can be estopped by the taxing authority from exercising any independence whatsoever. This is true both in

---

[38] The prime example in this treatise is, of course, when the once sovereign Union State decided to pay a tax to the United States it LOST its sovereignty as a matter of semantics.

the symbolic statement of paying the tax and in the practical effect of financially supporting the sovereign taxing party.

The concept of Dual Sovereignty is smothered in the concept of the "Balance of Power" between the two. Certainly the taxing of one sovereign by the other is a complete disruption of that "Balance of Power."

So, in our Constitutional structure, Union States may not tax each other, and they may not tax property of the Federal Government. The District of Columbia does not tax the property owned by foreign governments, and New York does not tax the property owned by the United Nations. Consequently, in our Republic where dual sovereignty is the defining feature of our Republic's Constitutional blueprint (see *Federal Marine Commission (FMC) v. South Carolina State Ports Authority*, 535 U.S. 743 (2002)) the Federal Government (The United States) does not have the constitutional authority to tax New York or any one of the other 49 sovereign Union States. See also Appendix B for a treatise on the Constitutional Dual sovereignty between the Union States and the Federal Government.

In the same Supreme Court case used in Appendix A as providing the authority to conclude that the People of the Union States enjoy the status of sovereigns, Justice Iredell made a similar proclamation relative to the Union States, to wit:

> "Each State in the Union is **sovereign** as to all powers reserved. **It must necessarily be so**, because the United States have no claim to any authority but such as the States have surrendered to them." *Chisholm v. Georgia, 2 Da11 (U.S.) 419, 435, 1 LEd. 440 (1793) Iredell, J.* (Emphasis added)

In discussing the little known capacity of the United States' power to exclusively legislate only for all federal territory in the same manner as the Union State legislators legislate within their territories, a **truer word was never spoken** when Honorable

Supreme Court *Justice John Harlan* in the 1901 case of *Downes v. Bidwell, 182 U.S. 244 (1901)* stated:

> "The idea prevails with some, indeed it has expression in arguments at the bar, that we have in this country substantially two national governments; one to be maintained under the Constitution, with all its restrictions; the other to be maintained by Congress outside and independently of that instrument, by exercising such powers as other nations of the earth are accustomed to . . . I take leave to say that, if the principles thus announced should ever receive the sanction of a majority of this court, a radical and mischievous change in our system will result. We will, in that event, pass from the era of constitutional liberty guarded and protected by a written constitution into an era of legislative absolutism . . . It will be an evil day for American Liberty if the theory of a government outside the Supreme Law of the Land finds lodgment in our Constitutional Jurisprudence. No higher duty rests upon this court than to exert its full authority to prevent all violation of the principles of the Constitution."

Harlan offers **a foretelling predictive warning of what seemingly has already come to pass and the fundamental political (read power grab) cause of the matter at hand.** I might add that what Justice Harlan was alluding to is the fact that since the Constitution of the United States does not provide any power to interface directly with any the people of the Union States, it does, however, provide the power to interface directly with the Citizens whose situs is within federal territory through Article I, Section 8, Clause 17 and Article IV, Clause 3, Section 2. The substance of Justice Harlan's warning was a warning against EVER letting the Federal Government become a central government such as exists today in most European countries. **The destruction of Union State Sovereignty by taxation by the United States (Federal Government) removes any**

impediment to prevent the Federal Government from posing as the central and thus the only sovereign power.

Furthermore, a taxed sovereign no longer has the attribute of volition or will because it is under the will of another and loses any and all characteristics of sovereignty. Consequently, the notion of a sovereign taxing a sovereign is not only an oxymoron, the act itself cannot by definition occur in the nature or politics. The mere suggestion of the act causes the concept to implode into nothingness **and** that is why the notion of a sovereign taxing a sovereign is a conceptual contradiction and a linguistic and political absurdity. Consequently, the mere phrase of a "sovereign taxing a sovereign" is then itself conceptually self-destructive and therefore linguistically and politically unattainable.

One might question why a Sovereign Union State can't voluntarily volunteer to pay the subject tax to the Federal Government, since the above discussion clearly shows that Congress didn't even reference the territory of the Union States as an area over which Chapter 21 has application. If it did the issue could have been taken to the courts as being unconstitutional. But in the case of volunteering to federal law, which is in effect expanding and enlarging the scope of federal law, Supreme Court Justice Sandra Day O'Conner in the 1992 case of *New York v. United States, 505 U.S. 144 (1992)* has quite succinctly eradicated such a notion from our Republic's jurisprudence.

> "Congress exercises its confirmed powers subject to the limitations contained in the Constitution. If a state ratifies or gives consent to any authority which is not specifically granted by the Constitution of the United States, **it is null and void. State officials cannot consent to the enlargement of powers of Congress beyond those enumerated in the Constitution.**"

Justice O'Conner went on to say:

> Indeed, the facts of this case raise the possibility that powerful incentives might lead both federal and state officials to view departures from the federal structure to be in their personal interests. *Id @ 182*

In emphasizing the need for the indestructibility of both the Union of States and the States themselves, Justice O'Conner quoted Chief Justice Chase from an 1860 case

> "the preservation of the States, and the maintenance of their governments, are as much within the design and care of the Constitution as the preservation of the Union and the maintenance of the National government. **The Constitution, in all its provisions, looks to an indestructible Union, composed of indestructible States.**" *Texas v. White, 7 Wall. 700, 725 (1869). Id @ 162*

Now compare the above statement by Justice Chase with Justice Marshal's statement that "the unlimited power to tax involves the power to destroy," and any one should be able to, without a doubt, **conclude that the 50 Union States are no longer INDESTRUCTIBLE. Their sovereignty has for certain been DESTROYED.**

Since Justice John Marshal's decision in *McCulloch v. Maryland, 17 U.S. 316 (1819)*, it has become axiomatic, at least in this republic, that "[A]n unlimited power to tax involves, necessarily, a power to destroy." Now, considering that "[t]he Constitution and all its provisions, looks to an indestructible Union, composed of indestructible States," that the Union State officials are not at liberty to consent to the enlargement of powers enumerated in the Constitution, and that it is axiomatic in this Republic that inherent in the power to tax is the power to destroy, I think any rational competent mind would conclude that the Union States have no legitimate authority to consent to the forgoing discussed tax upon themselves.

As witnessed above, the imposed tax on Employers, § 3111, is defined in the statutes as an excise tax. And excise taxes are viewed by the law as a privilege tax. **It certainly goes without saying that the Union States in their Sovereign capacity and co-creator of the United States EXERCISE NO PRIVILEGE GRANTED BY THEIR CRATION, THE UNITED STATES!**

Nevertheless, this simple act of the Union States PAYING EXCISE TAXES to the United States creates the fact certain that the Union States have forfeited their participation in the Dual Sovereignty and have become mere APPENDAGES TO THE FEDERAL GOVERNMENT, thus DESTROYING THE DEFINING FEATURE OF THIS NATION'S CONSTITUTIONAL BLUEPRINT. This is the Unconstitutional act outlined at such great length in the Preface. And, again to re-emphasize here:

> **The Act of Sovereigns taxing Sovereigns is a linguistic and political absurdity and is, in and of itself, conceptually impossible.**

Accordingly, it naturally and logically follows that by this same doctrine the United States does not possess the Constitutional Power to tax any of the Union States (except by a Constitutional direct tax) or they become subservient to the United States, an outcome never envisioned by the drafters of the United States Constitution. In view of the fact that The United States was, in fact, was created by the Union States and the respective People of Union States thereof, the notion that a creation can subvert its creators by any means is also a linguistic, logical, and political absurdity.

This alone may appear very harmless, but an investigation of the cascading facts shows otherwise. Since only federally connected employers are subjected to the Chapter 21 FICA tax for being engaged in the act of employment, as defined, when Union States act as if they are instrumentalities of the United States, they create an inference and/or a prima facie unrebuttable presumption that they are federal territory and thus federal states and NO LONGER Union States. But by this one prima facie inference and/or unrebuttable presumption, the posing as a federal state and therefore federal territory, creates another inference and/or prima facie unrebuttable presumption that **ALL** employee/employer relations within said taxed Union State are "within the United States." (See above § 3121(b)(A)(i)) Thus satisfying and creating a third inference and/or unrebuttable presumption that ALL employee/employer relationships fall under the umbrella of "**employment**" as defined and therefore subject to the FICA tax making any and all wages subject to Subtitle A, Section 1 taxes as well. **The further nefarious meaning of this is that the United States (Federal Government) is silently and stealthily invading the Union State territories for the purpose of occupying them by and through the excise tax imposed by § 3111 of Chapter 21 to acquire total control over their citizens so that there can be no objection to the global takeover of this Constitutional Republic; and to think that We the People and our primary organ of government, the Union States, stood by and let it happen, nay, actually caused it to happen.**

Remember that Ben Franklin informed a woman in Philadelphia that "You have a Republic, if you can keep it." Well, are we in the throes of losing it?

So not only does the Union State's paying of the misapplied federal excise tax reduce its status from an Independent Sovereign agent of its Sovereign citizens to an instrumentality of the Federal Government subject to **ALL** its laws, it also destroys the sovereignty of its Sovereign People to serfs on the land subject to **ALL** the draconian control we declared our independence from under the **Declaration of Independence**. This too is now just a "God damned piece of paper." Maybe President Bush knew more than we give him credit for when he made the forgoing statement about the **Constitution of the United States**. And now there is only one sovereign to rule the roost, the federal now central government, ruler of all. **The ruling law replaced by ruling men! That could only occur by occupation!**

Invasion by any means for the purpose of occupation is an act of war setting the stage for a cause of action to try those, involved in aiding and abetting the demise of the Sovereignty of Union States and thus destroying the defining feature of our Constitutional blueprint of dual sovereignty, for Treason.

Let us hope that the 2nd Amendment doesn't end up being the vehicle used for the ultimate solution for this travesty

In the absence of its two creating Sovereigns keeping the Federal Government within the bounds established by the Constitution for the United States, there is no Federal Government with limited powers. Therefore there are no shackles on the federal bureaucracy limiting its powers against the once Sovereign We the People and as a result any and all entities are objects of control and taxation. This results in the United States politically simulating a socialist/communist country while economically simulating a fascist/international corporately controlled one. That's the TRUTH! Now, are you mad?

And we should now also be able to understand that the concept of Sovereigns taxing Sovereigns is an oxymoron and a political and linguistic absurdity!

In the final analysis, the structure of our Constitutional Republic left in our care by the Founding Fathers as a political mechanism designed to provide and protect our Liberties is BROKEN. The Sovereignty of the Union States has been DESTROYED and Congress is nothing more than a bureaucratic Tea Party get together to discuss who they want to incarcerate and whose property they think

they can confiscate/steal without creating an uprising. For without Sovereign Union States and their sovereign people representatives, THERE IS NO CONGRESS and therefore no legitimate passage of bills, including the nefarious communist healthcare bill. (See Appendix E and Part 3 below relative to the lack of voting rights in Congress for entities subservient to the Federal Government as if they were instrumentalities.)

Consequently, the only cure to return the Union States to their rightful and Constitutional Sovereign status and re-establish the defining feature of the Constitutional blueprint of our nation is for the Union States to CEASE PAYING THE CHAPTER 21 TAX. Anything and everything else will fail or lead to armed conflict which in and of itself is failure

RECAP:

From the above we learn that by law the act of employment exists when an employee providing a service for his or her employer does so within the United States as defined or on or in connection with an American vessel or American aircraft under a contract of service which is entered into **within** the **United States**[39] or working on a vessel or aircraft if it touches at a port in the **United States**[40], if the employee was on the vessel or aircraft when outside the **United States,** or if the employment occurred **outside** the **United States** by a citizen or resident of the **United States** as an employee for an **American employer** which is one of the following: The **United States** or an **instrumentality thereof**, an individual who is a **residence of the United States**, a partnership, if two-thirds or more of the partners are residents of the **United States**, a trust, if all of the trustees are residents of the **United States**,

---

[39] As defined
[40] As defined

or a corporation organized under the laws of the **United States** or of any [Federal] **State**. It's that simple, and those are the only **employers** subject to the § 3111 excise tax and the Union States are not included in that list as a matter of law, nor are the corporations organized under its laws, Period.

At the risk of being redundant, one should again note at this point that the definition of the term "**State**" does not encompass anyone of the 50 Union States, but is, instead, a definition of the various federal territories as "**States of the United States**" not, as a matter of law, to be confused with any of the intended sovereign Union States. "**States**" then, as defined, are instrumentalities of the United States (Federal Government) **BUT Union States** are not. Note also from the statutes that any employer involved in the act of "employment," as defined, is correspondingly somehow involved with the Federal Government and accordingly can, as a matter of fact, be designated as a "federally connected employer."

Further, we can legitimately conclude that the only individuals who are or can be involved in the act of "**employment**" are those who work for **federally connected_employers** thus defining them as **federal employees**. Such a conclusion is reached by and through a firm understanding of the semantics of the terms defined, used, and referenced to in §§ 3101, 3111, 3121(b), 3121(e), 3121(h)(1-5),

As an aside, notice also that anyone who voluntarily allows FICA/Medicare taxes to be withheld from his or her wages is also providing an unrebuttable presumption that he or she is a federal employee subject to all the federal laws and has by presumption, in due course, provided that he or she is transmogrifying their private sector rightful property wages received for the exchange of their labor into taxable income whether or not the wage earner is actually in fact knowingly aware of the definition of "**employment**" or not.

While the key subject matter addressed here is the Union State Sovereignty, it should also be apparent, however, that if, and only if, a private sector individual within a Union State permits a portion of his wages to be deducted as FICA taxes, regardless of whether or not said individual is engaged in the act of employment as defined, he has self-declared his wages to be taxable income and has concurrently taken up the legal posture of a federal employee. It's the actual FICA deduction from his or her compensation that creates the presumption that the individual is engaged in the act of "employment" by the statutes of Chapter 21, namely § 3101,[41] mainly due to the fact that he or she signed a W4 requesting withholding and thereby recognizing the event of an income tax being deducted from his pay. Therefore the individual's compensation is presumed to be taxable income measured by his wages, thus also allowing for the existence of a non-rebuttable presumption or inference that he is employed by a "federally connected employer," therefore making him a "federal employee," subject to the entire litany of federal law. Now we know why the judge gave his jury instruction that my "wages were income as a matter of law." The existence of a Social Security number on my pay stub together with the evidence, also on my paystub, that I had Social Security deductions taken out of my pay was used as prima facie evidence and/or an unrebuttable presumption that I was an employee as defined working for a federally connected employer as defined. Since I offered no evidence to the contrary, the Judge on his own just took judicial notice of what he saw.

Having a firm understanding of the concepts conveyed by Congress' convoluted legislation associated with the FICA taxes forms the basis for this whole thesis. Look at this exercise as a challenge to connect all the dots and still have legislation that passes Constitutional muster. Whether or not one maintains

---

[41] Remember the Judges Questions and his jury instruction.

their sanity in the process is a question that can't be answered here.

However, each and every one of the 50 Union States and their instrumentalities are paying § 3111 excise taxes_and dutifully collecting the § **3101** income taxes and turning it over to the Federal Government (IRS). As we now know from understanding the analysis above, and given the advice of the Supreme Court that Sovereigns cannot tax each other, there is no legal foundation and thus no excuse for any Union State actor to pay and collect FICA taxes. But what's the problem? The problem comes about from the fact that to be an employer subject to the tax, such an employer must possess the attribute(s) of one or more of the employers listed in § 3121(b) and § 3121(h), i.e., a **federally connected employer**. Due to the fact that the Union States are constitutionally intended to be legitimate sovereign organs of government, the most logical and likely conclusion to be drawn is that the **Union States** are mistakenly viewing themselves to be **"instrumentalities"** of the **United States**," which they most certainly are not. Consequently, the Union States are involved in the Misapplication of Federal Law. Only **"States"** as defined (i.e., federal States) could, as a matter of law, be instrumentalities of the United States. While we see from reading Appendix B and restated above that:

> "States, upon ratification of the Constitution, did not consent to become mere appendages [instrumentalities] of the Federal Government. Rather, they entered the Union "with their sovereignty intact." *Blatchford* v. *Native Village of Noatak*, 501 U.S. 775, 779 (1991)."

There, consequently, exist no Constitutional provisions for the Union States to voluntarily give up their sovereignty. By doing so they alter the Constitutional Blueprint of Dual Sovereignty thereby destroying the Constitutional Structure of our Republic and thus creating the unrebuttable presumption or inference that every employee/employer relationship within that Union

State's borders is an excise taxable act of employment, an act which can only be performed in federal territory or involving a "federally connected employer." So, to any alphabet soup federal agency, such as the IRS, the paying and collecting thereof of Chapter 21 taxes by any Union State, becomes, in their minds, prima facie evidence enough to presume that such Union State is an instrumentality of the United States and thus federal territory subject to the entire body of federal laws. In effect, that simple act of Union States paying an excise tax to the Federal Government as if they were an instrumentality thereto, destroys our Constitutional Blueprint of Dual Sovereignty, politically transmogrifies our Constructional Republic from a federation of Union States to a national central government of unlimited power, thus breaking the chain that binds our agents, both State and federal, firmly down to the "Rule of Law."

Don't like the Real Id Card? Stop letting your Union State act like a federal instrumentality.[42] Think the Patriot Act has no business in your Union State? Stop your Union State from paying and collecting the Chapter 21 taxes. Don't want federal military troops roaming the streets in your Union State? Insist that your Union State behave as the sovereign Union State that it, really in fact, was intended to be and force it to cease and desist paying and collecting Chapter 21 taxes. Don't want your sons in the National Guard going off to fight and be killed in international political police actions? Insist that your Union State **cease and desist** its unconstitutional behavior of acting like an appendage or instrumentality to the Federal Government by paying and collecting the Chapter 21 tax and further direct your representatives (your Senators) in the Senate to propose and pass legislation to take back control of (repatriate) the National Guard under the Union State's command rather than that of a misdirected (despotic) president. Don't want federal socialist health care? Stop letting your Union State act like a federal instrumentality. Don't want Cap and Trade? Insist that your

---

[42]   An appendage/instrumentality to the Federal Government.

Union State stop paying FICA and restore your Union State's Sovereignty. You get the idea.

A few comments are in order here relative to the structure of Congress and your Union States representation therein. It's of interest to note that the United States Congress is constitutionally made up of representation from the two sovereigns that created the United States (Federal Government) in the first place, they being the sovereign people and the sovereign Union States in which they live and labor. Proof of the existence of the aforementioned two sovereigns can be found in Appendix B and A respectively. While the 17th Amendment to the federal Constitution changed the method by which Senators as Union State Representatives are appointed, it did not in any way alter the duties they are constitutionally obligated to perform. Taking from the *Federalist Papers # 39* by James Madison (Appendix D) we see the following, first principles relative to the intent to maintain Union State sovereignty and then the first principle purpose of the Senate as the organ of Congress functioning as the representative for each of the Union States:

> Each State, in ratifying the Constitution, is considered as a sovereign body, **independent of all others**, and only to be bound by its own voluntary act. **In this relation, then, the new Constitution will, if established, be a FEDERAL, and not a NATIONAL Constitution**.

The next relation is, to the sources from which the ordinary powers of government are to be derived.

> The House of Representatives will derive its powers from the people of America; and the people will be represented in the same proportion, and on the same principle, as they are in the legislature of a particular State. So far the government is NATIONAL, not FEDERAL. The Senate, on the other hand, will derive its powers from the States, as political and

coequal societies; and these will be represented on the principle of equality in the Senate, as they now are in the existing Congress. So far the government is FEDERAL, not NATIONAL. Federalist Papers # 39 (emphasis added *Federalist Papers # 39* by James Madison*)*

Notice the subtle distinction that James Madison makes between NATIONAL and FEDERAL. When the source of power of the new government is derived solely from the people, the new government was termed NATIONAL, or, in other words, a central top down government controlling the people at large. When the source of power was derived equally from the people and the states (which, by the way, ultimately derived their power from the people as well) the two tier new government was termed FEDERAL.

Further reading to help cement the notion that the purpose of the Senate is the federal forum for each and every Union State to use for the management of its political concerns in the Republic can be found in Appendix D. Thus, from the above set out portions of the Federalist Papers and a comprehensive reading of Appendix D, it should be conclusively understood that the Senate was created for the sole purpose of providing the sovereign States with equal footing in Congress (the House of sovereigns) in concert with its companion sovereigns, the sovereign citizens of the respective Union States. Accordingly then, **nothing** set out in the 17th Amendment altered the character and purpose of the Senate by one iota as the Union States respective representation in Congress. Otherwise the 17th Amendment would have had to contain language in the Amendment relative to any such Constitutional alterations of duties as set out in Article I, Section 3. Consequently, each and every Senator is duty bound by the Oath of Office, to uphold both the federal and Union State's Constitutions to do the bidding of his or her respective Union State legislature which should by legislative resolution direct the conduct and voting direction of each of the two Union State Senators. Senators serve at the pleasure of the Union State legislatures. While the people elect them, the Union State, upon bad behavior, can have them replaced. However, the Senators, via their oath of office, have sufficient impetus on their own to steer the Senate in Congress to a position restricting federal agencies/ agents from unlawfully recognizing the Union States as instrumentalities of the United States. As will be seen below, without this correction, every Senator and House Representative is legally and constitutionally out of a job. Remember, a Senator performs according to an oath of office which is not significantly different than a witness who takes an oath to perform which is simply the telling of the truth. A Senator's oath should contain a promise to obey both the State and Federal constitution with a subpart that promises to deliver to the Senate of the United States the directions provide to the Senator by the Union State Legislature. If a witness fails to tell the truth as his or her oath promises, he or she may be prosecuted for perjury. So why is it not reasonable for the same to apply to all public officials who violate what their oath of office promises, to obey?

PART 3

Constitutional/Political Ramifications

Let's now look at some of the **ramifications** stemming from the unconstitutional behavior of the various now non-sovereign Union State Actors as a result of their misapplication of federal law causing them (the Union States) to imitate the characteristics of instrumentalities or mere appendages of the United States (Federal Government). To aid in the understanding of the following, we need to comprehend the existence of the three separate entities referred to as "States" as discussed above. First, there are the constitutionally recognized Sovereign independent **Union States**, 50 in number, each being represented in the House of sovereigns (Congress) in the Senate via two elected Senators. These are NOT instrumentalities of the United States. Second, there are the organized political entities situated in federal territory under the exclusive legislative power of Congress via Article I, Section 8, Clause 2 and Section IV, Section 3, Clause 2 of the federal Constitution. By legislative convention, Congress has chosen to name these territorial entities situated in federal territory also as "States," but they are, by definition, non-sovereign "States" and ARE instrumentalities of the United States with no representation in Congress. For clarification, we will use the moniker "**Federal States**" here to avoid confusion with and differentiate them from Union States. Federal States (instrumentalities) are invited to send elected members to the House of Representatives to engage in discussion with the main body of Representatives, but said members have no voting rights and are therefore merely a participating audience from the various instrumentalities of the United States. Now there's a third unconstitutional breed of "State" which is a transmogrified Union State which has been stripped of its sovereignty by paying an excise tax which in common parlance is the "employer's share of FICA & Medicare taxes" as discussed at length above. While an appropriate moniker for this entity may be a **"Bastard State,"** we will, for the sake of literary convenience, use the moniker **"Non-Sovereign Union State."**

So in abstract, we end up with three different types of "States" with grossly differing Constitutional characteristics: a **"Union State"** which is a Sovereign, shares in the Dual Sovereignty which is the defining feature of our Republics Constitutional Blueprint, and is NOT an instrumentality of the United States; a **"Federal State"** which is not sovereign but IS an instrumentality of the United States (Federal Government); and **"Non-Sovereign Union State"** which is not sovereign by its own action by the misapplication of federal law resulting in unconstitutionally paying an excise tax to the Federal Government, and will, by imperative necessity, need to restore its sovereign status to keep it from becoming a Federal State, thereby destroying the defining feature of our Republic's Constitutional Blueprint and completely destroying the founder's ingenious scheme of checks and balances to protect our liberties from all assaults both foreign and domestic. That, my friends, if it should ever happen, will be the creation of a despotic central government of subservient citizens with absolutely no Sovereign Union States to protect our Liberties.

The calling into question the validity of all Congressional legislation (See Appendix E).

First, probably the most pernicious and politically alarming consequence of the **Non-Sovereign Union States'** unconstitutional behaving as Instrumentalities of the United States is the fact that United States instrumentalities (Non Sovereign Federal States,) and now the **Non-Sovereign Union States**, technically, have no legitimate representation in either house of Congress. While the House receives representatives from each of the lawful instrumentalities of the United States which may be involved in discussions, they have no voting rights. On the other hand, the Senate receives no representatives from the federal instrumentalities whatsoever, which obviously calls into question all the legislation passed by Congress during the time in which all the **Non-Sovereign Union States** have been unconstitutionally acting as Federal States, i.e. acting as instrumentalities or mere appendages of the United States. Appendix E is presented for a review of the status difference in Congress between Union State representation and that of Federal States (instrumentalities) representation. Since none of the Union States **or** We the People have had valid representation in Congress because the Union State territories in which we all live have been transmogrified into **Non-Sovereign Union States** and fraudulently occupied by the Federal Government as implied instrumentalities thereof. We the People are now back to **taxation without representation, simply because the primary agents of We the People, the Union States have forfeited their sovereignty (and thus our representation) to the Federal Government.** Current representation in Congress is a façade and a fraud, because the Federal Government can't have it both ways. Either the Federal Government acknowledges the Union States as independent sovereigns as a matter of fact and law thus making them immune from taxation[43], or it loses its Constitutional foundation to exist at all for the lack of a Constitutionally valid Congress as so laid down in the federal Constitution made up of sovereign Union State representatives in the Senate and representatives of the sovereign People from said Union State territories in the House. Even the IRS agents who, in the process of implementing Chapter 21 taxes with any Union State, do in fact, "falsely assume or pretend to be an officer or employee **acting under the authority of the United States or any department, agency or officer thereof,** and acts as such, or in such

---

[43]   either by appropriate legislation or by prosecuting the unlawful acts of Union State actors for impersonating Federal employees along with federal employees for aiding and abetting.

pretended character demands or obtains any money, paper, document, or thing of value" are exposed to criminal sanctions as set out in Title 18, § 912. This is so because, as seen above, authority granted in the IRC, Chapter 21 only reaches territory over which Congress has exclusive jurisdiction, or in other words, federal territory. Such federal agents are also exposed to civil causes of action in Union State courts for damages for "abuse of process" to Union State Citizens[44] and in some cases "unjust enrichment."

The Destruction of our Constitutional Republic's Constitutional Blueprint

Second, and perhaps equally alarming, is the fact that by acting as a non-sovereign instrumentality of the United States, the Non-Sovereign Union States are destroying "the **defining feature** of our **Nation's Constitutional Blueprint of Dual Sovereignty.**"[45] It would seem logical and constitutionally appropriate to consider the destruction of **the defining feature of our Constitutional Blueprint** to be sufficient to classify such an act as an act of treason? Obviously there exists no Constitutional power having been delegated to any of our represented organs of government to restructure our Republic under any circumstances and certainly not by implication.

While Treason is constitutionally limited to levying war against the Union States, it should be noted that the general purpose of war is occupation. Since the Federal Government has successfully annexed (occupied) the Non-sovereign Union States by deceit, fraud, and patriotic devotion without openly firing a shot, the outcome is no different than the outcome of a successful armed invasion. Why then is the occupation or unlawful annexing by the Federal Government against the Union

---

[44]   This action may also reach Union State actors as well for the aiding and abetting of Federal actors.

[45]   See Appendix A

States not Treason per se? After all, there have been several cases of federal troops manning garrisons in the sovereign territory of Union States. They certainly weren't there in defense of said Non-Sovereign Union State. Their presence represents occupation. Occupation is an act of war and therefore Treason no matter what the method of materialization or causality.

Falling Under the Umbrella of Federal Territory, Subject to Congress's Exclusive Power to Legislate

Third, as mentioned above, the acts[46] portraying the status of an instrumentality of the United States are publicly stating that the Non-Sovereign Union States involved in such behavior have supplied sufficient grounds for the world to view them as Federal States and not as Union States, if only by inference. This accordingly provides an inference for the various federal agents and agencies to presume that all acts associated with employee/employer relationships (whether corporate or private) within said Non-Sovereign Union State boundaries are acts of "employment" as defined occurring in federal territory. Said inference finds its unconstitutional light of day from the combined relationship between § 3121(b)(A)(i) and § 3121(h) (1) when federal agents unlawfully infer that a Non-Sovereign Union State is a mere appendage of the United States by the mere unlawful acts of Non-Sovereign Union State Actors when they behave as if their Non-Sovereign Union State is an instrumentality of the United States (Federal Government).

Remember, it all starts with the definition of "employment."

§ 3121(b) Employment For purposes of this chapter, the term **"employment"** means any service, of whatever nature, performed, (A) by an employee for the person employing him,

---

[46] The act of unlawfully paying an excise to the United States

irrespective of the citizenship or residence of either, (i) within the **United States**[47].

§ 3121(h) American employer

For purposes of this chapter, the term "**American employer**" means an employer which is—

(1) the **United States** or **any instrumentality** thereof, ...

Absent the Non-Sovereign Union State Actor's behavior of paying and collecting Chapter 21 taxes, there could be no basis for any resulting inference propping up an excuse for plausible deniability for making the unrebuttable presumption that said Union State lies within federal territory over which Congress was given the Constitutional power to exclusively legislate.[48] That is to say, that only an true constitutional instrumentality of the United States lies "within the United States [federal territory];" and except for the unlawful actions of Non-Sovereign Union State actors, Union States are not included as a matter of Constitutional fact and law.

An interesting aside here creates a couple of disturbingly related facts. In the Social Security Act, which is IRC Chapter 21, Congress authorized the Federal States to tax their citizens presumably to provide a source of revenue to pay the "Employer's share" of the FICA tax imposed by IRC §3111. It should be noted here, that even the Non-Sovereign Union States which have instituted an "Income Tax," such tax is tied directly to the federal income tax law and returns. Consequently, only those submitting federal returns can legitimately complete a Non-Sovereign Union State Income tax return.

---

[47]   As defined and by acting as an instrumentality of the United States, the entire Union State territory can be presumed to be "within the United States" (Federal territory).

[48]   See Article I, Section 8, Clause 17 of the Federal Constitution.

Aside from the obvious budgetary impact that such behavior[49] causes, there are many concerns. First, there is the concern over who might be culpable for the pernicious attempt to restructure our Republic and for the damages suffered as a result. The magnitude of the depth of this concern warrants a Part all to itself and is covered in Part 4 following.

The 16ᵗʰ Amendment

Most people think that the 16ᵗʰ Amendment is the reason they are paying income tax, but is it really? The Supreme Court has been trying to hint for years that we are effectively providing a gift to the Federal Government (the United States) in the amount of a percentage of our revenue.

> "The provisions of the Sixteenth Amendment conferred **no new power of taxation** but simply prohibited the complete and plenary power of income taxation possessed by Congress from the beginning from being taken out of the category of indirect taxation[50] to which it inherently belonged . . ." *Stanton v. Baltic Mining Co.,* 240 U.S. 103 (1916)

But the coup de grace of the 16ᵗʰ Amendment can be found within the context of the Amendment itself.

Black's Law Dictionary defines **apportionment** as:

> "The **apportionment of a tax** consists in a **selection of the subjects to be taxed,** and in laying down the rule by which to measure the contribution which

---

[49]   The misapplication of Federal Law by paying an excise tax
[50]   Nor did it take income taxation power beyond the reach of Congress's Exclusive Power to Legislate within Federal territory and impose it in any territory among the several States as we will soon learn.

each of the subjects shall make to the tax." *Barfield
v. Gleason,* 111 Ky. 491, 63 S.W. 964. (Black's Law
Dictionary, Revised 4th Edition, p. 129)

The United States 16th Amendment states that:

"Congress shall have the power to lay and collect
taxes on incomes, from whatever source derived,
without apportionment among the several States,
and without regard to any census or enumeration."
(emphasis added)

Consequently, by incorporating the semantics of the above
definition of *apportionment,* a proper re-phrase of the 16th
Amendment should accurately be:

The Congress shall have the power to lay and collect
taxes on incomes, from whatever source derived,
without selecting any subjects to be taxed among
the several States, and without regard to any census
or enumeration.

Additionally, since the definition of *apportionment* was added
to Black's Dictionary in 1910 it can be presumed that Congress
was aware of the addition to the dictionary and capitalized on it
in forming the 16th Amendment.

WOW! So not only are the Union States, by and through
the elected officials, violating and extending the scope and
application of federal law beyond that which is defined in the
federal statutes themselves, they are violating the Constitution
by extending the taxing power beyond that which was granted
to the Federal Government by the 16th Amendment to the
federal Constitution.

The end game questions are:

1. Are the officers and elected officials of a sovereign organ of government (such as a Sovereign Union State) responsible for their actions when such behavior entails the misapplication and execution of the laws of a foreign sovereign or government (such as the Federal Government), which might also imply a jurisdictional transfer to the sovereign whose laws are being misapplied and executed? Such an implication of jurisdictional transfer may also imply the occupation and control of the people by the sovereign whose laws are unlawfully being misapplied. Since occupation and control of the people is the goal of all wars, it would seem that the stealthy take over a territory by nefarious means through the misapplication of laws of a foreign sovereign would constitute treason? Sanctions, like unlawful taxes, placed on one sovereign by another are acts of war to weaken or otherwise make an easy conquest of the sovereign upon whom the sanctions are placed. It matters not that no black powder or C4 was used to aid in the intended occupation. The intended occupation of another sovereign's territory is sufficient to be deemed an act of war and anyone aiding in its occurrence would seem to qualify as participating in an act of Treason.

2. When Non-Sovereign Union States forfeit their Constitutionally granted sovereignty by acting as if they are Instrumentalities of the United States, are all the laws passed by Congress void because Instrumentalities have no Constitutional standing or representation in Congress as instrumentalities of the United States, thus making any and all such Congressional acts void and inoperable as a

matter of fact and law[51]? Congress and the Federal Government in general can't have it both ways!

3.   In view of the fact that the Federal Constitution directs Congress to protect the Union States from invasion[52], isn't it quite obvious that Congress reneged on its mandate to prevent an invasion of the Union States when the Federal Government is the very invader that occupies the Union States by the misapplication of federal laws? Isn't the collection of federal taxes within the Union States further evidence of occupation stemming from the stealth invasion through the misapplication of federal law to pull it off? And wouldn't the elected officials involved in such a stealth invasion, both federal and Union State, be civilly and criminally responsible for the nefarious occupation resulting therefrom?

Summary

The misapplication of federal law includes first, the specific misapplication of the Social Security laws with respect to application of the taxes imposed therein; second, the notion of any tax attempted to be enacted by one sovereign upon another sovereign, in and of itself, destroys the sovereignty of the sovereign upon whom the tax is attempting to be levied, and third, the 16th Amendments prohibits the application of the federal income tax from being imposed upon subjects within any of the Union States. Now you know the **truth**. Are you mad yet?

---

[51]   See Appendix E

[52]   With absolutely no predicate provisions at Article IV, Section 4, Clause 1.

PART 4

Who Is Ultimately Culpable?

One more time; the rule prohibiting Sovereigns from taxing Sovereigns lies in the phrase itself; we know from the above discussions that the concept of Sovereigns taxing Sovereigns cannot exist in either theory or fact. Since the mere attempt of one Sovereign taxing another Sovereign is in fact the ultimate destruction of the once sovereign taxed entity, and since the destruction of a Sovereign is an unlawful act, even an act of war and thus treason, some person or persons must shoulder the culpability for the act.

Since we now know the cause of how the "defining feature of our Nation's Constitutional Blueprint" was blown to smithereens virtually destroying the very political structure of our Constitutional Republics,[53] it now also behooves us to understand who was behind the cause. Consequently we look for who may be culpable and why. Perhaps the first group who must shoulder the largest share of the culpability would be the elected official(s) responsible for drafting the budget for each Union State together with the budgets of the instrumentalities thereunder due to the fact that each and every such budget contains an expense line item for the employer's share of FICA/Medicare (§ 3111) to be paid to the United States (Federal Government). This is the fundamental un-Constitutional behavior by Union State actors that creates the problem of their lack of sovereignty in the first place and explicitly becomes a violation of any and all Union State actor's Oath of Office and thus perjury for failure to do due diligence in the promised performance of the duty taken under Oath to protect the Constitution for his or her respective Union State. Certainly, the protection of the Union State's sovereignty was a presumed fiduciary duty in

---

[53]   Union States

connection to the protection to the Union State constitution. From the above discussion, it is observed that Congress didn't (and couldn't due to our Republic's Constitutional Blueprint of Dual Sovereignty and the 16th Amendment) tax any Union State and/or its employees. Besides, as discussed above the notion that a Sovereign has the power to tax another Sovereign is a contradiction of the concept referred to by the term Sovereign and is likewise, as aforesaid, a political and linguistic absurdity.

Each and every member of the legislator who approved the budget must also shoulder a portion of the culpability because said member has an opportunity to vote against the budget on the grounds that the budget has an unconstitutional expense line item, the execution of which transmogrifies the Union State from a Sovereign Union State to an appendage (i.e., an instrumentality/subject) of the Federal Government and thus federal territory over which Congress was given the exclusive power to legislate under Article I, Section 8, Clause 17 and Article IV, Section 3, Clause 2 of the federal Constitution.

Any Union State or any instrumentality thereof actor(s) who aided and abetted any federal employee, agent, or official in the taking of private property[54] may be culpable to the private property owner(s) for the damages suffered for the unlawful taking of said property including, but not limited to, any and all income taxes imposed upon any and all Union State people.

Any Union State or any instrumentality (or corporation) thereof actor(s) who aided and abetted any federal employee, agent, or official in the misapplication of federal law wherein Congress or the Constitution strictly limited said application of federal law to the territory over which Congress was granted exclusive power to legislate, namely federal territory, may be culpable for damages to any and all persons damaged by said application, including but not limited to time spent in confinement, should

---

[54]   Such as honoring Federal tax liens against resident Citizens therein.

a jail term have been imposed. This would be particularly true where the Union State actors were members of any of the Union State agencies and/or any one or more of its instrumentality's law enforcement agencies (such as in counties, cities, towns or villages).

Almost every municipality within each and every Union State enlists the aid of legal counsel, the cost of which is covered by taxpayer funds budgeted and paid for out of the municipal treasury. It would then seem logical that said legal counsel, the municipal attorney, would be duty bound to advise his charge to stay within the bounds of maintaining the Constitutional structure of this Constitutional Republic, including, but not limited to, the advice not to pay a tax to another sovereign organ of government responsible for obliterating the Union State's Sovereign Status and violating the long standing prohibition of sovereigns taxing sovereigns or the property of sovereigns. Not to do so on the municipal attorney's own volition would seem to indicate malpractice, especially since federal law[55] has no application in the territory under his charge. Take notice of the fact that his bad advice affects each and every sovereign person of the entity under his charge who pays the taxes to support his advice of the bad counsel. In other words, the Union State sovereign persons are being taxed to pay the tax to the Federal Government, a tax on taxes, so to speak.

Remember, the Union States as sovereigns are immune from suites at law. Aside from the discussion as to whether they lose that immunity or not when they act as non-sovereigns, there are enough human agents to go around for all the damages suffered by the sovereign persons of the Union States for allowing the fungus of federal law to permeate within the territory of the Union States. Clearing out that fungus occurs through bringing

---

[55] Including, but not limited to, the Real ID Act, the Patriot Act, Federal Troops roaming the streets of Union States, National Guardsmen fighting undeclared wars compromising their ability to Guard the union State, Bailouts, etc.

causes of actions for claims for damages in the Union State's Courts caused by the treasonous actions by their representative agents to the Union State government and its instrumentalities.

The Loss of Liberty is certainly also an actionable damage. As argued above, the mere behavior of Union States by paying the §3111 Employer FICA tax creates an inference of federal territory, which also further creates an inference that all the Union State Citizens domiciled in that Union State are engaged in the act of employment as defined which further creates the inference that their compensation for labor becomes taxable wages as defined. The multiple layers of inference producing unrebuttable presumptions thereby causing the loss of Liberty are certainly actionable once the person or persons responsible for such are identified.

And how about those persons engaged in preparing "tax return" for a fee. Because of the complexity of the federal tax code, thousands of people have made a business living off the fear of said tax code. Those holding themselves out to be tax law experts have a legal duty to know and understand ALL aspects of the tax code, including that the federal FICA employee tax is only legislated upon those individuals involved in the act of employment[56] as defined as employees or employers.[57] Now, while every individual is responsible to know the law, in the case of tax preparers, it would seem that the very existence of any particular person seeking assistance from a tax preparer would suffice as prima facie evidence that the person seeking help is unfamiliar with the tax code. Otherwise the person would not be willing to shell out funds to the tax preparer for having the necessary knowledge to aid the person in computing and filing the necessary forms for the tax owed.

---

[56]   Which, as discussed above, is limited to Federal employees or others engaged in the act of employment as defined in Federal territory?

[57]   Which, as discussed above, are Federally connected employers.

While tax preparers are not required by law to ask any questions of the person seeking assistance, it is a foregone conclusion that the tax preparer must ask questions to ascertain the necessary information relative to a person's revenue and expenses to fill in the various forms for each tax year. So how can a tax preparer presume that anyone is required to file returns and pay taxes if the preparer doesn't ask enough questions to ascertain that the application of the tax is applicable to any person showing up at their doorstep? Now we've concluded that the person seeking assistance is ignorant of the tax code or the person wouldn't be seeking assist in paying the tax in the first place. Why then wouldn't it seem feasible that the person might also be ignorant of the application of the tax code? Ineffective professional aid for fees is tantamount to malpractice.

Consequently, every person seeking aid in filing and paying his or her federal tax should be, at a minimum, asked the following questions. In other words, the preparer should verify that the person seeking his or her aid can answer in the affirmative to at least one of the following questions:

1. At any time during the subject tax year were you ever employed anywhere in federal territory (D.C,. Puerto Rico, Guam, Virgin Islands, or American Samoa)? For which you received any revenue for such work?

2. At any time during the subject tax year have you ever worked on or in connection with an American vessel or American aircraft under a contract of service which was entered into within the United States or during the performance of which and while the employee is employed on the vessel or aircraft it touches at a port in the United States. Or if the employee is employed on and in connection with such vessel or aircraft when outside the United State?

3. At any time during the subject tax year were you a federal employee working for the United States (Federal Government) or any agency or instrumentality there of?

4.   At any time during the subject tax year were you
a resident of the United States (federal territory,
D.C. Puerto Rico, Guam, Virgin Islands, American
Samoa)?

5.   At any time during the subject tax year were you a
member of a partnership, two thirds of which were
residents of the United States (federal territory,
D.C. Puerto Rico, Guam, Virgin Islands, American
Samoa)?

6.   At any time during the subject tax year were you a
member of a trust, where all the members were
residents of the United States (federal territory,
D.C. Puerto Rico, Guam, Virgin Islands, American
Samoa)?

7.   At any time during the subject tax year did you work
for or do business as a corporation organized under
the laws of the United States or of any federal State,
such as D.C., Puerto Rico, Virgin Islands, American
Samoa, etc.?

8.   At any time during the subject tax year were you
ever involved in the performance of the functions of a
public office in federal territory?

Unless there is an affirmative answer to at least one of the
above questions, the tax preparer could then be liable to the
person seeking his or her aid for abuse of process, unjust
enrichment, and/or fraud.

PART 5

Some Necessary
Corrective Actions

What can be done?

Now that we know the cause, the cure becomes quite obvious.

1. Since the paying of the FICA tax to the Federal Government causes the Union State to be a Constitutional freak by forfeiting its own intended Sovereignty,[58]the first order of business, therefore, is to stop the Union States from paying the freaking tax! We, the Sovereign people of the Union States, together with each of the Sovereign Union States **MUST** become liberated from the FICA tax and any and all Federal Government control stemming therefrom, including, but not limited to, the federal income tax.

2. Aside from the actionable damages against those persons whose behavior renders them culpable as set out in Part 4 above, each and every Union State should by legislative enactment reestablish its Sovereignty by instantly making it unlawful to pay and collect any federal tax, or any other tax attempting to be levied by another entity, even mid fiscal year. This erases any and all doubt about what jurisdiction applies within the Union State territory and removes any unrebuttable presumption that the Federal

---

[58] See Appendix D where the Founders went to great lengths to verify their intentions that the Union States should never lose their Sovereignty.

Government and/or its agents have any power to execute federal law within the territories of any Union State unless Congress has explicitly expressed it to be so together with expressing what designated power Congress is relying on in the relevant federal legislation. In order to be a sovereign entity, said entity must first act like a sovereign and therefore reject, out of hand, any and all taxes from any alien entity whatsoever.

3. The legislation enacted in 2 above should further make it unlawful for any and all instrumentalities of said Union State to pay any taxes whatsoever and must immediately cease paying any taxes even in mid fiscal Year. This erases any and all doubt about what jurisdiction applies within the Union State instrumentalities and removes any unrebuttable presumption that the Federal Government and/or its agents have any power to execute federal law within the instrumentalities of any Union State unless Congress has explicitly expressed it to be so in the relevant federal legislation. This together with 1 above also eliminates the capability for any federal agent or employee from pleading plausible deniability for abuse of process or any other expansion of federal law within the territory of any one of the Union States.

4. Each and every Union State should by legislative enactment make it unlawful for any and all corporations organized under the laws of a Union State to pay or collect taxes from its employees or extort any money from them under the guise of a tax, again even mid fiscal Year. Said legislation should also contain a mandate requiring each such corporation as an employer to inform each old and new employee that it no longer supports Chapter 21 taxes and any employee wishing to participate in the so called Social Security scheme (scam) must deal directly with the Social Security Administration

for future payment arrangements required to so participate. Such legislation should also prohibit any Union State person, including corporations organized under the laws of Union State, from deducting and withholding any tax imposed by another sovereign, bar none.

5. Each and every Union State should by legislative enactment make it unlawful for any and all private sector resident persons of said Union State to pay or collect taxes or extort any money from its employees under the guise of an income tax, again even mid fiscal Year. This erases any and all doubt about what jurisdiction applies within the Union State private sector territory and removes any unrebuttable presumption that the Federal Government and/or its agents have any power to execute federal law within said private sector property and further prevents the federal sump from sucking any more private sector funds from the said Union States free market.

6. In other words, each and every Union State must make it unlawful for ANY foreign jurisdiction to tax itself, its corporations, any corporations organized under the laws of any other Union State operating within its territorial boundaries, and any and ALL persons pursuing their right to their pursuit of happiness within that Union State or any sister Union State.

7. Each and every Union State should by legislative enactment make it illegal to file liens in a form not providing the proper verification or signed affidavits under Union State due process, such as federal tax liens where the County Clerks convert unsubscribed paper documents to a negotiable instrument. Only contracts consummated by consideration and witnessed signatures or Court orders are legally required to process a lien on property and/or the taking of private property.

8. Each and every Union State should by legislative enactment make it a crime in their Union State for any person, including, but not limited to, law enforcement personal, to attempt, in any way, to compromise the sovereignty and the exclusive jurisdiction of said Union State. Said law should make civil damages available to any victims of any such compromise. The background of the Chapter 21 debacle is not known to this author, but the fact that it caused a great deal of pain and suffering to the private people of the various Union States, such pain and suffereing is known and is therefore certainly actionable. While the total amount of damages suffered because of said debacle resulting from the tremendous amounts of money/property confiscated and unlawfully turned over to the Federal Government is immeasurable, it should not hinder any efforts for retribution of those injuries.

9. While the 17th Amendment to the Federal constitution changed the method by which Senators are selected for service in the Senate, it in no way altered the task Constitutionally assigned to each Senator to represent the Sovereign Union States in the Senate house of Congress of the United States. Each and every Union State should by resolution instruct its Union State Senators to submit bills in Congress to make it a crime for any agent, official (elected or not), employee, or individual associated with the United States to aid and abet any official, agent or employee of a Union State in an attempt, in any way, to compromise the sovereignty of any Union State. Such legislation finds its legitimacy under Section IV, Section 4 of the Constitution for the United States wherein it instructs that "The United States shall guarantee to every State in this Union a Republican Form of Government, and shall protect each of them against Invasion" and that must, as

a matter of Constitutional law, include an invasion perpetrated by the United States government as in the matter at hand of divesting the Union States of their Sovereignty by Fraud or otherwise as well as interfering with the welfare of its people by literally stealing from these people under phony, colorable, and unconstitutional law.

10. Each and every Union State should by resolution instruct its Senators to make it a federal crime for any employee of the United States to participate in any way with Union State actors in the behavior that in any way causes a Union State to be subordinate to the United States. An example being, of course, the accepting of any FICA taxes by any agent of the Federal Government from any Union State Actor.

11. Each and every Union State should, by resolution, instruct its Senators to propose and pass a bill requiring the Senate to reexamine all federal legislation passed during the period of time when anyone of the Union States was acting as an instrumentality of the United States. This is necessary because neither the Senate nor the House were Constitutionally convened with representatives from Sovereign Union States capable of voting on any Bills before them. During the time that all the Union States were posing as instrumentalities of the United States, the passage of bills was simply a façade requiring the mass repeal of all such acts and any act deemed desirable must be resubmitted to a legitimate Congress composed of legitimate representatives from **Sovereign** Union States.

12. Each Union State should, by resolution, instruct its respective Senators to inform the Commissioner of the Internal Revenue Service that said Union State, its instrumentalities, its resident corporations organized under the laws of said Union State, and any and all resident private sector employers are being instructed

by law to cease and desist the paying and collecting of ALL foreign taxes as an unlawful practice within the territory of said Union State for the simple matter that a) Congress was never given the power to tax a foreign corporation such as the Union States[59], b) a reading of Chapter 21 using the definitions therein proves that Congress didn't in fact or in law impose a tax on any one of the Union States and any and all entities domiciled or existing as a legitimate sovereign person of said Union State or any of its sister Union States, and c) said Union State will not accept any direct tax bill for any of the debt incurred by United States through the Unconstitutional Federal Reserve debt created without substance together with any associated bailouts. I.e. all Union States must obey the Constitution and NOT make anything but Gold or Silver as payment for payment of debt.

13. For those Union States who fail to voluntarily move to reestablish their constitutional Sovereignty, the sovereign citizens of that Union State need by public ballot referendum to force the Union State to enact the proper legislation in the flavor of the above set out recommendations.

10th Amendment Resolutions

Many Union States are passing 10th Amendment Resolutions in an effort to restore their Sovereignty. However, all the ones that I have reviewed amount to nothing more than a whining or bitch session to the Federal Government containing absolutely no change in Union State actor behavior. I just recently learned of an appropriate quip relating to the research for a solution to

---

[59]   "The United States Government is a Foreign Corporation with respect to a State." 19 Corpus Jurus Secundum §884, In re: Marriam's Estate, 36 N.Y. 505, 141 N.Y. 479, Affirmed in United States v. Perkins, 163 U.S. 625

any problematic matter that "You cannot expect the problem to fix the problem." Since the Federal Government is ultimately the problem here, it makes no sense to seek aid from the problem, the ballooning Federal Government, which simply wants to achieve more and more power until it replaces both We the People and the Union States to become the residual ultimate power over the entire territory we call the United States of America as the omnipotent Central government. In other words occupy all the Union States and each of the Sovereign People attached there to. The first rule of sovereignty is that he who professes to be sovereign must first act like a sovereign. A sovereign may acquire his sovereignty in many ways. He can gain sovereignty by force (war), he can gain it by popular vote, he can gain it by inheritance, or he can gain it, as in our Constructional Republic, by its mere existence as being created by We the People for the purpose of guarding and preserving our Life, Liberty, and the pursuit of Happiness (Property). In all cases, no matter how created, the sovereign is solely responsible to protect his Sovereign Status. It fundamentally goes with the territory. It just so happens that We the People created two Sovereigns as a means of providing two sets of counter opposing powers for the sole purpose of providing for a self-regulating balance of powers assuming each would diligently protect its powers and thus its sovereignty. The problem, as it turns out, is that the Union States failed to properly protect their powers and lost their sovereignty as a result (and, in the process, has allowed the Federal Government to overstep its Constitutional bounds while attempting to occupy the sovereign people in the process).

The Tenth Amendment Center (Tenth Amendment Center [info@tenthamendmentcenter.com]) posted a proposed 10th Amendment Resolution by the Governor of Wyoming. First, we need to understand that from the mere wording of the first 10 Amendments, they do NOT grant any rights, whatsoever. They are merely prohibitions against the newly created Federal Government from the infringement of any declared rights under the umbrella of the unalienable Rights to Life, Liberty, and

Pursuit of Happiness (property) or those rights/powers granted to the Union States by We the People. In other words, **THERE ARE NO CONSTITUTIONALLY GRANTED RIGHTS**, only Constitutional Probations[60] against infringements by the United States of any of those already in existence.

The 10th Amendment Resolution by the Governor of Wyoming is offered here as an example of a non-functioning resolution that will accomplish absolutely nothing in the way of reestablishing the Union State of Wyoming's Sovereignty. Following the posted proposed Resolution is my reply and what I think is the necessary additions to the proposed resolution showing what needs to be added to the resolution in order to actually alter the Union State of Wyoming's behavior in such a manner as to cause the Union State of Wyoming to begin acting like a Sovereign. In other words, put some teeth into the resolution that extends far beyond the purpose of displaying smiles. The next step is to lay the necessary political foundation for the ongoing behavior required to protect that sovereignty.

Draft of Wyoming's proposed 10th Amendment proposal posted on the 10th Amendment Center on or about July 28th, 2009

Wyoming Governor Dave Freudenthal today transmitted the following memorandum and proposed resolution on state sovereignty to the Wyoming Legislature's Management Council.

(h/t Mike Johnson, EverythingCody.com)

Freudenthal, a Democrat, was previously a US attorney for the Clinton administration, and is currently serving his 2nd term as Governor of Wyoming. He endorsed Barack Obama

---

[60] See the "Bill of What" at poorclydesalmanac.info for an analysis of the so-called Bill of Rights.

for president and is commonly referred to as one of the most popular governors in the country.

MEMORANDUM

To: Management Council Members
From: Dave Freudenthal, Governor
Date: July 28, 2009
Re: Sovereignty Resolution

As you know, individual states have been adopting Sovereignty Resolutions over the past few years. Such resolutions have been considered by the Wyoming Legislature over the years as well. Representative Illoway is working on one for this session.

The attached version expands slightly on the versions currently circulating. The resolution includes a list of specific federal laws and a reference to the idea that retaining lands in federal ownership runs afoul of the "equal footing" doctrine. I am enclosing a possible resolution for your consideration. Clearly this is ultimately a legislative prerogative.[61]

From time to time we all wonder whether sending resolutions to Washington, DC really does any good. On the other hand, it's nice to at least get our view on the record.[62]

---

[61] True, but the budget proposals of an expense item tax is initiated by the Governor.

[62] Isn't that your Senator's job?

DRAFT

A JOINT RESOLUTION requesting Congress to cease and desist from enacting mandates that are beyond the scope of the enumerated powers granted to Congress by the Constitution for the United States.

WHEREAS, the Tenth Amendment to the Constitution of the United States reads as follows: "The powers not delegated to the United States by the Constitution, nor prohibited by it to the States, are reserved to the States respectively, or to the people"; and

WHEREAS, the Tenth Amendment defines the total scope of federal power as being that specifically granted by the Constitution of the United States and no more; and

WHEREAS, the scope of power defined by the Tenth Amendment means that the Federal Government was created by the states specifically to be an agent of the states; and

WHEREAS, today, in 2010, the states are demonstrably treated as agents of the Federal Government; and

WHEREAS, many powers assumed by the Federal Government and federal mandates are directly in violation of the Tenth Amendment to the Constitution of the United States; and

WHEREAS, the Tenth Amendment assures that we, the people of the United States of America and each sovereign state in the union of states, now have, and have always had, rights the Federal Government may not usurp; and

WHEREAS, section 4, article IV, of the Constitution provides, "The United States shall guarantee to every State in this Union a Republican Form of Government," and the Ninth Amendment provides, "The enumeration in the Constitution, of certain rights, shall not be construed to deny or disparage others retained by the people"; and

WHEREAS, the United States Supreme Court has ruled in New York v. United States, 505 U.S. 144 (1992), that Congress may not simply commandeer the legislative and regulatory processes of the states; and

WHEREAS, the Congress of the United States frequently considers and passes laws, and the executive agencies of the Federal Government frequently promulgate regulations, the constitutional authority for which is either absent or tenuous, including, without limitation, the Real ID Act (which imposes significant unfunded mandates upon the states with respect to the traditional state function of driver's licensing), the Endangered Species Act (which, as construed by the United States Fish & Wildlife Service, authorizes a federal executive agency to require specific legislation related to the traditional state function of wildlife management), the Clean Water Act (which, as construed by the Environmental Protection Agency, authorizes a federal executive agency to exercise regulatory jurisdiction over waters which are not subject to federal regulation), the Federal Land Policy and Management Act (which implements a policy of federal lands retention in derogation of the "equal footing" doctrine); and[63]

WHEREAS, a number of proposals from previous administrations and some now pending from the present administration and from Congress may further violate the Constitution of the United States;

NOW, THEREFORE, BE IT RESOLVED BY THE MEMBERS OF THE LEGISLATURE OF THE STATE OF WYOMING:

---

[63]   Like the Chapter 21 scope, most of these listed enactments are carefully written to be applicable only in Federal territory.

Section 1. That the Wyoming Legislature claims sovereignty under the Tenth Amendment to the Constitution of the United States over all powers not otherwise enumerated and granted to the Federal Government by the Constitution of the United States.

Section 2. That this resolution/Bill shall serve as notice and demand to the Federal Government, as our agent, to cease and desist, effective immediately, from enacting mandates that are beyond the scope of these constitutionally delegated powers.

Section 3. That all compulsory federal legislation that directs the states to comply under threat of civil or criminal penalties or sanctions or that requires states to pass legislation or lose federal funding be prohibited or repealed.[64]

Section 4. That the Secretary of State of Wyoming transmit copies of this resolution to the President of the United States, the President of the Senate and Speaker of the House of Representatives of the United States Congress and to the Wyoming Congressional Delegation, with a request that this resolution be officially entered in the congressional record as a memorial to the Congress of the United States of America.

The following is this author's additions necessary to cause the Union State of Wyoming to regain its sovereignty

The restoration of Union State Sovereignty is the single most important political problem We the People are faced with in these turbulent difficult times. It is the ultimate and only solution to the current runaway power and financial mismanagement of the Federal Government. However, the necessary first step

---

[64]   Sovereigns are independent thus the acquisition of a dependence on outside funding is in and of itself a forfeiture of sovereignty. Only a spoiled brat receives funds absent conditions.

is to recognize that the cause is exemplified by Pogo; the cartoon character's profound discover that "We have met the enemy and he is us!" The first step to sovereignty is to act like a sovereign. Currently, as shown above, the 50 Union States are all behaving as if they are subservient instrumentalities of the Federal Government, the United States. Consequently, that is what has to be fixed.

From this work come the following additions to the governor's resolution which will enable the Union State of Wyoming to once again act as if it were a Sovereign as Constitutionally intended and to begin taking the necessary steps to protect it:

WHEREAS, while The Constitution for United States mandates that Congress, at Article IV, Section 4, "shall protect each of them [Union States] from invasion" and while the Supreme Court has ruled that the "The United States Government is a Foreign Corporation with respect to a [Union] State." (see 19 Corpus Jurus Secundum §884, In re: Marriam's Estate, 36 N.Y. 505, 141 N.Y. 479, Affirmed in United States v. Perkins, 163 U.S. 625), any attempts by any agent of the Federal Government to misapply federal law promulgated by Congress under Article I, Section 8, clause 17 powers (the exclusive power to legislate within federal territory) within anyone of the Sovereign Union States is, in fact and law, an invasion from a foreign Corporation with the intent to cause the occupation of the territory of our Union State and its sovereign people; and

WHEREAS The Supreme Court reaffirmed Union State sovereignty in 2002 in its opinion in Federal Marine Commission (FMC) v. South Carolina State Ports Authority, 535 U.S. 743 (2002), wherein Justice Thomas writing the opinion for the Court expresses the abstract of a long chain of legal opinions regarding Union State sovereignty: "Dual sovereignty is a defining feature of our Nation's constitutional Blueprint." See Gregory v. Ashcroft, 501 U.S. 452, 457 (1991). **States, upon ratification of the Constitution, did**

not consent to become mere appendages of the Federal Government. Rather, they entered the Union "with their sovereignty intact;" and

WHEREAS the Congress is really the "House of Sovereigns," the Senators in the Senate representing each of the Sovereign Union States (the 17th Amendment to the federal Constitution notwithstanding) and the Representatives in the House representing the Sovereign people of each of the Union States in the House of Representatives, it therefore is incumbent upon each representative to take his or her direction explicitly from the party for which he or she represents and that his or her free will is to have no influence on his or her voting positions taken and further may incur penalties for doing so; and

WHEREAS the supremacy clause in the Federal Constitution at Article VI, clause 2 declares that "this CONSTITUTION [not the Federal Government], and the [legitimate] Laws of the United States which shall be made in Pursuance thereof . . . shall be the supreme Law of the Land;" and

WHEREAS the notion held in the minds of federal agents, including, but not limited to, federal prosecutors and the President that federal law trumps Union State Law is a treasonous lie; and

WHEREAS accepting money from any foreign corporation compromises Union State Sovereignty with respect to said corporation; and

WHEREAS the attempted act of one sovereign taxing another sovereign is a political and legal impossibility. First the phrase "sovereigns taxing sovereigns" self-destructs by the mere concepts represented by the semantics involved. It is an oxymoron and a linguistic and political absurdity. There is a distinction between constitutionally separate "sovereigns." For one sovereign entity to tax another leaves the taxed one subservient to the taxing authority of the other. Consequently the act of taxing a sovereign fundamentally destroys the sovereignty of the one being taxed. This is true both in the symbolic statement of paying the tax and in the practical effect of supporting the sovereign party. So, in our constitutional structure, states may not tax each other, and they may not tax property of the Federal Government. The District of Columbia does not tax the property owned by foreign governments, and New York does not tax the property owned by the United Nations. Certainly this principle carries through to the fact that the Federal Government Sovereign, the United States, may not tax any of the Union State Sovereigns; and

WHEREAS paying a tax to a foreign corporation, in this case the United States, together with collecting same on behalf of a "foreign Corporation" from employees further compromises Union State sovereignty and unlawfully burdens the employees and the sovereign people of said Union State; and

WHEREAS Sovereignty only exists if the Sovereign protects and enforces it, otherwise the Sovereign compromises its Sovereignty by dependence and subordinate obedience to another Sovereign, i.e., a sovereign is only a sovereign if it in fact behaves as one; and

WHEREAS the Legislature for the Union State of Wyoming finds that the body of Federal Law is promulgated under Congress's power to legislate exclusively only within and relative to the territorial jurisdiction of the United States (Federal Government) as granted by Article I, Section 8, Clause 17 and Article IV, Section 3, Clause 2;[65] and

WHEREAS the Legislature for the Union State of Wyoming finds that during the Eisenhower administration a committee was

---

[65]   See Appendix C

formed to study the Jurisdiction Over Federal Areas Within the [Union] States and that said committee formulated a two part report titled REPORT OF THE INTERDEPARTMENTAL COMMITTEE FOR THE STUDY OF JURISDICTION OVER FEDERAL AREAS WITHIN THE STATES of which Part I, *The Facts and Committee Recommendations,* was submitted to the Attorney General and transmitted to the President in the month of April, 1956 and Part II, *A text of the Law* of Legislative Jurisdiction, was submitted to the Attorney General and transmitted to the President in the month of June, 1957; wherein The Union State of Wyoming Statutes for ceding jurisdiction to the United States for the property owned by the United States for Constitutional purposes is found on pages 224 to 225 of said Part I; and

WHEREAS the 17th Amendment for the United States upon ratification altered the manner in which Senators sitting in the Senate of Congress were to be appointed. It did not, however, in any way alter the function and duties of the appointed Senators which were to represent the Sovereign Union State from which they were elected in the Senate House of Congress; and

WHEREAS Federal Law at 26 U.S.C. §7701 (a)(9) specifically defines the term United States to be:

> **(9) United States:** The term "United States" when used in a geographical[66] sense includes only the States and the District of Columbia; and

WHEREAS Federal Law at 26 U.S.C. §7701 (a)(10) specifically defines the term States to be:

> **(10) State:** The term "State" shall be construed to include the District of Columbia, where such

---

[66]   Geographical means Territorial which means Jurisdictional

construction is necessary to carry out provisions of this title;[67] and

WHEREAS the Legislature for the Union State of Wyoming finds that the 14th amendment[68] applies strictly to Federal territory (defined as the United States).

"It is claimed that the plaintiff is a citizen of the United States and of this State. Undoubtedly she is. It is argued that she became such by force of the first section of the Fourteenth Amendment, already recited. This, however, is a mistake. It could as well be claimed that she became free by the effect of the Thirteenth Amendment, by which slavery was abolished; for she was no less a citizen than she was free before the adoption of either of these amendments. No white person born within the limits of the United States, and subject to their jurisdiction, or born without those limits, and subsequently naturalized under their laws, owes the status of citizenship to the recent amendments to the Federal Constitution. The history and aim of the Fourteenth Amendment is well known, and the purpose had in view in its adoption well understood. That purpose was to confer the status of citizenship upon a class of persons domiciled within the limits of the United States, who could not be brought within the operation of the naturalization laws because native born, and whose birth, though native, had at the same time left them without the status of citizenship. These persons were not white persons, but were, in the main, persons of African descent, who had been held in slavery in this country, or, if having themselves never been held in slavery, were the native-born

---

[67] This is a Federal State NOT a Union State. It does not include Union States.

[68] See analysis below at page 126

descendants of slaves. Prior to the adoption of the Fourteenth Amendment it was settled that neither slaves, nor those who had been such, nor the descendants of these, though native and free born, were capable of becoming citizens of the United States. (Dread Scott v. Sanford, 19 How. 393.) The Thirteenth Amendment, though conferring the boon of freedom upon native-born persons of African blood, had yet left them under an insuperable bar as to citizenship; and it was mainly to remedy this condition that the Fourteenth Amendment was adopted . . .

"This is recent history—familiar to all . . . pp. 46-47.

". . . each state was a sovereign and independent state, and the states had confederated only for the purposes of general defense and to promote the general welfare . . . p. 49.

"This circumstance [privilege of elective franchise] has given rise to a notion in some quarters that the privilege of voting and the status of citizenship are necessarily connected in some way—so that the existence of the one argues that of the other. But the history of the country shows that there was never any foundation for such a view." p. 50. [Brackets original.] *Van Valkenburg v. Brown, 43 Cal. 43 (1872)*

WHEREAS Federal Law at 26 U.S.C. §7701(a)(30) specifically defines a "U.S. Person" to be:

(a)   When used in this title, where not otherwise distinctly expressed or manifestly incompatible with the intent thereof—

(30)   **United States person** The term "United States person" means—

(A)   a citizen or resident of the United States,

(B)   a domestic partnership,

(C)   a domestic corporation,
(D)   any estate (other than a foreign estate, within the meaning of paragraph (31)), and
(E)   any trust if—

    (i)   a court within the United States is able to exercise primary supervision over the administration of the trust, and,

    (ii)   one or more United States persons have the authority to control all substantial decisions of the trust; and

WHEREAS Federal Law at 8 U.S.C. 1101(a)(3) specifically defines an alien to be:

(a)   As used in this chapter—
(3)   The term "alien" means any person not a citizen or national of the United States;

WHEREAS Federal Law at 26 U.S.C.7701 (b)(1)(B) specifically defines Nonresident Alien to be:

(B)   Nonresident alien:

An individual is a nonresident alien if such individual is neither a citizen of the United States nor a resident of the United States (within the meaning of subparagraph (A)[69]);

WHEREAS, the Supreme Court has opined that "The United States Government is a Foreign Corporation with respect to a [Union] State." *19 Corpus Jurus Secundum §884, In re: Marriam's Estate, 36 N.Y. 505, 141 N.Y. 479, Affirmed in United States v. Perkins, 163 U.S. 625*; and

---

[69]   Which is the definition of a Resident Alien.

WHEREAS, a Union State government, by Constitutional law and legislative definitions, is a Foreign Corporation with respect to the United States Government;

WHEREAS instrumentalities of the United States have no voting representative power in Congress, (see Appendix E) the entire body of legislation passed during the submission of Union States, including the State of Wyoming, as instrumentalities of the United States is called into question by the mere consequence that Congress could not have been in session during these times for the simple reason that no legitimate representatives from the Sovereign Union States were seated during that time.

Section 5. That henceforth, the Union State of Wyoming shall reassert its Constitutionally recognized Sovereignty by appropriate legislation for each of the following: 1)that hereinafter, no Agency or other instrumentality of the State of Wyoming will be authorized under State Law to accept any funds whatsoever from the Government of the United States (Federal Government); and 2) that hereinafter, no Agency, instrumentality, or Corporation created by and/or under the authority of the Union State of Wyoming will by authorized under any State Law to pay any tax or collect any tax on behalf of any foreign corporation, including, but not limited to, the Government of the United States (Federal Government) such as the FICA and income taxes.

Section 6. That henceforth, any and all federal officers attempting to enforce any federal legal process in the territory of the Union State of Wyoming against any citizen of the Union State of Wyoming must file suit and gain authority for extradition from the Courts of the Union State of Wyoming whereupon The Union State of Wyoming law enforcement agents/officers shall take care of all necessary legal process ordered by an appropriate Wyoming Court to be executed within the Union State of Wyoming.

Section 7. That the Union State of Wyoming will henceforth consider any and all federal agent's direct actions or involvement with any and all citizens and residents of the Union State of Wyoming without a Court Order from an appropriate Court of the Union State of Wyoming to be considered a criminal "Abuse of Process," invasion for occupation,[70] and prosecuted as such, including, but not limited to the removal of any Union State citizen or resident from the jurisdiction of the Union State of Wyoming absent a lawful extradition process conducted in the Courts of the Union State of Wyoming.

Section 8. That each Senator's Constitutional task and duty is to represent the Union State from which he or she was elected, therefore, each Senator from the Union State of Wyoming shall henceforth, in all matters undertaken in Congress, take his or her explicit direction from the Legislature of Wyoming by applicable resolution based on reviews conducted with each Senator and officially documented as voting and legislative instructions for said Senators. (This shall be included in the Senator's Oath of Office before taking his or her seat in the Senate, the breach of which will stand as evidence of perjury.) Furthermore, anyone, including a Senator, found to have tampered with the aforesaid officially documented instructions shall, if convicted, be incarcerated for no less than 5 years but not more than 10.

Section 9. That each Senator from the Union State of Wyoming shall henceforth be directed by the Legislator of said State of Wyoming to jointly sponsor a Senate Bill putting the United States on NOTICE of the change in the Union State of Wyoming's status and that it is now taking its

---

[70]   Attempted occupation by any means can be considered an act of war and thus an act of trreason

constitutionally proper place as a peer Sovereign next to the United States as an integral part of the Dual Sovereignty which is the defining feature of our Nation's Constitutional Blueprint. (See Appendix B)

Section 10. That the Union State of Wyoming henceforth presumes that the entire body of Federal Statutes applies only within and relative to Federal territorial jurisdiction as specified in Article I, Section 8, Clause 17 or Article IV, Section 3, Clause 2 unless and until the Union State of Wyoming is specifically named in a Federal statute (act of Congress) together with the specific power granted by the Constitution which is being exercised to grant jurisdiction in said statute within the Union State of Wyoming and such presumption includes Federal Titles 1 through Title 50 excepting only those conditions enumerated in the REPORT OF THE INTERDEPARTMENTAL COMMITTEE FOR THE STUDY OF JURISDICTION OVER FEDERAL AREAS WITHIN THE [UNION] STATES (Available from http://www. constitution.org/liberlib.htm. in digital form downloadable as HTML, WP, Text.)

Section 11. That henceforth every Law Library associated with or within the Union State of Wyoming will contain a copy of the *Report Of The Interdepartmental Committee For The Study Of Jurisdiction Over Federal Areas Within The [Union] States* and made available to anyone enlisting the services of such Library. If it was appropriate for President Eisenhower, it is certainly appropriate for the litigators in the Union State of Wyoming. (See the source and web address for reprinted copies above on page 78)

Section 12. That each Senator from the Union State of Wyoming shall in due course jointly sponsor a Senate Bill which mandates that all federal laws promulgated or enacted shall specify explicitly which Constitutional power the law is calling upon for its authority and enforcement without which said enactment cannot, as a matter of law, have any influence, impact, or application within the territory of the Union State of Wyoming.

Section 13. That in due course a communication mechanism be established throughout the Union State of Wyoming for each Congressional District providing a method by which each and every Sovereign person of the Union State of Wyoming can input his or her political desires to their respective Representatives and resulting input from the Sovereign people of Wyoming shall by law be the only influence the respective Representative may use in determining how he votes; all other input notwithstanding, including by lobby, and his or her own volition.

Section 14. That in due course a new position be established within each Representative District to catalogue and compile input from the sovereign people of such District to be interpreted and constructed as a set of official documents of instructions served on each Representative directing his voting and legislative behavior. Any skullduggery or interference with the integrity of said official instructions will be a criminal felony punishable for no less than 5 years but no more than 10.

Section 15. That henceforth all Acts, Regulations, and agency instructions shall be repealed which instruct the sending of Union State of Wyoming sovereign people data to any foreign jurisdiction, including, but not limited to, the United States (Federal Government) and peer Union States.

Section 16. That henceforth all Acts, regulations, and agency instructions which mimic federal law and/or regulations which in any way abrogates personal Liberties and essentially throws Union State of Wyoming sovereign people under the runaway train of federal law shall be Repealed or nullified by the now Sovereign Union State of Wyoming.

Section 17. That having eliminated its subservient status to its peer sovereign, the United States (Federal Government) and reaffirmed its Union State Sovereignty, the Union State of Wyoming will henceforth Repatriate itself by Official Proclamation and also reaffirm its mandated Duty to provide, protect, and maintain each and every Union State of Wyoming emancipated sovereign person's Rights to Life, Liberty, and property.

Section 18. That in view of the fact that the Citizens of the Union State of Wyoming are aliens to the United States they are in turn Nonresident Aliens as defined in federal Law and therefore not subject in any way to federal law.

Section 19. That in consequence of the sovereign people of the Union State of Wyoming being repatriated, such repatriation must include a resolution (proclamation, declaration or statute) to publically recognize that the now repatriated sovereign people of Wyoming from this time forward will have in their possession the full unalienable rights of a king granted by and through the Declaration Independence where they are dutifully protected from the federal government by the first 10 Amendments of the federal Constitution. (See Appendix B)

Section 20. Said repatriation of the sovereign people of the Union State of Wyoming shall include that henceforth in any and all records designating residence or citizenship to be that of the United States will be changed to reflect that the person is a repatriated sovereign person of the Union State of Wyoming.

Section 21. The legislature for the Union State of Wyoming shall enact a law for the purpose of protecting the repatriation of the people of the Union State of Wyoming from any force whatsoever in attempting to stealthily alter said person's citizenship without his or her consent upon the condition of full disclosure.

Section 22. That having expelled its Subservient status relative to its companion Sovereign, the United States (Federal Government) and reaffirmed its Union State Sovereignty, the Union State of Wyoming shall henceforth Repatriate ALL State sovereign people of the Union State of Wyoming by rescinding their unintended and errant Citizen Status of the United States thus removing the yoke of the federal income tax and provide aid and assistance for each repatriated individual sovereign person of the Union State of Wyoming to have all their Social Security Money AND Federal income tax paid returned on the basis of fraud minus any benefits paid to said persons. The foregoing procedure is started by first filing SSA Form 521 with the appropriate verbiage to rescind each person's SSN and revert back to the status of a Union State sovereign person status which was Constitutionally intend from the very beginning. The Union State of Wyoming will further modify its voting records and all other records containing references to the individual as a "Citizen of the United States," to that of a repatriated "Citizen of the Union state of Wyoming." These steps are necessary as a token of apology to the people of the Union State of Wyoming's Constitutional error for allowing the Federal Government to essentially occupy the Union State of Wyoming destroying the defining feature of our Nation's Constitutional Blueprint of Dual Sovereignty by paying and collecting Chapter 21 excise taxes.

That's this author's recommendations for the Tenth Amendment Resolution for the Restoration of Sovereignty for the Union State of Wyoming. Other Union States can certainly benefit from the suggestion herein made for the Union State of Wyoming The reference to the REPORT OF THE INTERDEPARTMENTAL COMMITTEE FOR THE STUDY OF JURISDICTION OVER FEDERAL AREAS WITHIN THE [UNION] STATES is an extremely important study on the constitutional split between Federal and Union State Sovereigns making up the Dual Sovereignty which has been ruled by the Supreme Court in 2002 as the "defining feature of our Nation's Constitutional

Blueprint." While the REPORT is far too lengthy to undertake a review here, everyone interested in the REAL Constitutional jurisdictional boundaries between their Union State and the Federal Government should do themselves a great service and read the REPORT. Reprinted copies of the REPORT can be found at the Constitutional Research Associates, P.O. package 550, So. Holland, Illinois 60473 with the link found on page 78.

In my mind it is the political Bible for the understanding of the proper jurisdictional boundaries between the United States (the Federal Government) and one's Union State. This author would even go so far as to recommend that it should be taught in the public schools. There, for sure, should be a copy in every Union State's Legislative Library. Appendix B is an abstract of that study and should prove enlightening for those inclined to pursue the study.

PART 6

Why Union State Sovereignty?

Benefits stemming from the Reformation of Union State Sovereignty by abating the payment and collection of Chapter 21 (FICA), etal., taxes include:

1. Rids the Union States of any hint of federal jurisdiction except as expressly stated under the authority of the Constitution that Congress intended the federal legislation to be applicable within Union State territory utilizing an appropriate power specified in the Constitution for the United States authorizing Congress to so do.

    a. Eliminates the Chapter 21 tax thereby removing any lawful application of the federal income tax on Union State employees and the employees of their instrumentalities, Union State chartered corporation employees, and any and all private sector contractors within the Union State territories, etc.

    b. Ditto for all private sector employees working for Union State Corporations and/or any other private sector business not organized under the "laws of the United States."

    c. Eliminates the interference of any Union State functions including Law Enforcement by any federal agents or agencies such as the FBI, ATF, DEA, etc.

2. Restores the legitimacy of Congress as the House of Sovereigns which also restores Congress' power to enact enforceable laws.

3. Eliminates any ability for the Federal Government to enforce the Real ID card, the Patriot Act, Homeland Security, Gun Control, or any other federal legislation

wherein the act itself limits its enforcement to strictly federal territory.

4. Eliminates any exposure to any and all federal health care legislation.

5. Restores the integrity to Congress's Constitutional and proper purpose assuming the Union State legislators again direct their Senators' action while they sit in Congress. The restoration of the Union States to their sovereign status removes the question of the validity of all future Congressional Legislation.

6. Reduces the Union State and local budgets for labor costs by 15.3 percent off the top, that's 7.65 percent for the employee's share of FICA together with 7.65 percent for the employer's share. Since most all contracted service by the Union States and their instrumentalities are now protected from federal Chapter 21 taxes, the 15.3 percent reduction in contracted service cost should carry through to the budget's bottom line as well. Since most income taxpayers average around an additional 20 percent of their wages given up to income taxes, if the employees, Union State wide, were to split that advantage, 10 percent to themselves and 10 percent given back to the Union State, each such employee would have an additional 10 percent of his or her existing wages to spend in his or her local community and the Union State could also see the 10 percent savings the employees plus the 15.3 percent savings from the elimination of the Social Security tax. The Union State and its instrumentalities could then begin to see a total budget reduction in the neighborhood of 25 percent and there would be a mass increase in the spendable revenue throughout the territories of the Union States. It is a realization of the lessons learned from both the Henry Ford model and Austrian Economics. At the same time, each Union State would benefit from a legislative enactment forbidding any contractor who chooses to pay any tax to the

Federal Government from participating in any of the bidding for offerings put forth by the Union State or any of its instrumentalities.

7. Uncouples the Union State sovereign people from the phony imaginary debt created by the fiat artificial currency put into circulation by the private (unconstitutional) Federal Reserve, the brain child of Congress when it reneged on its constitutional mandate that it mint coin and regulate the value thereof and likewise punish for the act od=f conversion. By the establishment of a private central bank in 1913, Congress allowed the central bank to create trillions of phony and fraudulent debt created without consideration. That is to say, Congress and the Federal Reserve created this enormous debt by leveraging valueless phony money through the leverage of fractional reserve loans which piled valueless money upon valueless money, offered to member Banks all to be loaned out without any consideration. The debt is simply a façade of debt allowing banks to loan bookkeeping entries without consideration but will be collecting payments against the phony loans from productive Citizens using their labor and production to provide consideration to attempt to extinguish the debts created by such phony transaction, both private and public. Let Congress now divulge its plan to get itself out of its debt burden. The Union States need to exert their Constitutional sovereignty and refuse to be pawns of the Federal Government and its Central Bank to be duped into voluntarily contracting to help "bail out the private international banks" with which the members of Congress conspired to fleece the citizens of the Union States by unconstitutionally delegating its constitutional mandated duty to a bevy of already super rich private bank owners willing to trade a little bribe money for mass power in the first place.

8. One can expect that the above increase of the disposable revenue of Union State citizens will spark an economic boom which will materialize as a drastic decrease in unemployment, making room in the process for Union State employees to seek more productive jobs due to the fact that the Union State services should atrophy along with the decrease in Union State services needed to be provided.

PART 7

Unfinished Business

Sublata causa tollitur effectus.

Remove the cause and the effect will cease. 2 Bl. Com. 203. As discussed and analyzed in detail, the cause of the loss of Union State sovereignty is the paying of an excise tax to the Federal Government, The United States. However the period for which Union State Sovereignty did not exist created other problems for which removing the cause does not automatically cure.

Repatriate the Union State Sovereign People.

In view of the fact that a great majority of Union State people believe (from fraud and/or indoctrination) that the Federal Government has eminent power over them, they may find themselves in a confusing quandary torn between allegiance to the United States and its taxes and the emancipated lifestyle of Liberty, Independence, and Responsibility. It therefore becomes incumbent upon the now Sovereign Union States to formulate a turnkey process permitting the bewildered people to take up his or her place as a now Sovereign person among his or her fellow Sovereign people relying on the now Sovereign Union State to provide and protect his or her Liberty and Sovereignty.

This includes having the Union States conduct the re-naturalization process for all immigrants wishing to make their first residency citizenship in that Union State. This is necessary to help each and every new Union State person to understand the technical difference between a federal, U.S., citizen from that of a Union State person. In earlier days the Union States had a naturalization process which an immigrant could opt for in the very beginning and the Supreme Court has suggested it, therefore, each Union State by searching its archives should be able to re-implement that process again to allow our immigrants the choice between a Sovereign person of one (and therefore all) of our Sovereign Union States or a subject class citizen of the United States (Federal Government) and at the same time solve the 14th Amendment problem.

As for the majority of existing Union State people they have, by fraud and/or indoctrination, been misled to unknowingly becoming Citizens of the United States by various nefarious means in contradistinction to sovereign people of the Union State in which they chose to live. Consequently, one of the most pressing tasks needing to be addressed immediately following or in conjunction with the Union States restoration of its Sovereignty is the **Repatriation of Its own People**. To most, this will seem strange and foreign. However, We the People, the holders of the Ultimate Political Power, are going to have to study this issue in detail, if they want their Liberty back as this is of paramount importance in the restoration of their own Sovereignty as well. It starts with each Union State designing a turnkey process to file the necessary affidavits and memorandums of law to restore each human individual's Sovereign status to that of a Sovereign Union State person. That turnkey process must include the filing of the form SSA 521 to rescind the form SSA-5. Also the records of all repatriated individuals must be revamped so that the notation appearing on each and every record of the individual that contains the words "Citizen of the United States" needs to be purged and replaced with the words "People of the Union State of _____."

The following is a few authorities to help individuals start to gain the knowledge needed to be able to understand the significant differences between a Citizen of the United States and a person of a Union State. The two are in no way the same. Observe what the courts have to say:

>"We have in our political system a government of the United States and a government of each of the

several States. Each one of these governments is distinct from the others, and each has citizens of its own . . ." *United States v. Cruikshank*, 92 U.S. 542 (1875)

". . . he was not a citizen of the United States, he was a citizen and voter of the State, . . ." "One may be a citizen of a State and yet not a citizen of the United States".

McDonel v. The State, 90 Ind. 320 (1883)

"That there is a citizenship of the United States and citizenship of a state, . . ." *Tashiro v. Jordan*, 201 Cal. 236 (1927)

"A citizen of the United States is a citizen of the Federal Government . . ."

Kitchens v. Steele, 112 F.Supp 383

"The governments of the United States and of each state of the several states are distinct from one another. The rights of a citizen under one may be quite different from those which he has under the other".

Colgate v. Harvey, 296 U.S. 404; 56 S.Ct. 252 (1935)

"There is a difference between privileges and immunities belonging to the citizens of the United States as such, and those belonging to the citizens of each state as such".

Ruhstrat v. People, 57 N.E. 41 (1900)

"The rights and privileges, and immunities which the fourteenth constitutional amendment and Rev. St. section 1979 [U.S. Comp. St. 1901, p. 1262], for its enforcement, were designated to protect, are such as belonging to citizens of the United States as such, and not as citizens of a state." *Wadleigh v. Newhall* 136 F. 941 (1905)

". . . rights of national citizenship as distinct from the fundamental or natural rights inherent in state citizenship". *Madden v. Kentucky*, 309 U.S. 83: 84 L.Ed. 590 (1940)

SUI JURIS. One who has all the rights to which a freeman is entitled; one who is not under the power of another, as a slave, a minor, and the like.

2. To make a valid contract, a person must, in general, be sui juris. Every one of full age is presumed to be sui juris. Story on Ag. p. 10.

A little research will reveal that Citizens of the United States are a subject class of citizens, while Union States Citizens are, by State constitutional decree, **Sui Juris** Citizens.

Nonresident Aliens

Since the Supreme Court has opined that:

"The government of the United States is a foreign corporation with respect to a [Union] state."

It therefore conceptually follows that the Union States are foreign corporations to the United States. Consequently, a citizen of the United States is a nonresident alien when living in one of the Union States. The drawback of that is that nonresident aliens are unable to sit on juries because juries are required to be a collection of the Defendant's peers and a peer would have to be a Citizen of the jurisdiction in which the matter was being litigated.

Additionally, what else might cement the proper Citizenship status of the people of the Union States, restore their constitutionally intended Sovereignty, and preserve for all time this intended Sovereignty as inhabitants of various Sovereign Union States?[71] In Appendix B we exhaustively analyzed the Constitutional relationship between the Union States and the Federal Government. In the context of that Dual Sovereignty what then is the Constitutional jurisdictional relationship between a Union State and the Federal Government in federal legislation?

Since each governmental sovereign organ has constitutionally delegated powers, the fundamental first principle question is what is the scope and sphere of said delegated powers? The answer is that each is sovereign within the boundary(s) of its assigned and/or acquired territory(s); the United States being sovereign over all territory ceded to it by the [Union] States and the [Union] States remaining sovereign over their own territory "as to all powers reserved."

The conduit through which all constitutionally delegated powers flow is jurisdiction. As to what jurisdiction remained with the Union States, the Supreme Court asked and answered the question:

> "What then, is the extent of jurisdiction which a state possesses? We answer, without hesitation; the jurisdiction is co-extensive with its territory; co-extensive with its legislative [sovereign] power." _United States v. Baevans_, 16 U.S. (3 Wheat) 336, 386, 387.

---

[71]   See Appendix A.

Since the sphere and scope of the delegated powers for each Union State and the United States (Federal Government) is co-extensive with the jurisdiction of its legislature, coextensive with its territory, it remains to be shown just what basis one uses to determine such jurisdiction as a first principle issue of Constitutional law. The whole concept of dual but mutually exclusive jurisdictions between the United States and the States of the Union was further ratified by an *Interdepartmental Committee for the Study of Jurisdiction over Federal Areas within the States*, convened in 1957[72], and chaired by the then Assistant Attorney General, Mansfield D. Sprague during the Eisenhower administration. The Committee published the text of their findings and recommendations in two volumes, the first designated as *Part I, The Facts and Committee Recommendations* and the second as Part II, A Text of the Law of Legislative Jurisdiction. It is in Part II that the Committee ratifies the concept of dual but separate sovereignties," to wit:

> **"The Constitution gives express recognition to but one means of Federal acquisition of legislative jurisdiction—by [Union] State consent under Article I, section 8, Clause 17 . . . . Justice McLean suggested that the Constitution provided the sole mode of jurisdiction and that if this mode is not pursued, no transfer of jurisdiction can take place.** *Id @ 41* (emphasis added)

> "It scarcely needs to be said that unless there has been a transfer of jurisdiction (1) pursuant to clause 17 by Federal acquisition of land with [Union] State consent, or (2) by cession from the [Union] State to the Federal Government, or unless the Federal Government has reserved jurisdiction upon the admission of the [Union] State, the Federal

---

[72] This is also incorporated into the suggested additions to the Wyoming 10th Amendment resolution at page 100 above, along with the necessary instructions to obtain a copy of the findings.

Government possesses no Legislative jurisdiction over any area within the [Union] State,—such jurisdiction being for the exercise by the Union State, subject to non-interference by the [Union] State with Federal functions. *Id @45*(emphasis added).

"The Federal Government cannot, by unilateral action on its part, acquire legislative jurisdiction over any area within the exterior boundaries of a [Union] State." *Id @46* (emphasis added).

"On the other hand, while the Federal Government has power under various provisions of the Constitution to define, and prohibit as criminal, certain acts or omissions occurring anywhere in the United States [of America], it has no power to punish for various crimes [such as drugs firearms, etc], jurisdiction over which is retained by the [Union] States under our Federal-State system of government, unless such crime occurs in areas as to which legislative jurisdiction has been vested in the Federal Government." *Id @ 107*. (Insertions added by the author)

The last paragraph of the Committee's findings parallels exactly what Thomas Jefferson had to say opposing the "Sedition Act" when he wrote *The Kentucky Resolutions* addressing Congress's authority to punish such crimes, to wit:

"2. Resolved, That the Constitution of the United States, having delegated to Congress a power to punish treason, counterfeiting the securities and current coin of the United States, piracies, and felonies committed on the high seas, and offenses against the law of nations, and no other crimes whatsoever . . . ." (emphasis added)

In the context of the Dual Sovereignty we see that each has their separate and distinct jurisdictional territories over which their respective legislatures are constitutionally responsible for. And the Supreme Court further adds that:

> "The United States Government is a Foreign Corporation with respect to a [Union] State." *19 Corpus Jurus Secundum §884, In re: Marriam's Estate, 36 N.Y. 505, 141 N.Y. 479, Affirmed in United States v. Perkins, 163 U.S. 625 (1896).*

Consequently, if the United States Government is a Foreign Corporation with respect to a Union State, it follows, conversely, that a Union State is foreign entity with respect to the United States and its Government. Since the United States Government's legislation has no authority in a foreign land, it therefore has no authority in a Union State which is foreign to the United States Government.

Congress was fully aware of its limited ability to tax Union State Citizens because of their foreign status, so they created a term of art called a Nonresident Alien (NRA). Because Congress was aware of their dilemma that the majority of people living on the North American Continent (as Union State Citizens) were basically untouchable for taxing purposes, they propagandized the Union State Citizens into thinking they were domestic to the United States, i.e. United States citizens, and were therefore subject to the morass of federal taxing laws. But, at the same time, Congress had to behave legally but hide this NRA status or at least make believe it didn't apply to Union State Citizens by writing convoluted laws that properly treated such a Status as the NRA but used many new "words of art" to do so. So in the course of this treatment Congress had to make all NRAs exempt from all federal taxes and the Treasury Department even created a special 1040 form labeled as the 1040NR to permit NRAs to apply to the Treasury Department for funds erroneously withheld from the NRAs lawful remuneration.

In the analysis above in the taxing statutes defined by Congress at 26 USC, Chapter 21, §3101-3121, the first presumption is that Congress is legislating within its own territory over which it was granted exclusive legislative jurisdiction because there is no hint, much less any legal intent shown, that Congress intended the Internal Revenue code to apply in any territory other than federal territory.

> "'**All** legislation is prima facie territorial.' _Ex Parte Blain_, L.R. 12 Ch Div 522, 528; _State v. Carter_, 27 N.J.L. _499_; _People v. Merril_, 2 Park Crim. Rep. _590_, 596." _American Banana Co. v. United Fruit Co._, 213 U.S.347 (1909) (emphasis added)_.

Additionally, it is well settled that all legislation of Congress is presumed to be territorial unless a contrary intent appears in the Act(s).

> "We thus apply '[t]he canon of construction which teaches that legislation [acts] of Congress; unless contrary intent appears, is meant to apply only within the territorial jurisdiction of the United States.' _Foley Brothers v. Filardo_, 336 U.S. 281, 285, 93 L.Ed 689, 69 S.Ct. _575 (1949)_; See also _Weinberger v. Rossi_, 456 U.S. 25, 32 (1982)." _Argentine Republic v. American Hess_, 488 U.S. 428, 440 _(1989)._

Therefore, when federal statutes fail to show any intent that said statutes apply outside the territorial jurisdiction of the United States, the Federal Government and its agents accordingly fail to possess the required authority to enforce such statues and are thus constitutionally prohibited from doing so. In point of fact, Congress explicitly passed a law articulating such.

TITLE 26 > Subtitle F > CHAPTER 79 >§ 7701
§ 7701. Definitions

(B) Nonresident alien

An individual is a nonresident alien if such individual is neither a citizen of the United States nor a resident of the United States (within the meaning of subparagraph (A)).

Just to be certain that the reader truly understands the existence of the Dual Sovereignty between the United States and the Union States, I offer the following definitions of the "United States" and "State" while we are addressing § 7701 definitions. To wit:

(9) United States

The term "United States" when used in a geographical[73] sense includes only the States and the District of Columbia.

(10) State

The term "State" shall be construed to include[74] the District of Columbia, where such construction is necessary to carry out provisions of this title.

Notice that the definition for the term "State" is not yet available when the term is used in the preceding definition. This is the modus operandi throughout all federal code when dealing with these two terms which this author suspects is done to keep the

---

[73] Territorial sense, thus jurisdictional

[74] If this wording leaves the reader to conclude that the use of the word "includes" means that the definition is merely adding an additional concept to the definition, please read Appendix C for clarification.

common wrong understanding that a Citizen of a Union State is also a citizen of the United States alive and well.

So if you are a resident of say the Union State of New York, and you have never resided in federal territory, you are, by definition, a Citizen of New York, NOT the United States and thus an NRA (Non Resident Alien) in Federal Law. In fact, since Citizenship is an official Individual status, this author is of the opinion that, technically, one must go through some sort of naturalization process to be a Citizen of the United States which calls into question how the Federal Government drags Union States Citizens into its courts without first pleading and proving their citizenship as the facts necessary to provide the jurisdiction for the Federal Courts to hear the matter in the first place. When the Federal Government drags Union State Citizens into Federal Courts by silent presumption for acts committed in Union State territory of United State citizenship, the case is void for want of the Court's jurisdiction.

Consequently, the Union State of Wyoming will henceforth develop a plan to insulate the Citizens of Wyoming from foreign sovereigns and/or corporations and provide a barrier to anyone attempting invoke the 14th Amendment.

The 14th Amendment

Like the entire body of Federal Law, the 14th Amendment is not well understood by the Union State Citizens; nor is it well understood by the people they elect to either Federal or Union State political positions; and the same is likewise true for the instrumentalities of the Union States. Section 1 of the 14th Amendment states that:

> **Section 1.** All persons born or naturalized in the United States and subject to the jurisdiction thereof are citizens of the United States and of the State wherein they reside. No State shall make or

enforce any law which shall abridge the privileges or immunities of citizens of the United States; nor shall any State deprive any person of life, liberty, or property, without due process of law; nor deny to any person within its jurisdiction the equal protection of the laws.

Question: From Section 1, how do we know that the 14th Amendment relates to only federal territory? The first sentence tells us because only Federal territory can contain citizens of the United States and Federal States wherein they could legitimately live. And in the second sentence, only Federal territory over which Congress has exclusive jurisdiction can interface with Citizens of the United States. Thus, the 14th Amendment relates exclusively to Federal territory and Citizens of the United States

This chain of logic points to the fact that a Union State person is an alien to all foreign territory and therefore must, as a matter of legal fact, be a NRA with respect to all Federal legislation. This is covered below in greater detail in Unfinished Business.

Lawful Currency

While the path back to the proper Constitutional structure will solve a great deal of our current political and financial problems, there is still a financial one looming off stage and that is the issue of money. While the Union States are Constitutionally prohibited from issuing Bills of Credit,[75] which are the only thing in circulation today, and required to maintain that nothing but gold or silver can be used to settle debts, the Union States are faced with a "Catch 22" quandary. Since the resurrection of Union State sovereignty will measurably improve the disposable wage revenue for the Union State citizens derived from the funds released to them absent the Federal FICA and income

---

[75]   Article I, Section 10, Clause 1, U.S. Constitution

tax burdens, it can justifiably be foreseen that that economic wellbeing will soon return to the citizens of the Union States. But in order to repair the existing economic infrastructure, the Union States will need to provide some means of lawful currency perhaps other than the gold or silver coin in order to satisfy the Constitutional mandate that they cannot "make any Thing but gold and silver coin a Tender in Payment of Debts."[76] In other words, the hinge pin for valid contracts is the existence of consideration. This may call for the Law of Necessity. It would seem that the Constitutional path to the solution would be for the Union State Legislatures to charter private banks and allow them to issue "bearer bonds" against gold and silver on deposit in these banks.

All methods of "Fractional Reserve lending" will be made unlawful, i.e. a dollar lent will be backed one to one by a lawful dollar (in gold or silver) on deposit. Union State Legislatures could sanction private mints by license as the source for silver and gold coin. No bank would be allowed to be affiliated with any private mint and visa versa. While punitive measures will, by necessity, need to be established for fraud and other nefarious behavior, any concern of jumping ship and hiding in another Union State could be handled in the same manner in which the Union States deal today with interstate matters associated with motor vehicle regulations. To be sure, there are other proposals for the remedy of the *consideration* quandary which need to come to the light of day to fill the void of the Federal Government's treasonous reneging of its Constitutional mandate to provide silver and/or gold coin and regulate the value thereof. The valueless paper notes today issued by private banks, owners of the private Federal Reserve, are not capable of providing consideration for contracts, thus voiding almost all contracts attempting to be consummated within each of the 50 Union States and which, together with Fractional Reserve banking, is the primary cause for the recession/depression of 2008 and 2009 in the first place.

---

[76]   Article I, Section 10, Clause 1, U.S. Constitution

One possible solution could be to have all Union State Banks convert their assets to silver and gold coin and require them to exchange Federal Reserve (paper tokens) for these silver and gold coins. The Federal Reserve notes acquired by this process would be used to purchase additional coins. Additionally, the Union States could, by law, sanction legitimate mints to participate in the banking scheme. At the same time, no bank should be sanctioned to act as the mint, i.e., there should be an arm's length association between the banks and the mints, including any and all paths of ownership between them.

This author's background includes being born during the Great Depression on a small farm in New Jersey. On the occasions of his mother being asked how they were able to survive during 1930's depression, she always replied that the family, being on a farm, was self-sufficient and had no notice of any change in the family's financial environment. This same environment of self-sufficiency can be emulated by Sovereign Union States. The current economic catastrophe has the potential of ripping to shreds the economic infrastructure that allowed this Constitutional Republic to flourish in the first instance. However, the Reformation of Union State Sovereignty has the potential to save a major portion of said infrastructure by becoming self-sufficient with the assistance given by other Union States in their ability to trade among them. We the People of each and every Union State must also realize that the bed rock of any economic infrastructure is the production of food, (farming), clothing (textile mills), and shelter (carpentry, etc.) in that order. Therefore, any and all of these privately owned and operated necessity industries must be completely tax exempt from any and all taxes. On the other hand, Corporations involved in these necessity industries and all other types of industries should shoulder the normal corporate taxes for the privilege of existence.[77] After all, they exist at the pleasure of We the People. While the size of Union State governments may shrink out of necessity, with the maintenance of the respective

---

[77]   Any Court decisions to the contrary notwithstanding.

infrastructures, new jobs, from the return of manufacturing, will appear to take up the employment slack created by the shrinking of the Union State municipal governments. Additionally, with a stable monetary system not based on debt, the Union States will experience a paramount return of the private unincorporated farms. Private Citizens will no longer seek the dependent shelter of corporate employment. They all will enjoy the fruits of their Liberty and correspondingly the fruits of their Labor. Generally, house wives, if they so desire, will be permitted economically to return to the sanctity of the home to concentrate on child rearing.

Also, the Union States in all fairness should by resolution instruct their Senators to notify Congress in session that the line item revenue from Chapter 21 taxes will not contain revenue from his or her Union State or its Union State affiliate employers and employees. Such employers and employees include all instrumentalities and corporations **not** incorporated under the laws of the United States or any (Federal) State, all private individual employers and employees, all professional employers and their employees, and any legitimate private business employers and their employees, of any class, operating a lawful business in this Union State.

In addition, each Union State, by legislation enactment, needs to take total control of all its Law Enforcement agencies and by law make them each superior to any agents of foreign jurisdictions, including, but not limited to, the Federal Government. Of course, it would also be imperative to maintain the superiority of the Sheriff of the County as being the highest ranking Law Enforcement officer in all of the Union State Counties. This should be codified in Union State Law.

Other Meaningful Corrective Measures

Repatriate the National Guard

In view of the evidence that the Federal Government not only failed in its Constitutional mandate to protect the Union States from invasion, it became the invader whether for plunder or occupation and it matters not what the objective. Since the offense of Treason requires one to commit and act of war and since occupation by any means is and overt act of war, any federal elected official, agent, appointee, or employee engaged in the act of invasion by entrapping Union State legislatures AND Union State Citizens to inapplicable federal taxes has been an accessory in fact to the warlike offense of occupation and thus guilty of treason.

Consequently, under the Law of Necessity, once Sovereignty is reestablished, each Union State should repatriate its National Guard to help protect the boundaries of each Union State. In so doing, the Legislatures need also to prohibit the use of the National Guard by the Federal Government for ANY purpose whatsoever except for the protection of the territories and boundaries of the 50 Union States or any one of them, but in no case shall the National Guard be used to prevent secession or be sent off shore to occupy foreign lands. Further, the repatriation should include provisions for a Switzerland like militia where all legal aged male (and perhaps female) inhabitants of the Union State possess an appropriate firearm for defense and attend yearly educational classes for its use.

Prevent the Execution of All Federal Law Within a Union State Not Specifically Permitted by the U.S. Constitution

Each Union State Legislature should make it a crime for any person, no matter their status, to aid and abet the application/

execution of any federal law within said Union State against any Union State Citizen not specifically designated as drawing on a power delegated by the Constitution of the United States for such purposes and so specified in said federal law wanting to be applied.

Apprising the Citizens and Their Union State Agents of the Limitations of Authority of Federal Law

For decades Congress has been redefining the term "State" to include only that territory over which it has been granted exclusive jurisdiction from Article I, Section 8, Clause 17 and Article 4, Section 3, Clause 2 of the Federal Constitution. However, such a definition is generally obfuscated in such a manner so as to leave the reader with the impression that the legislation in question was being directed to be operative in the Union States as well. Such an example is evidenced herein in Part 2. Consequently, it should be a Constitutional Mandate that each and every Union State be required to inform its Citizens and their agent representative from time to time by proclamation or otherwise that federal law has no application within the territory of their Union State unless the statute specifically names their Union State as being territory over which the statute has application and the federal Constitution designates the power being applied in such federal law.

State the Primary Mission of the Sovereign Union States

Since the foundation of the ethics in our political system is the Declaration of Independence (and Sovereignty) wherein we declared the source and therefore the existence of our Unalienable Rights to Life, Liberty, and the Pursuit of Happiness (Property), it would be exceedingly appropriate for each Union State to acknowledge, by proclamation and so include same in its Union State Constitution, that their sole purpose for existence, stems from the charter from We the People, is the absolute protection of Life, Liberty, and the Pursuit of Happiness (Property). The protection of Life can be assisted, certainly, by the Repatriation of the National Guard.

This author believes that the proper recognition of Liberty comes first from the recognition that *Freedom is the absence of detention,* while *Liberty is the absence of Control.* Correspondingly, Liberty and Sovereignty are companion concepts; the existence of one presupposes the existence of the other. In a society in which Liberty prevails, rights break down into 2 categories, the Rights we have and the Rights we don't have. Correspondingly, in the ethics of Liberty we can find two fundamental behavior traits associated with Rights for which we can establish two Doctrines titled the *Liberty Doctrines.* 1) Liberty Doctrine of Rights which, simply stated, is that *everyone has a right to do or act or conduct his affairs in any manner he chooses so long as he does not interfere with the life of another without the other's consent.* And 2) The Liberty Doctrine of Non-Existing Right is the antithesis of the first Doctrine and defined to be that *no one has the right to interfere with or influence the life of another without his consent.* That covers the sum total of all human intercourse of each and every person in a society where Liberty and Sovereignty prevails.

Sovereignty, as you have read in Appendix 1, was Devolved to us in the Declaration of Independence and as you no doubt have observed in your every life, Individual Sovereignty is a disappearing commodity. We as We the People must put our nose to the grind stone and educate ourselves to the Common Law in order to guarantee to ourselves of the sanctity of our Sovereignty. When we firmly reestablish our individual sovereignty, we will be remembered as the generation of the Reformation Founders who brought our individual Sovereignty to the fore for the posterity of our Republic. You Common Law education can start at 1215.org. For most of us, that's the beginning of our knowledge that we are in fact the Sovereigns of our Republic, Sovereigns without subjects. And what a joyful ride that will be.

Since the Pursuit of Happiness has been deemed to also include the right to Property, the protection of the Pursuit of Happiness entails the protection of private property and a Free Market. The concept of protecting the free market includes the understanding that any and all private transactions between un-enfranchised humans cannot be interfered with in any way except upon complaint by either of the parties. This also means that such transactions are not valid objects of taxation such as a sales tax. On the other hand, artificial entities engaged in the Market are valid objects for taxation because their mere existence is at the pleasure of We the People and our Union State.

Repatriation of the National Parks

Since there is no delegation of power to the Federal Government by and through the federal Constitution to confiscated Union State lands for the purpose of establishing and maintaining National Parks, the Union States need to take back the land by instructing their agent, the elected Senators representing them, to put forth the necessary bills to reclaim the territory.

Reclaim all Territory Donated or Otherwise Providing Occupation to a Foreign Political Entity, such as the U.N. Biospheres.

The Union States have every right and duty to take back these lands because, like National Parks, there was never any Constitutional provision for either the Union States or the Federal Government to allow any Alien Political Power to occupy lands within the territories of any of the Union States. In other words, there exists no Constitutional provision to allow the

Union States to sell, trade, or give land or territory to any foreign sovereign or entity except the United States and only then for Constitutionally specific purposes and by specific methods.

Provide a Method for Direct Communications between We the People and Their Congressional Representatives.

In light of the fact that Union State representation in Congress is under their direct control by and through the elected Senators, it seems fitting that We the people should have a direct interface to communicate with our Representatives in like manner. In this age of the Internet, such a website could be established by District and manned by a Citizen Action group, independent from any political party, to provide a forum to keep the populace of each district informed and, at the same time, provide a vehicle for We the People to present input and instructions for each respective Representative as to how to vote on any given issue and also bring to the fore the issues that need to come under consideration in Congress. Since there may be some risk of skullduggery in such a function, some type of oversight may be needed. This will allow each Union State representative to get explicit instructions from whom he or she is representing as to how to vote on issues before Congress for its consideration. At the same time it should be made illegal for any representative, Senator, or District Representative to supplant their instruction with their own will, whether from emotions, lobbying, or political party. Such a violation of trust should carry a criminal penalty and the representative should be so advised via the oath of office.

Additionally the unfinished business is very fertile ground to be plowed by various liberty minded "think tanks" with ample opportunity to come up with additional "cause and effect" solutions for the saving of the Republic and by and through the true Reformation of Union State Sovereignty.

Lobbying

Since lobbying interferes with the duty of legislators to represent the wishes of their constituents, it becomes a foreign third party influence to the workings of our constitutional governments and a destruction of the law making process to accurately perform the wishes of We the People. It provides very fertile territory for skullduggery and temptations to public officials to be available to special interests for a price. Therefore, lobbying at all levels of government should be made unlawful with criminal sanctions for both the lobbyist and the representatives involved.

Oaths

Rodger Clemens, an ace pitcher for Major League Baseball (MLB) was indicted for perjury by the federal government. Forget for the moment, that the federal government has no business in this Constitutional Republic of Sovereign Union States while attempting to protect the Sovereign Union State people to police the goings on of the MLB players within the Union States. If you will note, perjury is violating your oath to "tell the truth, the whole truth, and nothing but the truth," essentially a promise to perform. So in essence, Roger is being accused of violating his oath. Now it strikes me as quite odd that when we swear in our public servants why they don't expose themselves to the same risks that Rodger did as being a witness. While "perjury" is testifying to something that isn't true by saying that it is a person violates his oath by telling the falsehood. He promised to tell the truth and didn't. In other words, he breached his verbal contract to tell the truth. Why isn't it then that a person's Oath of Office is also a verbal contract to be administered as such on the same parameters as perjury? The answer lies in the words. As you will observe below, we offer these Oaths that are nebulous inferences with no meaningful substance.

Presidents Oath:

> **"I do solemnly swear (or affirm) that I will faithfully execute the office of President of the United States, and will to the best of my ability, preserve, protect and defend the Constitution of the United States."**

It might do us, We the People, a better service to us and our heirs to have the word **<u>obey and enforce</u>** in the second line, i.e. "preserve, protect, defend, obey, and enforce the Constitution of the United States."

Senators Oath:

> **"I do solemnly swear (or affirm) that I will support and defend the Constitution of the United States against all enemies, foreign and domestic; that I will bear true faith and allegiance to the same; that I take this obligation freely, without any mental reservation or purpose of evasion; and that I will well and faithfully discharge the duties of the office on which I am about to enter: So help me God."**

The question is, does any Senator who votes for an unconstitutional Bill violate his oath of office. I don't think he does because the terms "support and defend" are too nebulous and wishy washy to provide any grounds to prove the negative of them. Again, I would much prefer that the words **<u>obey and enforce the Constitution and its directives and probitions</u>** found its way in that oath.

Oaths for the House of Representatives:

> I do solemnly swear (or affirm) that I will support
> and defend the Constitution of the United States
> against all enemies, foreign and domestic; that
> I will bear true faith and allegiance to the same;
> that I take this obligation freely, without any
> mental reservation or purpose of evasion; and
> that I will well and faithfully discharge the duties
> of the office on which I am about to enter: So help
> me God.

Again, the oath is in want of the terms **obey and enforce the Constriction and its directives and prohibitions**. Actually in a political sense, just what do the terms *support and defend* connote? Since the members of the Senate and House of Representative have identical oaths, they need something more in their oaths than "support and defend the Constitution." What is not supporting or not defending? What specific facts would support the charge of perjury or Breach of Contract for not supporting and not defending? When a person tells a lie when he swore to tell the truth, the transcript of the lie proves the act of perjury, Breach or Promise to perform. What are the acts of not supporting and/or not defending?

The exact same thing is true for New York State oath for employees taking office or positions of authority. The "one size fits all oaths" for such new officials is as follows:

> Section 1. Members of the legislature, and all
> officers, executive and judicial, except such
> inferior officers as shall be by law exempted, shall,
> before they enter on the duties of their respective
> offices, take and subscribe the following oath
> or affirmation: "I do solemnly swear (or affirm)
> that I will support the Constitution of the United
> States, and the Constitution of the State of New
> York, and that I will faithfully discharge the duties

of the office of . . . . , according to the best of my ability;"

New York State feels that supporting the Constitution is sufficient. Supporting the Constitution(s) does not anywhere near come close to obeying enforcing the directives and prohibitions of a constitution. The problem I have is that I can't figure out how an officer of New York State can be found guilty of **NOT** supporting a document. I'm supporting the Constitution if I put a pocket edition in my pocket and, at the same time, I'm defending it if I have a copy in my lockbox. So, if I'm an officer of New York, for the life of me, I can't figure out how you are going to put me in jail for not supporting or defending the Constitution for the United States or any one of the Union States even if I go about my business saying that the United States of America is a democracy. That's why each and every State and Federal Oath needs to be revamped to include the terms "obey and enforce the Constitution and its directives and prohibitions" with respect to becoming an officer/representative for the Citizens of our Republic. Supporting connotes an audience like secondary involvement; a role of no direct involvement, if you will. On the other hand, "obey and enforce the directives and prohibitions" connotes a direct involvement of the matter at hand and leaves no doubt about what's expected. In fact, I will go so far as to suggest that the wording of the oath for any and all agents of government prior to their elected or appointed position include the terms: "I solemnly swear (or affirm) to obey and enforce the Constitution for the United States (and the Constitution of Union State of _____) and all the directives and prohibitions associated thereto." That verbiage or language leaves no wiggle room due to interpretation or volition. Man, watch the weeping and wailing and gnashing of teeth to stop these oaths from becoming a reality.

As an aside, I just looked up the oath of Office for the state of Wyoming prescribed by the Wyoming Constitution., To wit:

OATH OF OFFICE

PRESCRIBED BY THE CONSTITUTION
OF WYOMING

I do solemnly swear (or affirm) that I will support, defend and **obey** the Constitution for the United States, and the constitution of the state of Wyoming; including all the directives and prohibitions associated with each of them and that I have not knowingly violated any law related to my election or appointment, or caused it to be done by others; and that I will discharge the duties of my office with fidelity.

_____

Signed

What a surprise! What a fantastic job they have done. Now I'm off the hook to go back and add the Oath issue to my **additions necessary to cause the Union State of Wyoming to regain its sovereignty proposed as a 10th Amendment Resolution.** The Citizens of Wyoming should be proud of their Constitution and the levers it gives them to suspend and eliminate skullduggery in their state government.

Flags

This topic of Flags deserves a book all unto itself. While there isn't a lot of information available to the public on this topic a lot can be gleaned from the law and common practice. Unlike the other topics in this book, I've been able to support the conclusion drawn by factual proof. Here, I must confess, the discussion and the conclusions, for a large part, will be based on logic, reason, common sense, and observations. First, let's take a gander into the law. The first place to look is Title 4,

Section 3, **Use of flag for advertising purposes; mutilation of flag**.

Any person who, **within the District of Columbia**, in any manner, for exhibition or display, shall place or cause to be placed any word, figure, mark, picture, design, drawing, or any advertisement of any nature upon any flag, standard, colors, or ensign of the **United States of America**; or shall expose or cause to be exposed to public view any such flag, standard, colors, or ensign upon which shall have been printed, painted, or otherwise placed, or to which shall be attached, appended, affixed, or annexed any word, figure, mark, picture, design, or drawing, or any advertisement of any nature; or who, **within the District of Columbia,** shall manufacture, sell, expose for sale, or to public view, or give away or have in possession for sale, or to be given away or for use for any purpose, any article or substance being an article of merchandise, or a receptacle for merchandise or article or thing for carrying or transporting merchandise, upon which shall have been printed, painted, attached, or otherwise placed a representation of any such flag, standard, colors, or ensign, to advertise, call attention to, decorate, mark, or distinguish the article or substance on which so placed shall be deemed guilty of a misdemeanor and shall be punished by a fine not exceeding $100 or by imprisonment for not more than thirty days, or both, in the discretion of the court. The words "flag, standard, colors, or ensign", as used herein, shall include any flag, standard, colors, ensign, or any picture or representation of either, or of any part or parts of either, made of any substance or represented on any substance, of any size evidently purporting to be either of said flag, standard, colors, or ensign of the **United States of America** or a picture or a representation of either, upon which shall be shown the colors, the stars and the stripes, in any number of either thereof, or of any part or parts of either, by which the average person seeing the same without deliberation may believe the same to represent the flag, colors, standard, or ensign of the **United States of America**.

The question is in what territory is the sanctity of the flag of the United States protected. The answer, of course, is in the District of Columbia, which as you know, is Federal Territory. So if you alter the Flag of the United States of America for advertising or mutilate the Flag of the United States of America in Washington D.C. you're going to jail. Remember all the fanfare the press and the Federal Government created about mutilating the United States Flag. Did it leave you with the impression that the law covered all the territories within the Union Sates as well? Now you know it was vicious propaganda and any law associated with the Flag of the United States of America applies only within Washington D.C.

Now, that brings up the question as to who protects the sanctity of the Flags of the Union States and where do the flags of Union States fly? Certainly, Title 4 does not go into any discussion of Union State Flags, and since Title 4 is isolated entirely to federal territory by the definition of the term "State" and "Federal area" at Section 110 and does not make mention of any of the "Union States" we are left on our own to conclude that we should look to Union State Law for the proper behavior for dealing with Union State Flags.

However, having searched the New York State Laws for references to the Flag and how it should be displayed, I concluded that the matter is not covered for the New York State Flag and am left then to also conclude that the matter has probably not heretofore been discussed in legal or political circles. Consequently, we are left to draw parallels from our Federal Flag and the facts associated thereto in order to form an opinion relative to Union State Flags and their relationship to Union States Sovereignty. First, all ships on the high seas sourced from the United State displays the flag of the United States of America. The same is true for all other ships found bobbing around on the oceans. But the flag most likely does not so much represent the country to which it belongs as it does to designate the laws of the Sovereign from which it is governed and subject to. Upon reading USC Title 4 we learn that the United States of America Flag is held to designate Federal Territory only and says nothing about the Union States. Federal territory, as we know, is the Sovereign territory over which the United States has exclusive legislative jurisdiction, a position, I would suggest, is one of the conditions and designations of Sovereignty.

As you read in Appendix B, you learned that the Supreme Court has opined that the Union States are constitutionally also meant to be Sovereign as well, where their laws are exclusive within their established boundaries. This at least implies that the Union States have a right to expect their State Flag or Banner to designate the Sovereign territory of their state. From a very cursory search it would appear that none of the Union states have ever made an effort to make this a reality. I proffer that this should change in the course of events leading up to the reformation of Union State Sovereignty.

Union State law should be altered or added to include the declaration of the Union State Flag to designate the Sovereign territory of the said Union State. In addition there needs to be a section of Union State law which mirrors USC 4, Section 7 which outlines the Position and Manner of Display of the Union State Flag(s). It should be the primary flag for that Union State territory and all other flags are to take up an inferior position, including the Flag of the United States of America because Union State territory is not part of the of the federal territory of the United States and cannot attempt to hold a superior position or even a peer position to the Union State.

Along with this there is an implied need for each Union state to provide its school system with a modified Pledge of Allegiance. It would need to go something like this:

> I Pledge Allegiance to the Flag of the of the Union state of _____ as well as to the Flag to the United States and to the republics for which they stand, one nation under God, indivisible, with liberty, and justice for all.

Above, we pointed out that Justice O'Conner quoted Chief Justice Chase from an 1860 case that:

> "the preservation of the Union States, and the maintenance of their governments, are as much within the design and care of the Constitution as the preservation of the Union and the maintenance of the National government. **The Constitution, in all its provisions, looks to an indestructible Union, composed of indestructible States."** *Texas v. White, 7 Wall. 700, 725 (1869). Id @ 162*

In appendix B we observed that the Supreme Court stated that the dual sovereignty [of the Union States and the federal Government] was the defining feature of our nation's constitutional blueprint.

> "[d]ual sovereignty is a defining feature of our nation's constitutional blueprint." Federal Marine Commission (FMC) v. South Carolina State Ports Authority, 535 U.S. 743 (2002)

We point out the notion of "dual sovereignty" to justify the wording proffered in the now Sovereign state's Pledge of Allegiance and the notion of the Constitution provisions which "looks to an indestructible Union, composed of indestructible States" to allow the education system of each Union State to foster the notion of indestructibility creating a generation with an infinitely more genuine base set of political first principles than is prevalent today in an effort to install the need for each of them to guard against the destructible components in our politics. With this and the modified Oaths of office, that generation will have at their disposal a much better set of tools to maintain political order than we do today. If this all comes about, I doubt that the Citizens of this Country will need to worry about the issue of the Reformation of Union State Sovereignty 20 years from now.

AND THAT'S THE ISSUE OF THE FLAG, AS I SEE IT

A Couple of Surprises Found in Title 4

§ 110. Same; definitions

As used in sections 105-109 of this title—

(d) <u>The term "State" includes any Territory or possession of the United States.</u>

Congress is up to its misapplication of terms to maintain confusion in federal statutes. To wit:

"(4) the term 'State' means a State of the United States, the District of Columbia, or a territory or possession of the United States."

Using the semantics of the Supreme Court when they said "the most natural meaning of "of the United States" is "belonging to the United States" Ellis v, United States, 206 U.A. 246; 27 S. Ct 600 (1907) Therefore the term "State in this instance means a Federal Territory

(e) The term "Federal area" means any lands or premises held or acquired by or for the use of the United States or any department, establishment, or agency, of the United States; and any Federal area, or any part thereof, which is located within the exterior boundaries of any State, shall be deemed to be a Federal area located within such State.

§ 106. Same; income tax

(a) No person shall be relieved from liability for any income tax levied by any State, or by any duly constituted taxing authority therein, having jurisdiction to levy such a tax, by reason of his residing within a Federal area or receiving income from transactions occurring or services performed in such area; and such State or taxing authority shall have full jurisdiction and power to levy and collect such tax in any Federal area within such State to the same extent and with the same effect as though such area was not a Federal area.

(b) The provisions of subsection (a) shall be applicable only with respect to income or receipts received after December 31, 1940.

No comments except that this just reaffirms the analysis found in Part 2.

PART 8

Epilogue

One thing that should appear obvious to the reader at this point is that this has really been an exercise in deciphering and understanding what has been written in statutes and the authorities of the Courts in their interpretation. In other words, it has been an exercise in legal linguists, understanding and fully comprehending what actually is written in the statures as opposed to what we have been lead to believe by various means, such as government supported schools, misguided media outlets, the government agents themselves, and the deliberate convolution of the English language in many cases to capitalize on the speed reading scans of the readers which are in some cases extremely inefficient when measured by actual comprehension. This has been an analysis of fundamentals. What the law says is fundamental as well as what derived power was used by the legislature to formulate it. I dearly hope that every reader was able to make it to here. The understanding of this material could be a life changing event for most, certainly a life and structural change for our Constitutional Republic back to the first principles of Liberty and Sovereignty which we and our ancestors inherited but have collectively done an inferior job of protecting. Additionally, it is hoped that one of the comprehended first principles of our Constitutional Republic is that the concepts of individual Liberty and Sovereignty are inseparable companion concepts and that the existence of one presupposes the existence of the other.

While the Grass Roots effort in the support of Ron Paul has outlined a large number of misdeeds and raised many Constitutional issues relative to the many incumbents who, contrary to their oaths of office, have failed to heed their Constitutional obligations, little has been done heretofore because most of the intellectual residue from that Grass Roots effort has been left to operate in a campaigning mode by orchestrating public demonstrations in a continuing effort to convince the public to come over to our way of thinking in order to produce a majority. Therefore, in a Republic whose founders left us with the Rule of Law, it is the dictates of the Rule of Law that must be demonstrated rather than striving for any sort of majority. We should each look to the Common Law for our remedy for a lasting solution.

There are several conscientious groups which have been formed as outcrops of the Grass Roots movement who are looking for some guidance or purpose which will lead us to the return of the Rule of Law as a protector of Liberty rather than the constraint of inalienable rights. Rather than trying to convince Charlie Six Pact and Sally Housewife how they should vote, we need to demonstrate to them the Rule of Law and what remedies are available to us and how they are achieved and satisfied when an agent of ours strays from that Rule of Law.

This can hopefully be accomplished better by demonstrating in the Union State Court rooms using actionable causes with the Common Law rather than demonstrating in the streets and being clobbered by adrenalin fed, mind controlled, policemen funded by the Federal Government. Some of the actionable suites available to us are listed in Part 4. Those residual Grass Roots organizations which have a lawyer or lawyers sympathetic to the cause should be able to create additional actionable suites relying on the facts and law presented herein and any additional research they find verifying what has been herein presented. Of course, the first order of business is to get the Union States back to their Constitutional Sovereign status. After that, there's the issue of various damages from the abuse of process of federal law within the territories of the Union States. In the pursuit of remedies for these damages it would seem appropriate to seek reparations in the Union State courts. Additionally, Union States legislatures by resolutions need to declare that Union State law enforcement is completely detached from any and all federal control and in light of the fact that the accepting of funds is indicative of dependence and/ or servitude the Union State legislatures should also further mandate that the Union State and all local governments (the instrumentalities of the Union State) must also cease and desist accepting any and all funds from the Federal Government.

To error on the side of caution

This author once had a legal dispute with the counsel for one of his clients relative to the income tax deductions and their dispersion. Even though considerable time was spent with said counsel reviewing the law and he having been shown exactly where his interpretation was incorrect, his only defense was that as counsel, he'd rather error on the side of caution than take on the Federal Government. One of the early 40's movies of "Our Gang" had a scene where this well dressed gentleman drove up in his shinny 1934 Packard convertible at the curb where the group of "Our Gang" happened to be hanging out. One of the lads bellowed out, "Watch your car for a quarter, Mister?" The gentleman rejected the offer and upon his return to his car, there it sat with 4 flat tires. Now, while that may be good for comic relief, it is, in fact, the very essence of the "**protection racket**". Had the Gentleman handed over the quarter, it would have shown that he was willing to error on the side of caution. However, recognizing the offer for what it was, a classic example of the "**protection racket,**" and therefore extortion," he chose to ignore it and fight any adverse effects in a lawful manner on a latter date. How many people cough up between 40 and 50 percent of their compensation to pay income taxes because they would rather **error on the side of caution** rather than take the time to fully understand the law?

While the connecting of the dots exposing the holes in the current implementation of the Rule of Law is extremely complex and sometimes convoluted, it is the hope of this author that the complexity and the convolution has been unraveled in such a manner and to such an extent as to be comprehensible by the average high school graduate.

Anyone who thinks this is hogwash, whether a legal professional or otherwise, must come to grips with the oxymoron that a sovereign can remain a sovereign while at the same time paying homage and pledging allegiance to another sovereign by and through the paying of a tax. A taxpayer, pure and simple, is a subject. While, the Union States are agents for the people, by virtue of the fact that the people are their creators, they are proclaimed sovereigns with respect to the Federal Government and to each other as stated above quoting Federalist Paper # 39. A sovereign acts like a sovereign in its sphere of power and a subject acts like a subject in his sphere of servitude and never the twain shall meet in the same sphere.

While we inherited a well-founded bottom up power structure to protect our Liberty, Sovereignty, and a Free Market, what we are witnessing today in practice is an effort to replace it with a transmogrified top down central power system which politically is more akin to a socialist/communist system and an economic system which is more akin to a fascist corporate dictatorship. With the Central Banking System working in concert with the huge gaggle of powerful corporations, We the People may just be waking up to the realization *that We have allowed private banks to control the issuance of our currency, first by inflation and then by deflation and that the banks and corporations that have grown up around these private banks will deprive We the People of all our Property until our Children may one day wake up homeless on the continent their Fore Fathers conquered*[78]. There is talk of secession in many circles throughout the Union,

---

[78]   Paraphrased from a Quote by Thomas Jefferson: "If the American People allow private banks to control the issuance of their currency, first by inflation and then by deflation, the banks and corporations that will grow up around them will deprive the People of all their Property until their Children will wake up homeless on the continent their Fathers conquered"

but secession from what? Secession from the Union seems unrealistic in view of the fact that none of the sister Union States is causing any problem to any of the other Union States. It is the out of control Federal Government that is causing all the problems for the Union States. By the mere act of taking the necessary political steps to implement the reformation of its sovereignty, a Union State is effectively succeeding from the control and unconstitutional behavior of the Federal Government and at the same time stemming the tide of the Federal Government's secret/stealthy invasion of the Union State's territory for the purpose of occupying it for worldwide control according to a "new world order." By the simple act of reasserting their Constitutional Sovereignty by ceasing to behave as an instrumentality of the Federal Government, the 50 Union States are therefore letting the Federal Government sink or swim in its own sewage of debt. The Federal Government is floating on an ocean of debt created by its own creation, the Federal Reserve, so the Reformation of Union State Sovereignty is simply cutting the 50 life lines to allow it to either come up with a solution to its monstrous debt or have its creation, the Federal Reserve who bilked the Union States people for trillions, excuse the debt.

Here's to the reformation of our 50 Union State's Sovereignty, our own individual Liberty and Sovereignty, the Rule of Law, and the preservation of each through the proper control over our representative agents.

PART 9

Afterword

While this work being based on the principles and concepts established upon the wisdom of our Founders may prove entertaining and worthy of a snicker or two to some of our more insincere[79] aristocratic minded politicians representing various regions of our Republic, it might, however, be prudent to point out to them why the remedies proffered herein might prove beneficial to their own self interests. The aristocracy[80] has throughout most of the industrialized periods of history viewed themselves as masters of all "inferior" humanity. As a consequence they find such concepts as individualism, independence, delegated powers, the Power of the People, Liberty, Rights in general, personal rewards, etc., repugnant to their whims and as a consequence view the existence of our Constitutional Republic as a threat to their power and control. To be sure, what we see transpiring before our very eyes today is an ever increasing choke hold on the very elements of our existence by the Bankers[81] and other aristocrats. This Treatise reveals a manageable way to break that choke hold and return to the business of maintaining a Sovereign independent society.

I am reminded of an anecdote rendered in the movie *The War of the Roses* by Danny DeVito. Question: "What do you call 300 lawyers at the bottom of the Pacific Ocean? Answer: "A Good Start." And so it is with this book and the herein proposed additions to the **Draft of Wyoming's 10th Amendment Proposal** in Part 5. There is, however, a huge effort ahead needed and, indeed, necessary to pull it off.

---

[79] Read tinhorn.
[80] Read the world wide gaggle of banks holding the majority of wealth
[81] Read Aristocracy

And while some of the aforementioned politicians may think they will be able to kiss up to the Aristocracy for having provided some of the handy work in facilitating the aforementioned chokehold on the middle class, they may be unpleasantly surprised to find out that if the chokehold works to bring down our Constitutional Republic, they will be the same as any of the other peasant slaves, whether they wear a tie or not. A medieval existence will be all that is left. So coming at the matter from the other side, the reward for having aided and abetted the destruction of this Republic is simply to be allowed to share in the peonage of the masses. We're talking about a two class society, the Aristocracy on the one hand and the peons/slaves on the other. I doubt that there are any of today's politicians close enough to the aristocracy to be included in the former so the only alternative is the latter. Consequently, every member of our Constitutional Republic MUST take notice that they have only one choice to maintain their comfortable middle class existence and **that is simply to understand the fundamental principles of individual Liberties and the methods proffered above to regain and preserve them.**

In choosing our representatives to accomplish this we need to know the difference between a Statesman and a Politician and it comes down to this. **Self-interest** is the distinguishing characteristic between a Statesman and a politician. Statesmen have none but duty, while politicians, by their own actions, signify that they consider themselves to have no duty but to guide themselves by their own volition to maximize their own self-interest. What's interesting is that a statesman's duty is to preserve and protect the commercial environment to allow his constituents to advance their own self-interest (Liberty and the pursuit of happiness), while in order for the politician to advance his own self-interest, he must strive to instill a duty in his constituents to work harder for less reward (in the name of patriotism) so that his own self-interests can be fulfilled.

Statesmen work to maintain the Republic while politicians, must, as a matter of necessity, destroy the Republic in order to cause it to migrate to anyone of a number of despotic forms of government that give him power. Take you choice, communism, feudalism, fascism, autocratic, democracy, there's no major difference. Each is a two (2) class system. The average people/citizens are then simply serfs on the land. The only differences are technical among the structure of the aristocracy, and are only studied by those concerned about how many angels dance on the head of a pin. They must all oppress the people for the sake of the leaders/aristocracy. So it simply boils down to only two forms of government determined by whether we allow politicians to run our governing body or **demand** that Statesmen to do so! However, we failed to provide the necessary footing for the most worthy Statesmen to come down the pike in the last 50 years, namely Ron Paul. So our record for putting Statesmen in office is not, as they say, too sterling.

Interestingly the Aristocracy is a contradiction in human existence. They produce absolutely nothing to support their existence. They then are dependent upon those who they maintain an absolute power over. In other words, the Aristocracy is 100% dependent upon those who they must violently force to submit to the frame of mind that the controlled are dependent on the non-productive controller. Stated another way, in a medieval society, the controller is, in fact, dependent on the controlled, thus the controller must revert to the whip to maintain the façade of the inversion. The inversion is only righted when the people finally break through the façade, which is exactly what our founders did, and become aware that the aristocracy is in fact dependent upon them for their existence. That's how and why our Fore Fathers created this Constitutional Republic in the first place. It's the John Lock's bottom up sovereign hierarchy versus Thomas Hobbs Top Down slave driven Aristocracy.

Bottom Line

Exonomics[82] is the study of exchange and recognizes as a first principle that each and every human being is a consumer wherein his total consumption is provided by the productive efforts of human producers. Secondly, every exchange (transaction) between humans is a zero balance transaction. That is to say, with respect to the parties involved in the transaction, each party provided something equal in value to that which he received back, i.e., to each party there was a debit and a credit of equal value thus the zero balance transaction. The intrinsic value of the items traded in the transaction is termed "consideration" and carries within its concept the element that each party was satisfied with the items(s) he or she received.

Money is most often the consideration used by one of the parties in a transaction, but in our society today the paper we call money has no intrinsic value and is, in fact, just evidence of debt, therefore it is not valid for consideration and thus creates a non-zero balance transactions. That is to say that a debt is created and the contract is left as unconsummated in the balance. This is precisely why our Forefathers were very careful to include the phrase in our Constitution that "No State shall . . . ; make any Thing but gold or silver Coin a Tender in Payment of Debts;." The Forefathers failed to complete the prohibition by adding the phrase "and neither shall the United States.

However, F.D. Roosevelt in 1933 proclaimed it necessary under the banking emergency to prohibit the hoarding of Gold, Gold bullion, or Gold certificates where "the term 'hoarding' means the withdrawal and withholding of gold coin, gold bullion or gold certificates from the recognized and customary channels of trade."[83] Now who do you suppose Mr. Roosevelt specified as

---

[82]   The term used for the study of Exchange coined by the Author.

[83]   Quoted from the legislation defining "hoarding" as an undesirable trait as an excuse to confiscate Gold and Gold Certificates but

the recipient for the Gold items? Would you believe the privately owned Federal Reserve Banks? Talk about unjust enrichment! And who do you suspect used their gigantic financial power to suck the necessary items of consideration right out of our Society? Under the theory of "follow the money," the answer is, of course, the same entity to which We the People turned in their gold, the privately owned Federal Reserve.

Since the essence of Liberty is valid contracts, and since valid contracts are based on consideration, without a money substance with intrinsic value to be used as consideration, We the People have no Liberty, thus no valid contracts. While it is common place, either by habit or indoctrination, for the populace to label Federal Reserve Notes as "money," these Notes are, in reality, "just God damn pieces of paper" in our society today.

Fractional Reserve banking is another little understood scheme of leveraged theft. At a 10% reserve requirement, the banks are raking in 10 times the going interest rate stemming from their "loans." On an interest rate of 18% the bank is getting 180% of the amount on deposit to cover the outstanding loans. So, for a $1000 deposit the bank hauls in $1800 every year in interest alone. Isn't debt wonderful? At what point does it become Unjust Enrichment?

With the confiscation of our gold and the lending practice of the Fractional Reserve banking system the owners of this private banking cartel have robbed the producers of this country for close to 100% percent of all that has been produced including the people's real property since the turn of the 19th century.

The question is "What are we going to do about it?" Some of the Grass Roots are looking to the Federal Government to give us back our Liberty. What impetus does a thief have in returning stolen property? The answer is, of course, none. This author

---

like the income tax statutes, it was only applicable in the United States.

believes that the only course worthy of success is to mandate through due diligence and our political representatives that the Union States restore their independent sovereign status as outlined above and at the same time resolve the lack of any money/currency which can be used for valid consideration as required for valid contracts and thus the essence of our inherited inalienable Rights to Life, Liberty, and the property of We the People. Otherwise, We the People and our heirs will, in the near future, wake up in a fascist medieval society right out of the life style of the Middle Ages.

How can I tell if I'm being represented by a Statesman or a Politician? Since banks rake in tons of money from debt, one fairly sure proof way is to discover if he wants to have the government pays its bills as they come due or create more debt. If he wants to create more debt and feign myopia relative to the outstanding long term debt then you most likely have elected a politician. If, on the other hand, he proposes to eliminate all bailouts, bring the troops home from foreign lands, whittle the fat out of the government entity he was elected to, get the total cost of government to no more than 10 % of the GDP including all levels and branches, and if he pulls the curtain back on ALL government activities including military operations allowing the public to ascertain what's going on, then you more than likely have elected a very good statesman. **CONGRATULATIONS!**

LONG LIVE LIBERTY

THROUGH

THE SPECIALLY

FORMULATED

50 CONSTITUTIONAL SOVEREIGN

REPUBLICS

CREATED BY THE FOUNDERS

TO PRESERVE IT!

M. Kenneth Creamer—12/2008, revised 7/2009,
10/2010, 7/2011, and 3/2013.

NOTES

NOTES

Declarations of Individual Sovereignty

Few people understand the concept of individual sovereignty as it pertains to citizenship and fewer still understand that it is the basic building block of Power within our own Constitutional Republic. Below is an early Supreme Court opinion written by Justice John Jay, the first Chief Justice to be appointed to the Supreme Court. I have been told by an attorney that the idea or concept of individual sovereignty was a "big lie" and that sovereignty devolved to the people as one body for the whole. While such a notion violates the existence theorem and has no precedent to protect it from being categorized as belonging to the class of fictions, I have footnoted the following passage to help the readers decide on their own whether Chief Justice Jay is referring to the body of individuals collectively as a whole or whether he is referring to the whole body as separate individuals.

> "The revolution, or rather the Declaration of Independence, found the people already united for general purposes, and at the same time, providing for more domestic concerns, by states conventions, and other temporary arrangements. From the crown of Great Britain, the sovereignty of their country passed to the people of it: and it was then not an uncommon opinion that the un-appropriated lands, which belonged to the crown, passed, not to the people of the colony or states within those limits they were situated, but to the whole people . . . 'We the people of the United States do ordain and establish this constitution.' Here we see the people acting as

the sovereigns[84] of the whole country: and in the language of sovereignty, establishing a constitution by which it was their[85] will that the state governments should be bound, and to which constitutions should be made to conform . . . It will be sufficient to observe briefly, that the sovereignties of Europe, and particularly in England, existed on feudal principles. That system considers the prince as the sovereign, and the people his subjects; it regards his person as the object of allegiance, and excludes the idea of his being on an equal footing with a subject, either in a court of justice or elsewhere. That system contemplates him as being the fountain of honor and authority; and from his grace and grant, derives all franchises, immunities, and privileges; it is easy to perceive, that such a sovereign could not be amenable to a court of justice, or subjected to judicial control and actual constraint . . . The same feudal ideas run through all their jurisprudence, and constantly remind us of the distinction between the prince and the subject. No such ideas obtain here; at the revolution[86], the sovereignty devolved on the people; and they are **truly the sovereigns of the country**[87], but they are sovereigns without subjects[88] . . . and have none to govern but themselves; the citizens of America are equal as fellow-citizens,

---

[84]   Here we see "People acting as sovereigns," a plurality of individuals. If the sovereignty devolved to the whole people and not to individuals, then Judge Jay would have said "the people acting as the sovereign."

[85]   Again, a plurality of individuals.

[86]   Or rather the Declaration of Independence as aforesaid.

[87]   The statement that "they are truly the sovereigns of the country," is, again, unmistakenly obvious that Judge Jay meant "they" to encompass a plurality of individuals as sovereigns or he would have said "they are truly the sovereign of the country.

[88]   Same analysis as 33 above.

and as joint tenants in the sovereignty. From the differences existing between feudal sovereignties and governments founded on compacts, it necessarily follows that their respective prerogatives must differ. In Europe, the sovereignty is generally ascribed to the prince; here it rests with the people; there the sovereign actually administers the government; **here never in a single instance; our governors are agents of the people; and at most stand in the same relation to their sovereign, in which the regents of Europe stand to their sovereigns. Their princes have personal powers, dignities and preeminence; our rulers have none but official; nor do they partake in the sovereignty otherwise, or in any other capacity, than as private citizens.**[89] Chief Justice Jay, *Chisholm v. Georgia*, 2 (US) Dall 419, 457, 1 LEd 440, 456 at 454. (1793) (emphasis added)

AND

From another equally succinct Supreme Court ruling we find the Individual Sovereignty issue laid out in quite clearly in extremely understandable terms.

"**Sovereignty itself is, of course, not subject to the law, <u>for it is the author of the law,</u>** but in our system, while sovereign powers are delegated to the agencies of government, sovereignty itself remains with the people, by whom and for whom all government exists and acts . . . For, the very idea that one man may be compelled to hold his life, or the means of living, at the mere will of another, seems intolerable in any country where freedom prevails, as being the essence of slavery itself." *Yick Wo v.*

---

[89]   "Partake of the sovereignty . . . . . as [individual] private citizens."

Hopkins, Sheriff, 118 US. 356 (1886) (emphasis added)

Now, is there any question as to who holds the reigns and/ or reins of **Sovereign Power** in this Constitutional Republic made up today of 50 Sovereign Union States created by **We the Sovereign People** through their related Constitutions? Thereafter, **We the Sovereign people** together with our territorial agents, the individual Sovereign Union States "in order to form a more perfect Union" created the federal, not National, government, the United States, as an agent to speak for its Creators in matters relative to international diplomacy, treaties, etc., together with local matters such as the value of coinage, duties of each of the 3 estates, Congress, President, and Judicial, etc., as well as other matters needed to keep the agency sovereigns (the Union States and the Federal Government) off the backs of **We the Sovereign People.**

The Dual Sovereignty
of America and its Ramifications
to Federal Jurisdiction

PREFACE

On May 28th, 2002, the Supreme Court in its decision written by Justice Clarence Thomas in <u>Federal Marine Commission (FMC) v. South Carolina State Ports Authority</u>, 535 U.S. 743 (2002), pointed out that "[d]ual sovereignty is a defining feature of our nations constitutional blueprint." The "dual sovereignty" to which Justice Thomas and the Supreme Court were referring was the sovereignty of each of the fifty (50) States of the Union together with the sovereignty of the United States, more typically referred to as the Federal Government. While the lead into this discussion touches on the dual sovereignty between the people and their respective State and Federal Governments, the author concentrates primarily on the dominions of the dual sovereignty between the States and the Federal Government as it relates to the Federal Government's Constitutional authority/power to prosecute offenses against federal laws for acts or conduct committed within the territorial boundaries of anyone of the several fifty (50) States of the Union.

The following analysis of the federal/State dual sovereignty isolates eight (8) distinct areas of law relating directly to the topic.

I.   **Territorial Jurisdiction** Shows the Constitutional genesis of the concept of dual sovereignty and how each (federal or State) derives its authority/power to prosecute crimes as well as when and where such power(s) prevails.

II. **Original v. Subject Matter/Territorial Jurisdiction**. Here the author dispels the myth espoused by various actors in the Federal Government that the statute that grants the federal **Territorial Jurisdiction** Shows the Constitutional genesis of the concept of dual sovereignty and how the (federal or Union State) district courts with original jurisdiction also grants these federal district courts with subject matter jurisdiction. The two are by no means the same animal.

III. **Territorial Tribunals** The Supreme Court has ruled that the United States District Courts are Article I, territorial Tribunals and as such can only take cognizance of offenses and affairs occurring within the territory over which Congress was Constitutionally granted exclusive legislative jurisdiction by Article I, Section 8, Clause 17 and Article IV, Section 3, Clause 2.

IV. **The Gate Keeping Affects of Rule 54**. Here it is pointed out that the Federal Rules of Criminal Procedure (FRCrP), promulgated by the Supreme Court and approved by Congress, in Rule 54, completely confines the United States District Court's jurisdiction to only those federal offenses occurring within the territory over which Congress was constitutionally granted exclusive legislative jurisdiction. Also, Congress gave Rule 54 together with all other FRCrP Rules with supersession authority, making all laws in conflict with said rules to be of no further legal effect in 28 USC 2072(b).

V. **Interstate Commerce**. The Constitution granted Congress with extraterritorial powers to regulate commerce between the several States, commonly referred to as "interstate commerce," and was the primary vehicle used by the "New Deal" judiciary to greatly expand the scope and nature of federal powers. However, Congress has since curtailed such expansion by various government actors by redefining the term "interstate commerce" to include only that commerce which occurs between states within the territory over which Congress has exclusive legislative jurisdiction, such as Puerto Rico, Guam, Virgin Islands, etc. Such redefinition reigns in the jurisprudence to prosecute offenses under Congress's extraterritorial powers to regulate interstate commerce to be entirely consistent with Rule 54, in that only acts or conduct associated with commerce occurring within the territory over which Congress possesses exclusive jurisdiction are cognizable in the federal courts.

VI. **Persons:** Black's Law Dictionary, Sixth Edition, page 773 articulates that "[p]ersons are the substance of which rights and duties are the attributes." Rights and duties flow from contracts. Contracts are the genesis of artificial entities whose names or monikers are presented in all capital letters. Also, the statutory definition of the term person" includes only artificial entities. This coupled with the fact that the defendant's name is presented in all capital letters on the indictment leads one to conclude that the charges on the indictment are levied on some artificial entity. However, the record is generally void of any contractual nexus between such artificial entity/ person and the human being who has been arrested and imprisoned.

VII **Principal of Interest** Indictments are brought, in the name of the United States of America but the Constitution created the entity "United States" and delegated to it certain powers and authorities. There exists no evidence in the Constitution or the statutes of the United States which defines just who or what the United States of America really is. Absent any contract or agreement with the defendant, the United

States of America is unable, as a matter of law, to state any claim upon which relief can be granted.

VIII. **Original Understanding** The federal judiciary was given life tenure and undiminished salaries as a means to establish its independence from any political influences whatsoever. Also, the federal judiciary takes an oath of office to uphold the Constitution, not stare decisis when stare decisis would seem to conflict with the original understanding of the Framers of the Constitution and those who ratified it. The original understanding of the Constitution also includes the concept that the people were themselves each sovereign over their own lives and the agents of government were accordingly their servants. Anything contrary to such original understanding, including the political and judicial travesty of justice called the New Deal, has no place in the jurisprudence of this nation and its independent and sovereign States.

Conclusion The Supreme Court on May 28th, 2002, ratified the concept of a dual sovereignty, herein espoused, by stating that "[dual sovereignty is a defining feature of our nation's constitutional blueprint." It doesn't get any plainer than that! Until the representatives or the agents for the Federal Government can point to the specific facts in the record that grant the United States of America with the authority/jurisdiction to prosecute acts and/or conduct committed by a defendant within the territorial boundaries of anyone of the fifty *(50)* States of the Union in a United States District Court, no such jurisdiction exists and all such prosecutions and judgments are void as a matter of law.

MOST FEDERAL INDICTMENTS FAIL TO RECOGNIZE THE DUAL SOVEREIGNTY AND THUS FAIL TO ESTABLISH FEDERAL JURISDICTION FOR A FEDERAL CAUSE OF ACTION

Probably the best place to start this discussion is Justice Rehnquist's opinion *in United States v. Lopez, 514 U.S. 549, 131 LEd. 2d 626, 115 S.Ct. 1624,* wherein the Court set the stage for an analysis of all Federal powers; i.e., powers granted by the Constitution to the newly created United States, to wit:

> "We start with first principles. The Constitution creates a Federal Government of enumerated powers. See Art. 1, §8. As James Madison wrote: 'The powers delegated by the proposed Constitution to the Federal Government are few and defined. Those which are to remain in the State governments are numerous and indefinite.' The Federalist No. 45, pp 292-293 "(C. Rossiter ed, 1961). This Constitutionally mandated division of authority 'was adopted by the Framers to ensure protection of our fundamental liberties.' *Gregory v. Ashcroft, 501 U.S. 452, 458, 111 LEd.2d 410, 111 S.Ct. 2395 (1991)* (internal quotation marks omitted)" Ibid at 552 (emphasis added).

However, from 1776 till the Constitution was ratified by the States in 1789, displacing the Articles of Confederation, there was no "Constitutionally mandated division of authority." While there was an attempt at a division of authority in the Articles of Confederation, many of the statesmen of the time realized that the authority delegated in said Articles was without teeth because all sovereignty, power, freedom, independence, and jurisdiction was retained by the States. Article II so stated:

> "Article II. Each state retains its sovereignty, freedom, and independence, and every Power, Jurisdiction and right which is not by this Confederation expressly delegated to the United States, in Congress assembled." *Articles of Confederation, (1787).*

Consequently, one of the main objectives at the Constitutional Convention in Philadelphia in 1787 was to provide the newly created United States with the necessary vehicle to enforce the powers granted to it. The Framers, after much debate and trepidation from the States convinced the Convention Delegates that the only means by which the newly created entity, the United States, could execute the powers delegated to it was to provide it with its own sovereignty. See *The Federalists Papers, Essay* # 43, written by James Madison.

This sovereignty of the United States was established through *Article I, Section 8, Clause 17*, which Lopez characterized as the "Constitutionally mandated division of authority." This "division of authority" uniquely created, in fact, a dual but mutually exclusive sovereignty in the United States of America; one being that of the United States and the other (albeit 50 in number) being each State of the Union.

I—TERRITORIAL JURISDICTION

On May 28th, 2002, the Supreme Court in its decision written by Justice Clarence Thomas in *Federal Marine Commission (FMC) v. South Carolina State Ports Authority, 535 U.S. 743* (2002), pointed out that "[d]ual sovereignty is a defining feature of our nation's constitutional blueprint." The "dual sovereignty" to which Justice Thomas and the Supreme Court were referring was the sovereignty of each of the fifty (50) States of the Union (Union States) together with the sovereignty of the United States, more typically referred to as the Federal Government. We concentrate here upon the dominions of the dual sovereignty between the States and the Federal Government as it relates to the Federal Government's Constitutional authority/power for Congress to legislate federal laws for acts or conduct exercised within the territorial boundaries of anyone of the several fifty (50) States of the Union.

Probably the paramount statement by Justice Thomas relative to the sovereignty of anyone of the Union States is exemplified in the following quote from his opinion in FMC case referenced above:

Dual sovereignty is a defining feature of our Nation's constitutional blueprint. See *Gregory* v. *Ashcroft*, 501 U.S. 452, 457 (1991). States, upon ratification of the Constitution, did not consent to become mere appendages of the Federal Government. Rather, they entered the Union "with their sovereignty intact." *Blatchford* v. *Native Village of Noatak*, 501 U.S. 775, 779 (1991). An integral component of that "residuary and inviolable sovereignty," *The Federalist No. 39, p. 245 (C. Rossiter ed. 1961) (J. Madison),* retained by the States is their immunity from private suits. Reflecting the widespread understanding at the time the Constitution was drafted, Alexander Hamilton explained,

"It is inherent in the nature of sovereignty not to be amenable to the suit of an individual *without its consent.* This is the general sense and the general practice of mankind; and the exemption, as one of the attributes of sovereignty, is now enjoyed by the government of every State of the Union. Unless, therefore, there is a surrender of this immunity in the plan of the convention, it will remain with the States . . . ." *Id.,* No. 81, at 487-488 (emphasis in original).

States, in ratifying the Constitution, **did surrender a portion of their inherent immunity by consenting to suits brought by sister States or by the Federal Government.** See *Alden* v. *Maine*, 527 U.S. 706, 755 (1999). Nevertheless, the Convention did not disturb States' immunity from private suits, thus firmly enshrining this principle in our constitutional framework. **"The leading advocates of the Constitution assured the people in no uncertain terms that the Constitution would not strip the States of sovereign immunity."** *Id.,* at 716. (emphasis added).

This analysis shows the Constitutional genesis of the concept of dual sovereignty and how each (federal or Union State government) derives its legislative power when and where such power(s) prevails.

Consequently, one of the main objectives at the Constitutional Convention in Philadelphia in 1787 was to provide the newly created United States with the necessary vehicle to enforce the powers granted to it. The Framers, after much debate and trepidation from the States convinced the Convention Delegates that the only means by which the newly created entity, the United States, could execute the powers delegated to it was to provide it with its own sovereignty. See *The Federalists Papers, Essay # 43*, written by James Madison.

This sovereignty of the United States was established through Article I, Section 8, Clause 17, which Lopez characterized as the "Constitutionally mandated division of authority." This "division of authority" uniquely created, in fact, a dual but mutually exclusive sovereignty in the United States of America; one being that of the United States and the other (albeit 50 in number) being that of each of the States of the Union.

Since each governmental sovereign organ has constitutionally delegated powers, the fundamental first principle question is what is the scope and sphere of said delegated powers? The answer is that each is sovereign within the boundary(s) of its assigned and/or acquired territory(s); the United States being sovereign over all territory ceded to it by the States and the States remaining sovereign over their own territory "as to all powers reserved."

> "Each State in the Union is sovereign as to all powers reserved. It must necessarily be so, because the United States have no claim to any authority but such as the States have surrendered to them." *Chisholm v. Georgia*, 2 Da11 (U.S.) 419, 435, 1 LEd. 440 (1793) Iredell, J. (Emphasis added)

The conduit through which all constitutionally delegated powers flow is jurisdiction. As to what jurisdiction remained with the States, the Supreme Court asked and answered the question:

> "What then, is the extent of jurisdiction which a state possesses? We answer, without hesitation; the jurisdiction is co-extensive with its territory; co-extensive with its legislative [sovereign] power." *United States v. Baevans, 16 U.S. (3 Wheat) 336, 386, 387.*

Since the sphere and scope of the delegated powers for each is co-extensive with the jurisdiction of its legislature, coextensive with its territory, it remains to be shown just what basis one uses to determine such jurisdiction as a first principle issue of Constitutional law. The whole concept of dual but mutually exclusive jurisdictions between the United States and the States of the Union was further ratified by an *Interdepartmental Committee for the Study of Jurisdiction over Federal Areas within the States*, convened in 1957, and chaired by the then Assistant Attorney General, Mansfield D. Sprague during the Eisenhower administration. The <u>Committee</u> published the text of their findings and recommendations in two volumes, the first designated as *Part I, The Facts and Committee Recommendations* and the second as <u>Part II, A Text of the Law of Legislative Jurisdiction</u>. It is in <u>Part II</u> that the <u>Committee</u> ratifies the concept of dual but separate sovereignties," to wit:

> **"The Constitution gives express recognition to <u>but one means</u> of Federal acquisition of legislative jurisdiction—by State consent under Article I, section 8, Clause 17 . . . . Justice McLean suggested that the Constitution provided the sole mode of jurisdiction and that if this mode is not pursued, no transfer of jurisdiction can take place.** *Id @ 41* (emphasis added)

"It scarcely needs to be said that unless there has been a transfer of jurisdiction (1) pursuant to clause 17 by Federal acquisition of land with State consent, or (2) by cession from the State to the Federal Government, or unless the Federal Government has reserved jurisdiction upon the admission of the State, the Federal Government possesses no Legislative jurisdiction over any area within the State,—such jurisdiction being for the exercise by the State, subject to non-interference by the State with Federal functions. *Id* @45(emphasis added).

"The Federal Government cannot, by unilateral action on its part, acquire legislative jurisdiction over any area within the exterior boundaries of a State." *Id* @46 (emphasis added).

"On the other hand, while the Federal Government has power under various provisions of the Constitution to define, and prohibit as criminal, certain acts or omissions occurring anywhere in the United States [of America], it has no power to punish for various crimes [such as drugs and firearms], jurisdiction over which is retained by the States under our Federal-State system of government, unless such crime occurs in areas as to which legislative jurisdiction has been vested in the Federal Government." *Id* @ 107. (Insertions added by the author)

The last paragraph of the Committee's findings parallels exactly what Thomas Jefferson had to say opposing the "Sedition Act" when he wrote *The Kentucky Resolutions* addressing Congress's authority to punish such crimes, to wit:

"2. Resolved, That the Constitution of the United States, having delegated to Congress a power to punish treason, counterfeiting the securities and current coin of the United States, piracies, and felonies committed on the high seas, and offenses against the law of nations, and no other crimes whatsoever . . . ." (emphasis added)

In the context of the Dual Sovereignty what then is the Constitutional jurisdictional relationship between a Union State and the Federal Government in federal legislation.

"The United States Government is a Foreign Corporation with respect to a State." *19 Corpus Jurus Secundum §884, In re: Marriam's Estate, 36 N.Y. 505, 141 N.Y. 479, Affirmed in United States v. Perkins, 163 U.S. 625*

Consequently, if the United States Government is a Foreign Corporation with respect to a State, it follows, conversely, that a State is foreign with respect to the United States Government. Since the United States Government's legislation has no authority in a foreign land, it therefore has no authority in a State which is foreign to the United States Government.

With respect to taxing statutes defined by Congress at 26 USC, Chapter 21, §3101-3121, the first presumption is that Congress is legislating within its own territory over which it was granted exclusive legislative jurisdiction.

"'**All** legislation is prima facie territorial.' *Ex Parte Blain, L.R. 12 Ch Div 522, 528; State v. Carter, 27 N.J.L. 499; People v. Merril, 2 Park Crim. Rep. 590, 596." American Banana Co. v. United Fruit Co., 213 U.S.347 (1909)* (emphasis added).

Additionally, it is well settled that all legislation of Congress is presumed to be territorial unless a contrary intent appears in the Act(s).

> "We thus apply '[t]he canon of construction which teaches that legislation [acts] of Congress; unless contrary intent appears, is meant to apply only within the territorial jurisdiction of the United States.' _Foley Brothers v. Filardo_, 336 U.S. 281, 285, 93 L.Ed 689, 69 S.Ct. _575 (1949)_; See also _Weinberger v. Rossi_, 456 U.S. 25, 32 (1982)." _Argentine Republic v. American Hess_, 488 U.S. 428, 440 _(1989)_.

Therefore, when federal statutes fail to show any intent that said statutes apply outside the territorial jurisdiction of the United States, the Federal Government and its agents accordingly fail to possess the required authority to enforce such statues and are thus constitutionally prohibited from doing so. In point of fact, Congress explicitly passed a law articulating such.

U.S.C. Title 40, Section 3112. Federal jurisdiction

(a) Exclusive Jurisdiction Not Required.—It is not required that the Federal Government obtain exclusive jurisdiction in the United States over land or an interest in land it acquires.

(b) Acquisition and Acceptance of Jurisdiction.—When the head of a department, agency, or independent establishment of the Government, or other authorized officer of the department, agency, or independent establishment, considers it desirable, that individual may accept or secure, from the State in which land or an interest in land that is under the immediate jurisdiction, custody, or control of the individual is situated, consent to, or cession of, any jurisdiction over the land or interest not previously obtained. The individual shall indicate acceptance of jurisdiction on behalf of the Government by filing a **notice of acceptance** with the Governor of the State or in another manner prescribed by the laws of the State where the land is situated.

(c)   Presumption.—It is conclusively presumed that jurisdiction has not been accepted until the Government accepts jurisdiction over land as provided in this section.

II—ORIGINAL V. SUBJECT MATTER &TERRITORIAL JURISDICTION

U.S. Attorneys like to argue that 18 USC 3231 provides the United States District Courts with "subject matter jurisdiction" over all criminal causes of action before it, but a simple reading of the statute and the definition of terms proves otherwise.

> "The district courts of the United States shall have <u>original jurisdiction</u>, exclusive of the States, of all offenses against the laws of the United States.
>
> Nothing in this title [18 USC §§ 1 et seg.] shall be held to take away or impair the jurisdiction of the courts of the <u>several states </u>under the laws thereof." <u>18 USC 3231 </u>(emphasis added)

Notwithstanding the fact that the district courts of the United States, as set out in 18 USC 3231, are not the same courts as the United States District Courts, as argued below, and notwithstanding the fact that the principal of interest is usually designated as the "United States of America" and **not** the United States, as set out in 18 USC 3231, also argued below, the simple fact of the matter is that 18 USC §3231 only grants the district courts of the United States with <u>original jurisdiction</u> once federal subject matter jurisdiction has been established.

Adapting the definition of the United States legislated at 18 USC §5;

> "The term "United States," as used in this title [*18 USC §§1 et seg.*] in a territorial sense, includes all places and waters, continental or insular, **subject**

> **to the jurisdiction** of the United States except the
> Canal Zone.' *18 USC §5* (emphasis added); it is first
> semantically obvious that section 3231 is a grant
> of original jurisdiction for offenses against the laws
> of the United States only in those areas which are
> "subject to the jurisdiction of the United States," i.e.,
> to be litigated in Territorial Tribunals. Such areas are
> set out, in toto, at 18 USC §§ 7 & 5 and are what
> Congress has defined as the area "subject to the
> jurisdiction of the United States."

"Original jurisdiction" of a court simply means the court in
which any cause of action is first litigated as opposed to a court
which possesses appellate or supervisory jurisdiction, once
the matter is determined to be a matter over which the court
and its legislature has the lawful power to adjudicate. Black's
Law Dictionary aptly depicts the delineation between "original
jurisdiction" and "subject matter jurisdiction."

> "Original jurisdiction—A court's power to hear and
> decide a matter **before** any other court can review
> the matter. Cf. "appellate jurisdiction." *Black's Law
> Dictionary* 7th Ed. p.899 (emphasis added)

> "Subject Matter Jurisdiction—Jurisdiction over the
> nature of the case and the type of relief sought;
> the extent to which a court can rule on the conduct
> of persons or status of the things." *Id. at p. 857*
> (emphasis added)

The "nature of the case"(i.e. subject matter) in the case of a
federal court could be due to its power to adjudicate either the
laws of Congress under its power to exclusively legislate within
the sovereign territory (territorial jurisdiction) of the United
States or one of Congress's enumerated powers set out in the
Constitution. But it is well settled that the federal courts do not

have a general jurisdiction, they are known to have only "limited jurisdiction."

> "Limited Jurisdiction—Jurisdiction that is confined to a particular type of case or that may be exercised only under statutory limits and prescriptions—also termed special jurisdiction. Cf. general jurisdiction.
>
> 'It is a principle of first importance that the federal courts . . . cannot be courts of general jurisdiction. They are empowered to hear only such cases as are within the judicial power of the United States as defined in the Constitution, and have been entrusted to them by a jurisdictional grant by Congress.' Charles Alan Wright, The Law of Federal courts §7 at 27 (5th ed. 1994)" Black's, supra. at p. 856 (emphasis added)

Consequently, from the above it is semantically obvious that just because 18 USC §3231 grants the district courts with original jurisdiction does not grant or establish the district court's jurisdiction over the "nature of the case," which, of course, is the court's jurisdiction over the subject matter, whether territorial or a Constitutionally enumerated power. In fact, since the District Courts of the United States are Article IV courts established by the Constitution for the United States @

At the risk of beating a dead horse, it should be pointed out that the phrase "exclusive "of the States," means exclusive of the States within the Federal Government's sovereign territory over which Congress was granted the power of exclusive legislative authority. However, the use of the phrase "the several states" in the second sentence of 18 USC §3231 establishes that the district courts of the United States are barred from taking away or impairing the jurisdiction of the courts of the 50 States under the laws of their respective legislatures.

III—TERRITORIAL TRIBUNALS

There exists a very interesting conflict of law with respect to the types of courts the Citizens of the Union States are being vacuumed into by an overzealous federal Justice Department attempting to misapply federal law within the Union States. The issue pertains to two federal court systems with similar titles but with completely dissimilar functions. The courts to which I refer are the *United States District Courts* and *the District Courts of the United States.*

The dissimilarity being that one is an Article III Court like the Supreme Court and the other is an Article I Court created as a territorial tribunal to adjudicate issues arising under Congress's Article I, Section 8, Clause 17 power to exclusive Legislate within the federal territory set aside for the Seat of government together with its power and duty to make all the needful rules and regulations respecting the Territory and other property belonging to the United States found at Article IV, Section 3, Clause 2.

In 1938, the Supreme Court further distinguished Article III and Article I courts, i.e. Territorial tribunals, to wit:

> "The term 'District Courts of the United States,' as used in the rules, without an addition: expressing a wider connotation has its historic significance. It describes the constitutional courts created under Article 3 of the Constitution. Courts of the Territories are legislative [Article 1] courts, properly speaking, and are not District Courts of the United States [i.e., not Article III courts]. We have often held that vesting a territorial court with jurisdiction similar to that vested in the District Courts of the United States does not make it a 'District Court of the United States.'" Mookine v. United States, 303 U.S. 201, 58 S. Ct. 543, 2 L.Ed. 748.

Previously, in 1922 the Supreme Court had explicitly stated that "[t]he United States District Court is not a true United States court under Article 3 of the Constitution to administer the judicial powers for: the United States therein conveyed." Balzac, supra

> "The United States District Court is not a true United States Court established under Article 3 of the Constitution to administer the judicial powers of the United States therein conveyed. It is created in virtue of the sovereign congressional faculty, granted under article 4, §3, of that instrument, of making all needful rules and regulations respecting the territory belonging to the United States. The resemblance of its jurisdiction to that of true United States courts, in offering an opportunity to non-residence of resorting to a tribunal not subject to local influence, does not change its character as a mere territorial court. Balzac v. Puerto Ric0, 258 U.S. 298, 312, 66 L.Ed. 627, 42 S.Ct. 343 (1922)

The above Supreme Court ruling posits an extremely important question. Where in the huge body of Congressional legislation did Congress grant the United States District Courts with the power (jurisdiction) to charge, try, accept guilty pleas from, convict, and sentence un-enfranchised human beings for acts or conduct committed outside Congress's sovereign territory, namely within the sovereign territory of any one of the 50 States over which Congress has no Constitutional power to punish? The answer is **nowhere.**

While 18 USC §3231 grants "original jurisdiction" to the "district courts of the United States," **it does not grant jurisdiction** to the "United States District Courts." Furthermore, the definition for "Courts" at 28 USC §610 lists only the following, to wit:

> "As used in this chapter the word "courts" includes the courts of appeals and the district courts of the United States, the United States District Court for

the Marianna Islands, the District Court of Guam,
the District Court of the Virgin Islands, the United
States Court of Federal Claims, and the Court of
International Trade." 28 USC §610

Except for the United States District Court of the Northern
Marianna Islands, there is no "United States District Court"
listed in 28 USC §610. This is further verified by 4 CFR §91.2
where it reiterates the 28 USC §610 definition. So what is a
"United States District Court?"

> "A United States District Court is an inferior court,
> i.e., inferior to the United States Supreme Court. The
> District Court is a tribunal created by Congress under
> the power given to Congress by Article 1, Section 8,
> Clause 9, of the United States Constitution, which
> provides that Congress shall have power to constitute
> Tribunals inferior to the Supreme Court.' _Romero v._
> _International Terminal OreratiOng Co._, 358 U.S. _354_,
> _3 LEd.2d 368_, _79 S.Ct. 468 1959J_. The creation
> and composition of the United States District Courts
> is presently set forth in Title 28 U.S.C. Sec. 132. A
> United States District Court has only such jurisdiction
> as the Congress confers upon the Court." _Eastern_
> _Metals Corporation v. Martin_, 191 F.Supp 245 (1960)

Thus, the United States District Courts are territorial Tribunals
to operate exclusively within the sovereign territory over which
Congress was granted exclusive legislative jurisdiction and
are therefore not Article III Courts of the United States. This is
entirely consistent with Rule 54, F.R.Cr.P., wherein, it states:
"Courts—These rules apply to **all** criminal 'proceedings in the
United· States District Courts . . . ." As argued below, Rule 54 is
the "gate keeper" which confines (by not granting otherwise) the
prosecution of any "Act of Congress" to only the territory over
which Congress was granted exclusive legislative jurisdiction.

Then it follows that any natural human being found guilty of violating a federal statute for acts occurring within the exclusive territory of anyone of the several 50 states of the Union was unlawfully prosecuted for acts or conduct occurring outside Congress's exclusive jurisdiction in a territorial Tribunal.

> "If we look at the place of its operation, we find it to be within the territory, and, therefore, within the jurisdiction of New York [or anyone of the other 50 States]. If we look at the person on whom it operates, he is found within the same territory and jurisdiction."
> *New York v. Miln*, 36 U.S. (11Pet) 102, 133 (1837).

To make matters even worse, the offices of the U.S. Attorneys are offices attached to the seat of government and therefore pursuant to 4 USC 72 and are prohibited from exercising their offices outside the District of Columbia "except as otherwise expressly provided by law." U.S. Attorneys are without any authority to convene or seek an indictment from a grand jury sitting in a territorial Tribunal for acts or conduct committed by natural persons in the sovereign territory of anyone of the 50 States, nor do they have any legislated authority to prosecute any person for said acts or conduct. The same is true for the Drug Enforcement Agency (DEA) and the Federal Bureau of Investigation (FBI). Consequently, when a Union State Citizen is arrested by an agent from any one of the said agencies, such arrests are unlawful because there exists no legislated authority to commence an action or make arrests within the sovereign territory of anyone of the 50 States.

It may be that any one of the 50 States has entered into some extra Constitutional arrangement with the United States or the United States of America which is unknown to the public at large, but is known to the Courts and other law professionals that the territorial jurisdiction of Congress was extended to include the sovereign territory of any one of the 50 States, possibly through Chapter 21 if the Internal revenue code, thereby creating a defacto state within the dejure State of any one of the 50 States. However, Article IV, Section 3, Clause 1 strictly prohibits such a concept.

> "New States may be admitted by the Congress into this Union but no new State shall be formed or erected within the jurisdiction of another state . . . ." *U.S. Constitution Article IV, Sec., C* (emphasis added).

While the government may be poised to suggest that criminal cases, because of the bankruptcy of the United States are being prosecuted under admiralty law, territorial Tribunals do not have the power, it will be noted, to adjudicate admiralty matters in the territorial courts within the sovereign territory of anyone of the 50 States. Only Article III courts have such jurisdiction.

> "Although admiralty jurisdiction can be exercised in the states in those courts only which are established in pursuance of the third article of the Constitution, the same limitation does not extend to the territories, and Congress may vest admiralty jurisdiction in courts created by a territorial legislature as well as in territorial courts created by act of Congress, and it has exercised this power in both instances. *[In re Cooper, 143 U.S. 472; The City of Panama, 101 U.S. 453; American Ins. Co. v. 356 Bales of Cotton, 26 U.S. 511 (1828)J" Vol. 1 Corpus Juris, 1914 eg, §11,* p. 1251.

Consequently, as a territorial court, the United States District Court has no Constitutional authority to charge, try, convict, and sentence anyone under the laws of admiralty for acts or conduct committed within the sovereign territory of anyone of the 50 States.

Accordingly, when one is tried, convicted, and sentenced in a territorial Tribunal with no Constitutional authority to adjudicate any claims against an individual for acts or conduct occurring within the sovereign soil of one of the 50 Union States, and since the U.S. Attorney likewise is without any Constitutionally legislated authority to prosecute such an individual for any such acts or conduct occurring within the sovereign soil of anyone of the 50 Union States [i.e. outside the District of Columbia], and since armed DEA agents are likewise without any Constitutionally legislated authority to arrest or restrain any such person, such a person would be unconstitutionally incarcerated. Thus such an incarcerated person would be a victim of abuse of process and false imprisonment in its most cynical and despotic political form.

Therefore, the prosecuting Court would be obligated under the Constitution to perform its Article III duty and grant the prisoner a Writ of error, returning him to his natural and inalienable right to Liberty on the Courts own Motion.

IV—RULE 54 AS TERRITORIAL GATE KEEPER

As pointed out by Justice Marshal *in United States v. Wiltberger, 5 Wheat (U.S.) 76, 95, 5 L.Ed 37, 46:*

> "The rule that penal laws are to be construed strictly, is perhaps, not much less old than construction itself. It is founded on the tenderness of the law for the rights of individuals; and on the plain principle that the power of punishment is vested in the legislature, not in the judicial department." *United States v. Boston & Me. R.R., 380 U.S. 157, 160, 85 S.Ct. 868, 870, 13 L.Ed.2d 728 (1965) and United States v. A&P Trucking, 358 U.s. 121, 127, 3 L.ED.2d 165, 78 S.Ct. 203 (1958); also quoted in United States v. Anzalone, 766 F.2d 676 (1st Cir 1985).*

Taking this into account, it would appear that when Congress gave the Supreme Court the power, pursuant to 28 USC §2072(a), to prescribe general rules of practice and procedure and rules of evidence for cases in the United States District

Courts (including proceedings before magistrates thereof), Congress also gave the Supreme Court the power to repeal all legislation contrary to said rules, pursuant *to 28 USC 2072(b)*, to wit:

> "(b) Such Rules shall not abridge, enlarge, or modify any substantial right. **All laws in conflict with such rules shall be of no further force or effect after such rules have taken effect**. 28 U.S.C. 2072(b) (Emphasis added).

From a simple reading of the Federal Rules of Criminal Procedure, it will be obvious that the Supreme Court has repealed all legislation which is to be litigated in the United States District Courts for any and all acts or conduct occurring outside the territory over which Congress has exclusive legislative jurisdiction, hence the moniker "gate keeper" as herein assigned.

Rule 54. Application and exception.

(a) Courts. These rules apply to **all** criminal proceedings in the United States District Courts[90] . . . . (emphasis added) c) Application of terms. As used in these rules, the following terms have their designated meanings.—

'Act of Congress' includes **any Act of Congress locally** applicable to and in force in the District of Columbia, in Puerto Rico, in a territory or in an insular possession[91]. (emphasis added)

---

[90]   I.e., Article 1, Territorial (Administrative) Courts

[91]   Only that legislation having application in Federal territory is an "Act of congress"

'State' includes the District of Columbia, Puerto Rico, territory and insular possessions[92]. (emphasis added)

'Law' includes statutes and judicial decisions."
Federal Rules of Criminal Procedure, Rule 54.

From a reading of Rule 54, several things come to light as self-evident conclusions from the rules themselves. First, the rules apply to **all** criminal proceedings in the territorial Tribunals, the United States District Courts. Second, the only legislation, "acts of Congress," recognized by the F.R.Cr.P. to be prosecutable in said territorial Tribunals are those acts which have application within the territory over which Congress possesses exclusive territorial jurisdiction. This, by the way, puts Rule 54 entirely consistent with the Supreme Court's ruling in Balzac, set out in III above. Third, the term "State" is limited for all criminal prosecutions to the territory over which Congress has exclusive legislative jurisdiction. And fourth, Congress has legislated that all laws (which includes statutes and judicial decisions as per F.R.Cr.P. 54(c)) in conflict with the Supreme Court's rules "shall have no further force or effect after such rules have taken effect." Notice that, pursuant to 28 U.S.C. § 2072(b), that F.R.Cr.P. also invalidate all judicial decisions, stare decisis, which are in conflict with said rules.

While the idea that the F.R.Cr.P. trump legislation, "acts of Congress," or judicial decisions may raise doubts in the minds of some, the idea that such was the intent of both Congress and the Supreme Court is reflected explicitly in the Commentary by David D. Seigal on the 1988 and 1990 Revisions of Rule 54 on page 534 of Title 28, section 2072 (USCA 1996), to wit:

"the Second sentence of the new subdivision (b) of §2072 ·was a key player in the 1988 act. It's

---

[92] No Union States listed here, therefore the term "State" includes only Federal States.

the famous **supersession clause**, purporting to
subordinate all "laws," including Acts of Congress,
to the rules promulgated under subdivision (a)."
(Emphasis added)

Under the rule that penal statutes are to be strictly construed,
including the Rule governing their effects, there can be no
remaining doubt that Rule 54 under authority of 28 U.S.C.
§2072 limits all criminal proceedings in the United States District
Courts to alleged criminal offenses committed in the territory
over which Congress has exclusive legislative jurisdiction. Such
territory being explicitly set out in 18 U.S.C. §§ 7 and 5. Thus,
conclusively proving that the United States District Courts are
in fact and in law strictly territorial Tribunals which have limited
jurisdiction over only those acts or conduct occurring within the
United States territorial jurisdiction as argued in III above. To
posit otherwise is to suggest that linguistics have no application
in law and that we are being ruled by men, not law.

Since the above set out portions of Rule 54 have been in effect
since 1944, anyone charged in federal court for acts or activity
occurring in any one of the 50 States has been forced to answer
charges which have no force and effect in the United States
District Courts. This is so because of Congressional legislation
and the rules promulgated by the United States Supreme Court.
Thus, two branches of the Federal Government have spoken
against the Executive branch exercising any authority outside
the territory over which Congress has exclusive legislative
jurisdiction. Are we witnessing the executive branch together
with the United States District Courts ignoring the dictates of the
Supreme Court and Congress and thus reducing the country to
the rule of man and not law? After all, this isn't rocket science.

V—INTERSTATE COMMERCE

Prior to any discussion relative to "interstate commerce," it
needs to be said that when Congress, in its legislation, elects

to redefine a term used in the Constitution, such as "State," "United States," "interstate commerce," etc., it does so only within its power of exclusive legislative jurisdiction within its own sovereign territory. To postulate otherwise would be to absurdly suggest that Congress could legislate itself unlimited power by simply redefining terms used in the Constitution.

For example, the term "State" when used in the Constitution means one thing and one thing only, and that one thing is a State of the Union of 50 Union States. As .aforesaid, a State of the Union enjoys a dual sovereign relationship with the United States, akin to a peer relationship. A "State of the United States" by its own terms (discussed below) has a subject relationship to the United States and exists within the territorial boundaries of the United States over which Congress has exclusive legislative jurisdiction. Remembering that the States of the Union assembled at Philadelphia to create the United States by Constitutional compact, it would be a logical and legal impossibility and a linguistic absurdity to suggest that one of the States of the Union as one of the creators of the United States could be a subject of its own creation, the United States.

The key for much of Congress's legislation is its redefinition of the term "State." The term "State" is redefined in federal statutes in some 800 places, 55 statutes in Title 18 alone. Since some of those redefinitions include the phrase "State of the United States," it is imperative that such phrase be understood as a matter of law. By examining Congress's redefinition of the terms "United States" and "State" together, it can be easily understood just what Congress intended the phrase "State of the United States" to mean.

At 21 USC §802(28), Congress redefined the United States for all offenses in Title 21, Chapter 13; to wit:

> "The term 'United States,' when used in a geographic (territorial) sense, means all places and waters, continental and insular, **subject to the jurisdiction of**

the United States." *21 U.S.C. §802(28)*. (emphasis added)

Removing the surplusage from the above redefinition, it takes on the more simple form:

> "The term 'United States' includes all territory subject to the jurisdiction of the United States."

We know, of course, that the phrase "territory subject to the jurisdiction of the United States" is semantically equivalent to the phrase "territory over which Congress has exclusive legislative jurisdiction." Therefore, a semantically accurate rephrased redefinition of the "United States" at 21 U.S.C. §802(26) in Constitutional terms becomes:

> "The term 'United States' includes all territory over which Congress has exclusive legislative jurisdiction.[93]"

Thus the phrase "State of the United States" in actual fact means "State of the territory over which Congress has exclusive legislative jurisdiction."

Now turning to the redefinition of the term "State" as set out at 21 U.S.C. §802(26), to wit:

> "The term 'State' means a State of the United States, the District of Columbia, and any commonwealth, territory, or possession of the United States.

Substituting the meaning of the United States in the above redefinition of the term "State," it becomes:

---

[93]   The power for Congress to exclusively legislate comes from Article I, Section 8, Clause 17of the Federal Constitution, which, of course, is all Federal territory.

> "The term 'State' means a State of the territory over which Congress has exclusive legislative jurisdiction, the District of Columbia, and any commonwealth, territory, or possession over which Congress has exclusive legislative jurisdiction."

Consequently, unless Congress's redefinition of the term "State" explicitly includes "the several States of the Union," or "the 50 Union States," or the "States of the Union," such redefinition excludes the 50 States of the Union and only includes those entities therein specifically defined.

> "It is the canon of statutory construction that the inclusion of certain provisions implies the exclusion of others. The doctrine *inclusio unius est exclusio alterius* 'informs "the court to exclude from operation those items not included in a list of elements that are given effect expressly by the statutory language.' In re TMI, 67 F3d 1119, 1123 (3rd Cir 1995)(Quoting Williams v. Wohlegemuth.540 F2d 163, 169 (3rd Cir 1976)" United States v. McQuilkin, 78 F3d 105, 108 (3rd Cir 1996)

Terms such as the "several States of the Union" and "States of the Union" are terms or phrases used in the Constitution and would thus be presumed to refer to the fifty (50) States, except that the phrase "the several States of the United States," while at best ambiguous, cannot refer to the 50 States of the Union for the exact same reason that the phrase the "States of the United States" does not. As aforesaid, the "States of the United States" exist only within the territorial jurisdiction of the United States regardless of whether they are referred to as the "several States of the United States," "the States of the United States," or "any State of the United States".

As shown above, "the most natural meaning of "of the United States" is "belonging to the United States." *Ellis v, United States 206 U.S. 246, S.Ct. 600 (1907).*

Title 21, section 801 suggests that one should presume that Congress was calling on its "power to regulate interstate commerce" when it enacted Chapter 13 offenses. But upon closer scrutiny it is easy to see that such is not the case.

First, Congress admits at 21 USC §801(5) that it lacked the capacity to call on its commerce clause power when enacting the drug laws by declaring:

> "[I]t is **not feasible** to distinguish, in terms of control [legislation], between controlled substances manufactured and distributed interstate and controlled substances manufactured and distributed intrastate."
> 21 U.S.C. *§801(S)* (emphasis added)

Federal Rules of Criminal Procedure rule 54 notwithstanding, Congress obviously, point blank, washed its hands of having any authority under its commerce clause power when it enacted the controlled substance offenses set out in Chapter 13. For when Congress admits/declares that it is unable to distinguish between interstate commerce and intrastate commerce in terms of control (that is its enacted statutes), it is telling the Executive Branch and the Judiciary that this legislation is not based on Congress's power to "regulate interstate commerce" but is instead drawing on is exclusive power to legislate in and over federal territory Under Article I, Section 8, clause 17 and Article IV, Section 3, Clause 2.

Second, it must be noted that Chapter 13, *The Controlled Substance Act of 1970* was an amendment to the *Federal Food, Drug, and Cosmetic Act of 1938,* which was an amendment to the Pure *Food and Drug Act of 1906.* In the *Pure Food and Drug Act*, Congress redefined interstate commerce to be confined to the territory over which it has exclusive legislative jurisdiction.

> "The term 'interstate commerce' means (1) commerce between any State or Territory and any place outside thereof, and (2) commerce within the District of

Columbia or within any other Territory not organized
with a legislative body." 21 U.S.C. 321(b)

While Congress, as aforesaid, is not at liberty to redefine a term
used in the Constitution, especially when it has a direct bearing
on an enumerated power, such as "interstate commerce," it is;
of course, at liberty to do so when legislating under its grant
of power to exclusively legislate within its sovereign territorial
jurisdiction. A reading of the redefinition of the term "State" will
make it more than obvious that Congress did not in fact call
upon its commerce clause power when enacting the drug laws,
but instead, indeed, and in fact redefined "interstate commerce"
to be solely within its own sovereign territory.

> "The term 'State,'" . . . means any State or Territory of
> the United States, the District of Columbia, and the
> Commonwealth of Puerto Rico." 21 U.S.C. 321(a)(1)

Remembering that a "State of the United States" is not one
of the States of the Union but a State within the sovereign
territory of the United States, by substituting the above
definition for State in the redefinition of "interstate commerce,"
it then becomes intuitively obvious that the above redefinition of
"interstate commerce" clearly relates only to commerce within
the sovereign territorial jurisdiction of the United States.

At the risk of being redundant, the word "state" refers to the
representative government of a territory. For example, New
York is the territory; the state of New York is the representative
government of the people of New York domiciled within
its territorial boundaries. Likewise, the State of New York
is said to have exclusive legislative jurisdiction within the
territorial boundaries of New York. The men who attended the
Constitutional Convention in Philadelphia were representatives
from their respective state governments and were therefore
representing the State of New York, etc.

Black's Law Dictionary defines "State" as:

1. "The system of rules by which jurisdiction and authority are exercised over a political organized body of people; the political organization or the body of people itself."
2. "An institution of **self-government** within a larger political entity." _Blacks Law Dictionary_, Pocket Ed. (2000)

Since the States of the Union and the United States enjoy a mutually exclusive sovereignty, the State of New York, for example, while it is "an institution of self-government," it is **not** "within a larger political entity." Therefore, the States of the Union are not States of the United States, no matter how many angels dance on the head of a pin.

Notice also that the term States of the Union refer to peer states in a Union of States, and, as aforesaid, is not within a larger political entity, while a State of the United States is.

To demonstrate that Congress knows how to include the States of the Union in its redefinitions of the term "State," consider following nearly identical redefinitions at 7 U.S.C. §§2009 and 2012, 42 U.S.C. §§ 618 and 619:

"The term 'State' means each of the 50 States[94], the District of Columbia, the Commonwealth of Puerto Rico, Guam, the Virgin Islands of the United States, American Samoa, the Commonwealth of the Northern Marianna Islands, or the Trust Territory of the Pacific Islands."

"Each of the 50 States" is not a "State of the United States," but the remaining of the entities above listed are.

---

[94]   In my opinion, even the term "50 State" is somewhat ambiguous where "the several States of the Union is not.

Furthermore, the fact that Congress knows how to include the 50 independent States in its drug legislation is verified at 21 U.S.C. 1007, to wit:

> "The term 'State' includes, in addition to the several States of the Union, the Commonwealth of Puerto Rico, the District of Columbia, ..." 21 U.S.C. 1007

Therefore, when Congress decided to get into the "drug and cosmetic" regulation business in 1906, it was well aware that such legislation was authorized under its delegated power under Article I, Section 8, Clause 17 of the Constitution which is the power of exclusive legislative jurisdiction within its sovereign territory. Even when using the term "interstate commerce," Congress limited such commerce to be solely within its own sovereign territory or commerce going between territory within its exclusive jurisdiction and without. In either case, the commerce must by Congress's own definition of "interstate commerce" go through the territory over which Congress has exclusive legislative jurisdiction. But commerce involving drugs between any States of the Union that doesn't contact federal territory, in some manner, is not actionable in the District Courts. So when Congress declared in 21 U.S.C. 801(5) that it "was not feasible in terms of control (legislation)" to distinguish between interstate and intrastate drug commerce it was due to the fact that Congress's own redefinition of "interstate commerce" contained both concepts of interstate and intrastate commerce therein.

While Congress redefined "interstate commerce" in many chapters and sections within Title 18, it threw a blanket definition over the entire title at 18 USC §10. To wit:

> "§10 Interstate commerce and foreign commerce defined.
>
> The term 'interstate commerce,' **as used in this title,** includes commerce between one State, Territory,

Possession, or District of Columbia and another State, Territory, Possession, or District of Columbia. (emphasis added)

The term 'foreign commerce' as used in this title, includes commerce with a foreign country."

The first thing to notice is that this redefinition of the term interstate commerce applies to the whole of Title 18 unless it is again redefined in an applicable statute as it has been in section 921. In Congress's "plug and play" definitions of terms; whenever we run into a redefinition for the term State, it thus must be plugged into the foregoing definition using the term to fully understand the original definition. While the term State is not redefined for Section 10, it is known by the company it keeps as a "State of the United States", and by the simple fact that Congress is redefining a term of power found in the Constitution, dictating the Section 10 has application only within the territory over which Congress has been granted exclusive legislative jurisdiction. This is also consistent with 18 USC §7 which is a total blanket over Title 18 limiting its jurisdiction to areas over which Congress has the power of Exclusive Legislative jurisdiction.

Take section 1030, for another example, where Congress at 18 U.S.C. §1030(e)(3) redefines state:

"(3) the term 'State' includes the District of Columbia, the Commonwealth of Puerto Rico, and any other commonwealth, possession or territory of the United States."

Looking back to the redefinition of interstate commerce at section 10, while the redefinition of the term "State" from 18 U.S.C. 1030(e)(3) plugged into 18 U.S.C. §10 creates some textural redundancy, it, nonetheless, limits interstate commerce to that which occurs between political subdivisions within the federal territory over which Congress has exclusive legislative jurisdiction as granted by the Constitution.

This is all consistent with Rule 54, the fact that the United States District Courts are territorial Tribunals, and the fact that in order to adjudicate a cause of action under Congress's commerce clause power would require it be commenced in an Article III Tribunal, and establishes even further that Congress's redefinition of "interstate Commerce" must, as a matter of law, be confined to territory over which it has exclusive legislative jurisdiction. Consequently, because Congress cannot possibly redefine a term used in the Constitution which has a direct bearing on a delegated power therefrom, except when legislating within its sovereign territory, it is a first principle issue that when it chose to redefine the term like "interstate commerce", "State", etal, it accordingly limited such legislation to be enforceable only within its own territory. Furthermore, the clear unambiguous wording of the redefinition itself restricts the term "interstate commerce" to the territory over which Congress has exclusive legislative jurisdiction. Therefore, the Federal Government has no jurisdiction to enforce its drug laws under Title 21, Chapter 13 within the territorial boundaries of any one of the several 50 States. So, even if an indictment had alleged an interstate commerce nexus for acts occurring in any one or more of the 50 States of the Union, it would have been superfluous since "interstate commerce" as it applies to Title 21, Chapter 13, is strictly commerce within the territorial boundaries over which Congress possesses exclusive legislative jurisdiction, and such territory does not include any territory over which one of the 50 States has exclusive legislative jurisdiction except when the commerce traffic travels through the territory over which Congress has exclusive jurisdiction.

The same can be said for other federal legislation. Take for example the firearm statutes. For Title 18, Chapter 44 offenses (firearms), the limitations on the definitions of the terms "interstate commerce" and "State" and their associated jurisdictional restrictions on Chapter 44 offenses, are much clearer than they might be on Title 21, Chapter 13 offenses. Even though Congress throw a jurisdictional blanket over Title 18 offenses regarding interstate and foreign commerce at §10, it redefined "interstate commerce" in subsequent legislation for firearms.

At 18 USC §5, the definition for the "United States" as it applies to the entirety of Title 18 is nearly identical to the definition of that term for Title 21, Chapter 13 offenses, namely:

> "The term "United States," as used in this title in a territorial sense, includes all places and waters, continental or insular, **subject to the jurisdiction of the United States**, except the Canal Zone. *18 U.S.C. 5* (emphasis added).

Here again, we see Congress limiting the definition of the "United States" in the entirety of Title 18 to the territory over which Congress has exclusive legislative jurisdiction "unless a contrary intent appears" in the alleged offended statute. See Foley Brothers, supra, infra, at p. 5. It remains to be shown whether Congress intended for Chapter 44 offenses to be prosecuted outside of its territory under its commerce clause power or not. Looking at the redefinition for the term "interstate commerce" together with the redefinition for the term "State," at Section 921, it becomes semantically and linguistically obvious that Congress had no contrary intent for Chapter 44 offenses to be prosecuted beyond the territory over which it has exclusive legislative jurisdiction.

> "The term "interstate commerce" includes commerce between any place in a State and any place outside of that State, or within any possession of the United States (not including the Canal Zone) or the District of Columbia, but such term does not include commerce between places within the same State but through any place outside of that State. The term **"State" includes the District of Columbia,**

the Commonwealth of Puerto Rico, and the possessions of the United States (not including the Canal Zone).

In fact and in law, Congress's redefinition of the term "interstate commerce" specifically limits the scope of Chapter 44 offenses to the territory over which it has exclusive legislative jurisdiction. Consequently, even if the prosecution attempts to allege federal jurisdiction through an "interstate commerce" allegation, Congress has trapped such an allegation to be applicable only within the federal sovereign territory. Consequently, before any presumptions can be made relative to federal jurisdiction for the prosecution of criminal offenses, one must research Congress's redefinitions of various jurisdictional terms, such as "State," "interstate commerce," etc., before any conclusive presumptions relative to jurisdiction can be made.

Therefore, all conclusions drawn in the foregoing discussion also apply to all Title 18, Chapter 44 offenses, and any references to the term State within statutes defining an offense, do not include acts or conduct committed within any one of the fifty (50) States, but is, by definition, limited to the territory over which Congress has exclusive legislative jurisdiction. This line of reasoning, by legal necessity carries over and likewise applies to the term "prohibited person." A person who has committed an offense in anyone of the fifty (50) States does not become a "prohibited person" under the law in order to provide the Justice Department with a jurisdictional element for the express purpose of allowing the prosecutor to make an end run around the Constitution and Congress's intent.

However, an interesting conflict of law arises when a statute does actually convey Congress's intent to call on its commerce clause powers, such as in "mail fraud" and "wire fraud," 18 USC. §§ 1341 and 1343. Such statutes, it will be noted, are in conflict with the "gate keeping" effects of Rule 54. Remember, pursuant to 28 U.D.C. 2072, the Federal Rules of Criminal Procedure trump statutes in conflict thereto, and rule 54 limits the scope of "acts of Congress," statutes, to territory over which Congress has exclusive legislative jurisdiction. How such a conflict will be resolved in the courts remains to be seen. The courts need to be presented with the argument before any resolution of this conflict can occur. Perhaps the argument centers around the fact that the United States, as a corporation dealing in commercial paper, is bound by the Clearfield Doctrine, that the "United States does business on business terms." This limits the scope of its private corporate law to the territory over which it has the capacity under its corporate charter to establish commercial contracts with penal provisions under admiralty law. There has to be some reason for the presence of the President's flag (Commander in Chief, an executive officer) and symbolic oars in the federal court rooms.

Admittedly, there are a lot more questions than answers, but we need to formulate the questions before we are able to seek answers. Even then, there is no guarantee that the struggle to return to individual sovereignty will be realized, but for sure it can't happen without first **Restoring the Sovereignty of the Union States.** Therefore, at the outset be advised and warned that Liberty can only be enjoyed through eternal vigilance. Here's to our future.

Furthermore, since only an Article III court possesses the Constitutional power to litigate a cause of action under Congress's commerce power within the several 50 States, the United States District Court, consistent with the fact that it is solely a territorial Tribunal together with the "gate keeping" provisions of F.R.Cr.P. Rule 54 confining the United States District Courts to the territory over which Congress has exclusive legislative jurisdiction, could not and therefore did not possess the power to litigate a cause of action in any one of the 50 Union States under Congress's commerce clause power.

Therefore, interstate commerce does not provide a federal cause of action upon which relief could be granted in the case of either drug violations or firearm issues where the acts or activity allegedly violating federal law occurred outside the territory over which Congress was granted exclusive legislative jurisdiction, i.e., outside the United States. The lesson to be learned here is that things are not very often what they seem in federal statutes. One must read a statute in its entirety, including all the definitions dealing with the subject matter of any given chapter. It is in the definitions that one will find the key elements of federal jurisdiction. There are those who would propose a Constitutional Amendment to limit the range and scope of "interstate commerce" to the range and scope of the original understanding of the framers of the Constitution. It is this author's opinion that upon a thorough inspection of the statutes exercising control over interstate commerce, one will find that Congress has limited such power to the territory over which it has exclusive control and no such amendment would be meaningful or appropriate. In any case, any legislation which is overbroad in the use of Congress's interstate commerce power is throttled by F.R.C.P. Rule 54. Congress has done its job. It has written the law to stay within its own cocoon of power. It is the executive and the judicial branches which refuse to follow it but instead execute federal law when and where the individual Justice Department employees and Judges see fit. Thus, when individual government agents refuse to stay within the law, we no longer have the rule of law, we degenerate to the rule of men.

VI—PERSON

In many cases, the U. S. Attorneys attempt to use the definition of the term "person" to establish federal jurisdiction for criminal prosecutions. However, an analysis of the term "person" in federal legislation will soon reveal that such an attempt by federal prosecutors itself borders on criminal behavior. For example, in the Food and Drug Acts and subsequent amendments, the "term 'person' includes, individual, partnership, corporation, and association." Taking into account that an individual "may, in proper cases, include artificial persons," (Quoted form *Black's Law Dictionary*, Sixth Ed. page 773.) all the terms included in the definition of the term "person" are artificial non-human entities. Knowing a thing is characterized by the company it keeps, the definition of the term person in Title 21, Chapter 13, appears to relate to only artificial entities. Looking further, <u>Black's Law Dictionary</u> defines the term "person" as:

> "1. A Human being. 2. An entity (such as a corporation) that is recognized by law as having rights and duties of a human being. 3. The living body of a human being.
>
> 'So far as legal theory is concerned, a person is any being whom the law regards as **capable of rights and duties**. Any being that is so capable is a person, whether a human being or not, and no being that is not so capable is a person, even though he be a man.
>
> Persons are the substance of which rights and duties are the attributes. It is only in this respect that persons possess juridical significance, and this is the exclusive point of view from which personality receives legal recognition.' John Salmond <u>Jurisprudence </u>318 (Glanville C.Williams, 10th ed 1947)"

To reiterate, the **exclusive** point of view is that rights and duties are the attributes of a person in order for the being/person to receive any legal recognition. Rights and duties flow from contracts, whether they be the creation of the person, such as a corporation, or simply an agreement/contract between two or more persons, whether real or artificial. Therefore, all persons referred to in the statutes must possess the attributes of rights and duties, and thus must be a party to some contract or agreement with an agency of the government from which such rights and duties flow.

However, the record is usually, in federal cases, void of any pleading that a defendant is involved in any contract or agreement with government or the Plaintiff, the United States, from which there might flow any rights or duties beyond the duties of the Plaintiff to protect the defendant's inalienable rights to life, liberty and the pursuit of happiness as an emancipated human being. *Chisholm v. Georgia, 2 Dall (U.S.) 419, 454, 1 L.Ed440 (1793)* ("at the revolution, the sovereignty devolved on the people; and they are truly the sovereigns of the country, but they are sovereigns without subjects . . . and have none to govern but themselves") *Yick Wo v. Hopkins, Sheriff, 118, U.S. 356* ("Sovereignty itself is, of course, not subject to the law, for it is the author of the law, but in our system, while sovereign powers are delegated to the agencies of government, sovereignty itself remains with the people, by whom and for whom all government exists and acts.") *Hale v. Henkle, 201 u.s. 43, 50 L.Ed 652, 26 S.Ct. 370 (1906)* ("He owes no such duty to the state since he receives nothing therefrom.") Consequently, unless the record provides evidence that the defendant was a person recognizable by the federal statutes alleged to have been violated in an indictment, the federal courts have no power to proceed.

Notwithstanding the absence of any contract, agreement, or license creating the ens legis and conferring rights and duties thereto, the question also exists as to how and/or under what contract, agreement, or license did a criminal defendant become surety for this artificial entity designated by the representation of an all capital letters name arranged in the same sequence as the letters in the defendant's proper name? Now the primary question becomes, in what evidence exists in the record of any contract, agreement, or license making the defendant liable for any ens legis alter ego, straw man, person in which duties are one of its attributes? It must therefore be presumed that no such contract, agreement, or license exists and there is no legitimate cause of action or any valid claim upon which relief can be granted. For if there is such an adhesion contract, agreement, or license which imposes unspecified duties upon the person of the defendant through an ens legis transmitting utility, the government is required under the *Clearfield Trust Doctrine (Clearfield Trust Co. v. United States, 318 U.S 363-371 (1942))* to produce the document which establishes that the government corporation is the Holder in Due Course of some valid voluntary contract or commercial agreement binding the defendant to the specific performance or surety for said ens legis. Otherwise, the government corporation, the United States, by and through its probable transmitting utility, the United States of America, is attempting to enslave or subjugate such persons as the defendant by granting rights and duties in an ens legis being identified by all capital letters name arranged in the same order as the defendant's proper name by legislative, executive, and judicial fiat. While secret and unpublished in the record, this represents involuntary servitude which is strictly prohibited by the 13th Amendment to the Constitution.

Therefore, to secretly create some artificial entity with an ens legis in all capital letters arranged in the same sequence as a defendant's proper name for the purpose of creating a transmitting utility as a means of enslaving such person to be a subject slave of or to the bankrupt United States for the express purpose of servicing said debt is patently unconstitutional, unless the record has revealed some corporate contract, agreement, or license to show that the defendant knowingly and willingly in propria persona agreed to the creation of said artificial entity/strawman for said purposes.

Since the record usually evidences the existence of no such contract, agreement, or license, the ultimate jurisdictional question arises; which is, was the human being, the defendant, sitting at the defense table the same person named on the indictment or was the person named on the indictment merely a transmitting utility using the defendant's proper name in all capital letters to cunningly coerce the defendant into accepting the debt of said ens legis/transmitting utility thereby unConstitutionally enslaving him? Therefore, if the person named on the indictment is an ens legis and therefore not the same person as the defendant in propia persona, and the record contains no documentary evidence of any nexus between the defendant and said ens legis, the indictment has failed to make a claim upon which relief can be granted. Accordingly, the judgment, if the defendant is deemed to be guilty, is void and the Court must grant Writ of Error and immediately restore the defendant's rights to Liberty.

On the other hand, if the person named on the indictment is an ens legis and therefore not the same person as the defendant in propia persona and said ens legis is being used as a transmitting utility to involuntarily enslave the defendant in propia persona for whatever purpose, said involuntary enslavement is unconstitutional making any proceedings dependent thereto a fraud rendering the proceedings void for fraud and a violation of the defendant's inalienable right to Liberty. Accordingly, the judgment is void for fraud and the Court must grant a Writ of Error and immediately restore the defendant's rights to Liberty.[95]

While the government actors may have created an artificial/ legal fiction entity identified by the defendant's proper name in all capital letters as a "vessel" in order to proceed in admiralty, it is of no consequence for, as aforesaid, there is no Constitutional authority for territorial Tribunals, in this case the United States District Court, to take jurisdiction to adjudicate any case under maritime or admiralty law for acts or conduct committed within the territorial boundaries of anyone of the 50 States. See infra, page 11 & 12. Consequently, admiralty cannot serve as a lawful basis for the proceeding in the United States District Court in such a case and the judgment remains void for all the above argued reasons and this Court must dismiss all charges and restore a defendant's inalienable right to Liberty.

---

[95] It just may be that such a transmitting utility for purposes of contractual control over a person occurs when one pays the employee FICA tax analyzed in the of the article above, *The Reformation of Union State Sovereignty.*

VII—PRINCIPAL OF INTEREST

All Criminal actions are brought in the United States District Court in the name of the **United States of America**. However, Congress has never legislated that a cause of action of any kind can be brought in the name of the "United States of America" nor has Congress defined or legislatively created such an entity as the "United States of America."

In the Revised Statutes of 1878, Section 919, Congress legislated that:

> "All suits for recovery of any duties, imports, or
> taxes, . . . , and all suits arising under the postal laws,
> shall be **brought in the name of the United States**."
> (emphasis added)

This same Principal carries all the way to the present day legislation. The 1994 edition of Title 28, Section 566(c) is just one example:

> "(c) Except as otherwise provided by law or Rule of
> Procedure, the United States Marshals Service shall
> execute all lawful writs, process, and orders issued
> under authority of the United States . . . ."

Nowhere is there Constitutional or statutory authority for the "United States of America" to serve as principal of interest in civil or criminal causes of action in any of the States of the Union. A knee jerk response might be that the "United States" and the "United States of America" are one in the same, but such is not the case. Title 28 Code of Federal Regulations is just one of many examples that provide conclusive proof that the two are unique entities. The reader will notice that 28 CFR 0.96b clearly distinguishes one from the other.

Even 18 USC 3231 specifies original jurisdiction only "for offenses against the laws of the United States," not the "United States of America."

So how does the "United States of America" become the party to the action or Principal of Interest in criminal and civil proceedings against an accused person? Is the "United States of America" simply a legal fiction entity, created for the sole purpose to function as a transmitting utility for the United States due to the fact that the United States has declared bankruptcy, since a bankrupt corporation has no standing at law? (See House Joint Resolution 192 of June 5, 1933). Whether so or not, this issue should be raised at the outset of any commenced action because the "United States of America" has no Constitutional or legislated authority to bring a cause of action against anyone under the laws of the United States, whether in equity, common law, or admiralty. Consequently, all federal courts are duty bound to dismiss the action for failure of the U.S. Attorney to establish lawful standing to state a claim before the court.

VIII—ORIGINAL UNDERSTANDING

In *Lopez, supra*, Justice Thomas in his concurring opinion spoke of the concept of deciding cases based on the **original understanding**_of the Constitution by those who framed and ratified it and how far our jurisprudence has deviated from that **original understanding**_with respect to **interstate commerce**. Justice Robert H. Bork, in his book *The Tempting of America, The Political Seduction of the Law,"* 1st Touchstone ed. 1990, used the concept of **original understanding**_as his central theme. (Emphasis added)'

However, both Justice Thomas and Justice Bork lamented that to return our jurisprudence to such a basic and crisp purpose for our federal and State constitutions based on **original understanding**_would be a political impossibility. There are certainly very few legal scholars who would disagree with such an assessment based on the impact of stare decisis on current day rulings. But such a negative reservation raises a couple of questions. First, by giving appointed judges tenure and undiminished salaries, wasn't it the intent of the Framers of the Constitution to free the judiciary from **all** political pressures, or was their intent to design an appointment system to cause the judiciary to forever be beholding to the financial and political powers that made their lifetime appointment possible? Second, do our judges when appointed, take an oath to uphold the Constitution or do they swear to follow the path of **stare decisis**?

In 1818 the Supreme Court in Chisholm,. supra, the **original understanding** of the Constitution was recognized to be, that both the people and the states were sovereign and the offices of government were the servants of the people. Today, the federal servants take the position of sovereign and the people and the states are reduced to serfs on the land. The people pay an ever increasing percentage of their productivity to support the ever increasing aristocracy required to manage and control the ever increasing despotic bureaucracy's deviation from the **original understanding** of the Constitution.

The Constitution **commands** Congress to provide each state with a Republican Form of government, yet the federal oligarchy propagandizes that the United States is a Democracy. (This may be true in fact in the sense that Congress through its exclusive legislative power over its own sovereign soil has indeed created a Democracy rather than a Republic, contrary to the mandates of the Constitution wherein it states that "The United States shall guarantee to each State in this Union a Republican form of government.") And the people of the Union States believe it to be true also in their own territory. Justice Bork wrote "Constitutional jurisprudence is mysterious terrain for most people, who have more pressing things to think about. And a very handy fact that is for the revisionist." **Tempting, supra**, at 17. And so it is.

One should also notice that nowhere in this paper do we challenge the Constitutionality of **any**_of Congress's legislation. In fact, quite the contrary, on all occasions it is pointed out that Congress has in fact prevented the laws used as a claim against most defendants from being enforced within the sovereign territory of any one of the 50 Union States, either by statute or by the "gate keeping" effects of Rule 54 of the Federal Rules of Criminal Procedure, all fully within the principles of **original understanding** of the Framers and people ratifying the federal and Union State Constitutions.

In their **original understanding**_the Framers established a dual sovereignty between the States of the Union and the newly created United States. The above arguments show that with respect to Title 21, Chapter 13 drug offenses and firearm statutes (as well as others not referenced here) Congress did not in any way infringe upon that dual sovereignty. However, we witness the everyday process of the Executive branch through the Attorney General's office and the Judiciary through the District Courts arrogantly practicing federal law within the sovereign 50 states. While Congress may have been able to call on its **commerce clause** power, it chose not to by redefining **interstate commerce** to be commerce solely within the territory over which Congress has exclusive legislative jurisdiction. To further hold the line on the concept of dual sovereignty within the notion of **original understanding**, Congress **and** the Supreme Court created the territorial gate keeping function by the supersession phrase in 28 USC 2072(b) combined with Rule 54 of the Federal Rules of Criminal Procedure.

However, in spite of and contrary to the clear guiding light of Congress's legislation and the **original understanding**_of the Constitution, the Justice (sic) Department and the United States District Courts take the **revisionist** view that the sovereign territory of **any** one of the 50 States could be construed to be territory over which the laws of the United States could be prosecuted in a strictly territorial Tribunal, namely the United States District Court. Furthermore, for or under whatever revisionist pretext, the Justice Department seems to be able to get the Judge of said territorial Tribunal to recognize the "United States of America" rather than the "United States" as the principal of interest, contrary to any legislation or Constitutional authority allowing it.

The Supreme Court recognized early on that only Congress has the power to punish:

> "The rule that penal laws are to be construed strictly is, perhaps not much less old than construction itself. It is founded on the tenderness of the law for the rights of individuals; and on the **plain principle that the power of punishment is vested in the legislature, not in the judicial department.**" [or the **Executive through its Justice Department]** _United States v. Wiltberger_, 5 Wheat (U.S.) 76, 95, 5L.Ed 37, 46 (emphasis added).

When the United States District Court (USDC), a territorial Tribunal takes cognizance of a cause of action outside its territorial jurisdiction, when said USDC takes cognizance of a cause of action over which it has no subject matter jurisdiction, when said USDC ignores the Gate Keeping provisions of Rule 54, of the F.R.Cr.P., when said USDC ignores the limited scope of "interstate commerce" redefined by Congress for Title 21 legislation, when said USDC quite possibly takes judicial notice of the secret fact that a defendant is an ens legis using all capital letters in the same or similar sequence of this Petitioner's given name, and when said USDC recognizes the "United States of America" as the principal of interest in a criminal proceeding, said USDC is in all cases usurping the power of Congress to punish and, through its judicial power, is revising the very laws it was empowered to adjudicate to be what it felt the laws should be, not what they in fact really are.

It is against this practice of judicial legislation (judicial revisions of the law) that Appeals Courts and the Supreme Court should resolutely set their face. Otherwise, history will simply record that this great system of human sovereignty of the people in due time reverted right back to the very same feudal system, albeit much more centralized and controlled by a much larger corporate despotic oligarchy/aristocracy, from whence we gained our independence in the first place.

Accordingly, upon the foregoing, the body of Judges in the federal court system need to obey Congress's laws and ignore Stare Decisis when it conflicts with the clear language of Congress's statutes and/or the Constitution in an conscientious effort to restore a modicum of strict judicial integrity to the Federal Court system by refusing to entertain an action absent a clear and accurate jurisdictional pleading based in law when the cause of action is based solely on actions occurring within the territorial boundaries of one or more of the 50 states of the Union. Such action must be ruled coram non judice at the federal level, thus allowing the sovereign states to run their own affairs. When a federal court entertains a cause of action which Constitutionally should be resolved in the State courts, it is no different than if the Department of Justice attempted to enforce federal law in the District Courts for activity occurring in say Sweden.

CONCLUSION

In a most recent case, Justice Thomas in writing for the majority in *Federal Maritime Commission v. South Carolina State Ports· Authority*, 535 U.S. 743 (2002), (F.M.C.), decided May 28, 2002, wrote:

> "Dual sovereignty is a defining feature of our nation's constitutional blueprint. States, upon ratification of the Constitution, did not consent to become mere appendages of the Federal Government. Rather, they entered the union 'with their sovereignty intact." Id

The blueprint of the concept of dual but mutual exclusive sovereignties is precisely what has been argued above.

What was most interesting about this case was the wide disparity between the majority and the minority opinions relative to this issue of dual sovereignty and the fact that they are in fact mutually exclusive, except in rare specific circumstances. This pivotal issue surfaced loud and clears in both Justice Thomas's opinion for the Court and Justice Breyer's dissenting opinion. The latter of which unmasks the thesis upon which the revisionists have used over the years to revise our Constitution. This revisionism has plagued the jurisprudence of this County since at least the New Deal era. The point of contention among the legal professionals rests on the intent of the Framers as to whether the Federal Government, the United States, is constrained strictly to those powers delegated in the Constitution or whether the Federal Government is free to exercise the "required flexibility" it deems necessary to "keep up with the times" so long as such necessity does not include something "prohibited" by the Constitution. In other words, the debate is whether the Federal Government has enumerated powers or enumerated prohibitions. The real problem is that the Federal Government in fact has both. With respect to the States, it has enumerated powers, but with respect to its own sovereignty within its own territory, it has enumerated prohibitions, both in the body of the Constitution and in the first ten (10) amendments, known as the Bill of Rights, which should more aptly be viewed as a Bill of Prohibitions. But, be that as it may, James Madison in the Federalist Papers only wrote of enumerated powers. See Appendix D.

The fact that Justice Breyer and the minority, not unlike other Constitutional Revisionists, believes that the federal Constitution did not bind down the Federal Government can be found in their statement that the "majority **rejected** the 'basic understanding' reached during the New Deal era that the constitutional system requires **'structural flexibility sufficient to adapt substantive laws and institutions to rapidly changing social, economic,**

and technical conditions.'" Was this "basic understanding reached during the New Deal era" a result of the bankruptcy of the United States providing an excuse for expanding the sphere and scope of the Federal Government, or does the Minority really believe, as they wrote in *F.M.C.*, that "the Constitution created a Federal Government empowered to enact laws that would bind the states, and it empowered that Federal Government to enforce those laws against the states?" Where they find evidence of this belief is unexplained. In the Minority's view, the New Deal ushered in unconstrained Federal powers to do whatever it damn well pleased to adapt substantive laws and institutions to rapidly changing social, economic, and technical conditions. If this "walks, talks, and squawks very much like" unlimited power, perhaps the proof lies in what has transpired in the thirty (30) years between the New Deal era and the Vietnam War era where the Federal Budget ballooned to nearly one third (1/3), about thirty (30) percent of the Gross National Product (GNP), when, at the turn of the 19th Century, (1900), it was less than one percent (1%) of the GNP.

Since we have seen that Congress has stayed within its Constitutional authority and the word "adapt" means *to make fit as for a new use or for different circumstances*, this author would read the phrase "**structural flexibility sufficient to adapt substantive laws and institutions to rapidly changing social, economic, and technical conditions**" to suggest that Justice Breyer desires to legislate on the fly from the bench. That way he would have the opportunity to reshape the law as he sees fit and rule on the matter before the Court using his new customized law. Me thinks that Justice Breyer has just found a way to transform judges into kings.

History has witnessed far too many cases having been decided on the same premise that Justice Breyer and the minority espouses, namely, that if something is not prohibited by the Constitution, the Federal Government, through all three branches, is free to perform any function and pass any laws not so prohibited. While this is certainly true in its own sovereign territory, as aforesaid, it is certainly not true within the sovereign territory of anyone of the several fifty (50) states, party to the Union of States. A simple reading of the 9th and 10th Amendments should be enough to set the record straight for any intellectual on this issue, leaving no room for debate, any and all New Deal influences to the contrary notwithstanding.

Constitutional revisionists would do well to digest Justice Thomas's concluding statement:

> "While some might complain that our system of dual sovereignty is not a model of administrative convenience, that is not its purpose, Rather, the 'Constitutionally mandated balance of power' between the states and the Federal Government was adopted by the framers to ensure the protection of **'our fundamental liberties**.' By guarding against encroachments by the Federal Government on fundamental aspects of state sovereignty . . . , we strive to maintain the balance of power embodied in our Constitution and thus 'reduce the risk of tyranny and abuse from either front.'" Id. (emphasis added).

When the Supreme Court is ready to apply the same simple principle to the federal drug and firearm laws together with all other Sovereign State business in the very manner in which Congress has explicitly legislated them, as above argued, we will begin to return our federal jurisprudence to the "yellow brick road" to individual sovereignty and liberty.

> To this end, while rebuttable

> "'the presumption . . . is that the court below was without jurisdiction' unless 'the contrary intent appears affirmatively from the record.' *King Bridge Co. v. Otoe County*, 170 U.S. 225, 226 . . . (1887)" *Bender v. Williamsport Area School dist.*, 475 U.S. 534(1986)'

However, in the usual case, the record, including indictments, is grossly inadequate to rebut the presumption that the District Court's jurisdiction to charge, try, convict, and sentence a defendant does not exist. Consequently, the one and only remedy remaining to the government to prevent the presumption that the court below was without jurisdiction from becoming a conclusive presumption would be for the government to bring forth the "document of acceptance of jurisdiction" over the lands upon which the wrongful acts and/or conduct was alleged to have occurred, as per 40 U.S.C. 255 (now Section 3112). See Adams v. U.S., 319 U.S. 312-316 (1943). Absent such a document of acceptance of jurisdiction by the Federal Government, the hearing Court is duty bound to dismiss the action or deem the judgment void and immediately restore a defendant's right to Liberty.

Jurisdiction is the first principle issue in all federal suits, both criminal and civil. As aforesaid, if the Justice Department in concert with the District Courts refuses to stay within the law as Congress has written it, the rule of law has been lost and we in the 50 States are now being ruled by a privileged class of men.

On the Meaning of "Includes"

A Treatise on the Statutory Re-Definition of Terms

In order to know what Congress means when it uses the term "includes" we look first at what the Supreme Court and other Courts have to say regarding the term as well as other legal authorities such as Legal Dictionaries.

> It is the canon of statutory construction that the inclusion of certain provisions implies the exclusion of others. The doctrine inclusio unius est exclusio alterius 'informs "the court to exclude from operation those items not included in a list of elements that are given effect expressly by the statutory language.' In re TMI, 67 F3d 1119, 1123 (3rd Cir 1995)(Quoting Williams v. Wohlegemuth.540 F2d 163, 169 (3rd Cir 1976)" United States v. McQuilkin, 78 F3d 105, 108 (3rd Cir 1996)

"Inclusio unius est exclusio alterius. The inclusion of one is the exclusion of another. The certain designation of one person is an absolute exclusion of all others. . . . This doctrine decrees that where the law expressly describes [a] particular situation to which it shall apply, and irrefutable inference must be drawn that what is omitted or excluded was intended to be omitted or excluded." Black's Law Dictionary, 6th Edition.

It is axiomatic (and the law) that terms and phrases within a statute for which definitions are provided DO NOT have their common meanings as used therein.

"It is axiomatic that the statutory definition of the term excludes unstated meanings of that term." Meese v. Keene, 481 U.S. 465 (1987))

"Include or the participial form thereof, is defined to comprise 'within'; 'to hold'; to contain'; 'to shut up'; and synonyms are 'contain'; 'enclose'; 'comprehend'; 'embrace'." *Montello Salt Co. v. Utah, 221 U.S. 452, at 455, 466.*

This fact only underscores our duty to refrain from reading a phrase into a statute when Congress has left it out. '[W]here Congress includes particular language in one section of a statute but omits it in another . . . , it is generally presumed that Congress acts intentionally and purposely in the disparate inclusion or exclusion.'" *Russello v. United States, 464 U.S. 16, 23, 78 L Ed 2d 17, 104 S. Ct. 296 (1983).*

Possible the most direct opinion relative to the use of the term "including" was offered early on by Chief Judge Marshal in the following:

It [is argued that] the word "including" means "moreover", or "as well as"; but if this was the meaning of the legislature, it was a very embarrassing mode of expressing the idea." Chief Justice Marshall of the United States Supreme Court, United States v. The Schooner Betsey and Charlotte, 8 U.S. 443 (1808). Marshall proceeds to observe that the proposition that *"moreover" or "as well as"* is, in fact, what is meant by the legislative use of "including" (or, by extension, includes) **is nonsense**.

"Includes" is defined within the law as follows:

"Includes and including: The terms "includes" and "including" when used in a definition contained in this title shall not be deemed to exclude other things otherwise within the meaning of the term defined." Rev. Act of 1938 §901(b) (Codified at 26 USC 7701(c).)

The Department of the Treasury has helpfully clarified the meaning of this provision with the following regulatory language:

"The terms "includes and including" do not exclude things not enumerated which are in the same general class;" as has the United States Supreme Court:

"[T]he verb "includes" imports a general class, some of whose particular instances are those specified in the definition. This view finds support in § 2(b) of the Act, which reads:

"The terms 'includes' and 'including,' when used in a definition contained in this title, shall not be deemed to exclude other things otherwise within the meaning of the term defined." *Helvering v Morgan's, Inc, 293 U.S. 121, 126 fn. 1 (1934)*

The court refers to and re-iterates this observation in *Federal Land Bank of St. Paul v. Bismarck Lumber Co. 314 U.S. 95, 62 S.Ct. 1 U.S. 1941:*

"[I]ncluding . . . connotes simply an illustrative application of the general principle."(That is, the enumerated items in a definition in which "including" is deployed "illustrate"—identify, and thus establish—the contours of the class which the defined term represents—the "general principle" of its application).

The principle involved in the "includes" mechanism is largely that described by the Supreme Court in *Gustafson v. Alloyd Co. (93-404), 513 US 561 (1995)*:

> ". . . a word is known by the company it keeps (the doctrine of noscitur a sociis). This rule we rely upon to avoid ascribing to one word a meaning so broad that it is inconsistent with its accompanying words, thus giving "unintended breadth to the Acts of Congress."

That principle is clarified by these additional, related rulings:

> "When a statute includes an explicit definition, we must follow that definition, even if it varies from that term's ordinary meaning." *Stenberg v. Carhart, 530 U.S. 914 (2000)*.

> "It is axiomatic that the statutory definition of the term excludes unstated meanings of that term." *U.S. Supreme Court, Meese v. Keene, 481 U.S. 465 (1987)*.

> "Of course, statutory definitions of terms used therein prevail over colloquial meanings. *Fox v. Standard Oil Co., 294 U.S. 87, 95, 55 S.Ct. 333, 336.*" *Western Union Telegraph Co. v. Lenroot, 323 U.S. 490 (1945)*.

Am Jur 2d has an excellent abstract on the importance and supremacy of the legislature's redefinitions of terms used in statutes and their very narrow scope as it pertains to their use in the applicable in statutes.

73 Am Jur 2d § 146 Operation of legislative definitions, generally

Research References
West's Key Number Digest, Statutes 223.1

The lawmaking body's own construction of its language, by means of definitions of the term employed, should be followed in the interpretation of the act or section to which it relates and is intended to apply.[1] By the same token, the courts should not enlarge statutory definitions so as to include a situation or a condition which it might be assumed the legislature would have covered by an enlarged definition if its existence had been contemplated.[2] A statutory definition supersedes the common-law,[3] colloquial,[4] commonly accepted, dictionary or judicial definition.[5] In this regard, where statute itself contains a definition of a word used therein, the definition controls, however contrary to the ordinary meaning of the word it may be,[6] and the term may not be given the meaning in which it is employed in another statute, although the two may be in pari material.[7] **Where the legislature has defined words which are employed in a statute, its definitions are binding on the courts since the legislature has the right to give such signification as it deems proper to any word or phrase used by the statute, irrespective of the relationship of the definition to other terms.**[8] Furthermore, where a word that already has a definite, fixed, and unambiguous meaning is redefined in a statute, the definition must be taken literally by the courts.[9]

[1]*Curle v. Superior Court, 24 Cal. 4th 1057, 103 Cal. Rptr. 2d 751, 16 P.3d 166 (2001); State v. Olsen, 618 N.WE.2d 346 (Iowa 2000); Ohio Civil Rights Commission v. Parklawn Manner, Inc., 41 Ohio St. 2d 47, 70 Ohio Op. 2d 148, 322 N.E.2d 642 (1975); Devers v. Scranton City, 308 Pa. 13, 161 A. 540, 85 A.L.R. 692 (1932).*

[2]*Lenox Realty Co. v. Hackett, 122 Conn. 143, 187 A. 895, 107 A.L.R. 1306 (1936); Robertson v. Western Baptist Hosp., 267 S.W.2d 395 (Ky. 1954).*

[3]*Rayonier, Inc. v. Polson, 400 F.2d 909 (9th cir. 1968); 1137 18th Street Associates, Ltd. Partnership v. District of Columbia, 769 A.2d 155 (D.C. 2001).*

[4]*Western Union Telegraph Co. v. Lenroot, 323 U.S. 490, 65 S. Ct. 335, 89 L. Ed. 414 (1945).*

[5]*Stenberg v. Carhart, 530 U.S. 914, 120 S. Ct. 2597, 147 L. Ed. 2d 743 (2000); Driscoll v. General Nutrition Corp., 252 Conn. 215, 752 A.2d 1p069 (2000); Erlandson v. Genesee County Employees' Retirement Com'n, 337 Mich. 195, 59 N.W.2d 389 (1953); Appeal of Clayton-Marcus Co., Inc., 286 N.C. 215, 210 S.E.2d 199 (1974); Minnix v. State, 1955 OK CR 37, 282 P.2d 772 (Okla. Crim. App. 1955).*

[6]*Appeal of Clayton-Marcus Co., Inc., 286 N.C. 215, 210 S.E.2d 199 (1974).*

The general Assembly's own construction of its language as provided by definitions controls in the application of a statute, and such definition will be given great weight against any claim that application of the statutory definition defeats the general purpose of the statute. Ohio Civil Rights Commission v. Parklawn Manner, Inc., 41 Ohio St. 2d 47, 70 Ohio Op. 2d 148, 322 N.E.2d 642 (1975).

[7]*Davison v. F. W. Woolworth Co., 186 Ga. 663, 198 S.E. 738, 118 A.L.R. 1363 (1938).*

[8]*People v. Dugan, 91 Misc. 2d 239, 397 N.Y.S.2d 878 (County Ct. 1977).*

[9]*Young v. O'Keefe, 246 Iowa 1182, 69 N.W.2d 534 (1955); State v. Standard Oil Co., 61 Or. 438, 123 P. 40 (1912).*

But perhaps the best overview of the status of defined terms and their supremacy over other common meanings can be found in the following:

Statute Definitions Trump Common Usage

AS WE HAVE BEEN WELL-INSTRUCTED BY THE UNITED STATES SUPREME COURT AND OTHERS, once a word has been given a statutory definition, it loses its normal meaning and adopts a new one (see *Stenberg v. Carhart, 530 U.S. 914, 120 S. Ct. 2597, 147 L. Ed. 2d 743 (2000)*: *"When a statute includes an explicit definition, we must follow that definition, even if it varies from that term's ordinary meaning."* ; also see *Driscoll v. General Nutrition Corp., 252 Conn. 215, 752 A.2d 1p069 (2000); Erlandson v. Genesee County Employees' Retirement Com'n, 337 Mich. 195, 59 N.W.2d 389 (1953); Appeal of Clayton-Marcus Co., Inc., 286 N.C. 215, 210 S.E.2d 199 (1974); Minnix v. State, 1955 OK CR 37, 282 P.2d 772 (Okla. Crim. App. 1955)*). For example, the word "employee", once given a definition in the law such as that at 3401(c):

§ 3401(c)

"For purposes of this chapter, the term "employee" includes an officer, employee, or elected official of the United States, a State, or any political subdivision thereof, or the District of Columbia, or any agency or instrumentality of any one or more of the foregoing. The term "employee" also includes an officer of a corporation", no longer is 'employee'—the word as commonly used in everyday speech—but is now "statutorily-defined employee" (or "SDE" for short)—a unique term (assigned by the reader) meant to be understood only as specified by its new definition.

This principle applies regardless of any idiosyncrasy of the definition, such as whether that statutory definition deploys the term "means", or the term "includes", or both, or neither. That is, the principle applies because a special definition has been given, not because of how the definition is expressed or constructed. If the word being specially re-defined had been meant to retain its normal or otherwise specified meaning, it would not have been re-defined at all; that it WAS re-defined is inescapable evidence that it was NOT meant to retain that normal meaning.

Nor is the re-definition of the word a matter of its keeping its normal meaning but having additional items added to that meaning. The "employee" definition above exemplifies this, in that among the enumerated list of items providing the new, custom definition are "federal employees". Obviously, federal employees, like all other employees, would be within the normal definition of 'employee', and thus wouldn't need to be listed at all if the word had retained its normal meaning.

Here are a few other examples from Title 26 USC of statutory definitions that list as "included" things which would have been obviously within the common meaning of the word being re-defined, thus making clear that a re-definition is NOT the retention of the common meaning, plus the addition of other things:

§ 7701(a)

(7) Stock

The term "stock" includes shares in an association, joint-stock company, or insurance company.

(8) Shareholder

The term "shareholder" includes a member in an association, joint-stock company, or insurance company.

§ 3121

(g) Agricultural labor

For purposes of this chapter, the term "agricultural labor" includes all service performed—

(1) on a farm, in the employ of any person, in connection with cultivating the soil, or in connection with raising or harvesting any agricultural or horticultural commodity, including the raising, shearing, feeding, caring for, training, and management of livestock, bees, poultry, and fur-bearing animals and wildlife;

When Congress DOES wish to have a word retain its original meaning but have other things not within that ordinary meaning treated as though they are, it is perfectly capable of saying so directly, as in the following example:

26 USC § 7701(d) *Commonwealth of Puerto Rico*

Where not otherwise distinctly expressed or manifestly incompatible with the intent thereof, references in this title to possessions of the United States shall be treated as also referring to the Commonwealth of Puerto Rico.

IN LIGHT OF THE EFFECT OF RE-DEFINITION, the proper way to read statutory definitions is by substituting the new, accurate descriptor for what had been the common word that has been re-defined and stripped of its common meaning. For instance, by way of example, read the definition of "employee" at 3401(c) used as an example above as to what it really says:

> § *3401(c) Statutorily*-defined employee) **(SDE)**
>
> *For purposes of this chapter, the term "**SDE**" includes an officer, employee, or elected official of the United States, a State, or any political subdivision thereof, or the District of Columbia, or any agency or instrumentality of any one or more of the foregoing. The term "**SDE**" also includes an officer of a corporation."*

Immediately, any risk of confusion about the meaning and scope of the term vanishes.

Similarly, when we look at related provisions in the law and apply the same technique of accurate reading, we find clarity and confidence where otherwise we might have risked misunderstanding:

> § *3401*
>
> *(a) Wages*
>
> *For purposes of this chapter, the term "wages" means all remuneration (other than fees paid to a public official) for services performed by an **SDE** for his employer, including the cash value of all remuneration (including benefits) paid in any medium other than cash;*
>
> *(d) Employer*
>
> *For purposes of this chapter, the term "employer" means the person for whom an individual performs*

or performed any service, of whatever nature, as the **SDE** *of such person, except that—*

§ 3402(f)

(2) Exemption certificates

(A) On commencement of employment

On or before the date of the commencement of employment with an employer, the **SDE** *shall furnish the employer with a signed withholding exemption certificate relating to the number of withholding exemptions which he claims, which shall in no event exceed the number to which he is entitled.*

To read these provisions without at least mentally replacing "employee" with an alternative label not capable of being confused for the common word it merely mimics in appearance invites that confusion, especially when reading any significant volume of related law. The importance of avoiding such confusion even to one already educated on the subject of the tax is obvious, and it is much more important when presenting the law to those not already educated (indoctrinated).

IN FACT, although doing so would involve a bit of extra effort, it may well be that written material related to the tax—even extending to filings in litigation—would benefit from the substitution of more accurate descriptors for otherwise confusing words-of-art, after the inclusion of language designating that this will be the case. We have all seen that those invested in the mis-application of the "income" tax sometimes contrive to "misunderstand" what they find inconvenient. Anything that can be done to make such "misunderstanding" more implausible benefits those of us on the side of the truth.

Additional Reading Expressing the Purpose of the Senate

FEDERALIST PAPERS # 62 TO 66 INCLUSIVE

Followed by a Comprehensive List of Federalist Papers Dealing with the Sovereignty of the States

FEDERALIST No. 62
The Senate
For the Independent Journal.
Alexander Hamilton or **James Madison**

To the People of the State of New York:

HAVING examined the constitution of the House of Representatives, and answered such of the objections against it as seemed to merit notice, I enter next on the examination of the Senate.

The heads into which this member of the government may be considered are: I. The qualification of senators; II. The appointment of them by the State legislatures; III. The equality of representation in the Senate; IV. The number of senators, and the term for which they are to be elected; V. The powers vested in the Senate.

I. The qualifications proposed for senators, as distinguished from those of representatives, consist in a more advanced age and a longer period of citizenship. A senator must be thirty years of age at least; as a representative must be twenty-five. And the former must have been a citizen nine years; as seven years are required for the latter. The propriety of these distinctions is explained by the nature of the senatorial trust, which, requiring greater extent of information and tability of character, requires at the same time that the senator should have reached a period of life most likely to supply these advantages; and which, participating immediately in transactions with foreign nations, ought to be exercised by none who are not thoroughly weaned from the prepossessions and habits incident to foreign birth and education. The term of nine years appears to be a prudent mediocrity between a total exclusion of adopted citizens, whose merits and talents may claim a share in the public confidence, and an indiscriminate and hasty admission of them, which might create a channel for foreign influence on the national councils. II. It is equally unnecessary to dilate on the appointment of senators by the State legislatures. Among the various modes which might have been devised for constituting this branch of the government, that which has been proposed by the convention is probably the most congenial with the public opinion. It is recommended by the double advantage of favoring a select appointment, and of giving to the State governments such an agency in the formation of the Federal Government as must secure the authority of the former, and may form a convenient link between the two systems.

III. The equality of representation in the Senate is another point, which, being evidently the result of compromise between the opposite pretensions of the large and the small States, does not call for much discussion. If indeed it be right, that among a people thoroughly incorporated into one nation, every district ought to have a PROPORTIONAL share in the government, and that among independent and sovereign States, bound together by a simple league, the parties, however unequal in size, ought to have an EQUAL share in the common councils, it does not appear to be without some reason that in a compound republic, partaking both of the national and federal character, the government ought to be founded on a mixture of the principles of proportional and equal representation. But it is superfluous to try, by the standard of theory, a part of the Constitution which is allowed on all hands to be the result, not of theory, but "of a spirit of amity, and that mutual deference and concession which the peculiarity of our political situation rendered indispensable." A common government, with powers equal to its objects, is called for by the voice, and still more loudly by the political situation, of America. A government founded on principles more consonant to the wishes of the larger States, is not likely to be obtained from the smaller States. The only option, then, for the former, lies between the proposed government and a government still more objectionable. Under this alternative, the advice of prudence must be to embrace the lesser evil; and, instead of indulging a fruitless anticipation of the possible mischiefs which may ensue, to contemplate rather the advantageous consequences which may qualify the sacrifice.

In this spirit it may be remarked, that the equal vote allowed to each State is at once a constitutional recognition of the portion of sovereignty remaining in the individual States, and an instrument for preserving that residuary sovereignty. So far the equality ought to be no less acceptable to the large than to the small States; since they are not less solicitous to guard, by every possible expedient, against an improper consolidation of the States into one simple republic.

Another advantage accruing from this ingredient in the constitution of the Senate is, the additional impediment it must prove against improper acts of legislation. No law or resolution can now be passed without the concurrence, first, of a majority of the people, and then, of a majority of the States. It must be acknowledged that this complicated check on legislation may in some instances be injurious as well as beneficial; and that the peculiar defense which it involves in favor of the smaller States, would be more rational, if any interests common to them, and distinct from those of the other States, would otherwise be exposed to peculiar danger. But as the larger States will always be able, by their power over the supplies, to defeat unreasonable exertions of this prerogative of the lesser States, and as the faculty and excess of law-making seem to be the diseases to which our governments are most liable, it is not impossible that this part of the Constitution may be more convenient in practice than it appears to many in contemplation.

IV. The number of senators, and the duration of their appointment, come next to be considered. In order to form an accurate judgment on both of these points, it will be proper to inquire into the purposes which are to be answered by a senate; and in order to ascertain these, it will be necessary to review the inconveniences which a republic must suffer from the want of such an institution.

First; it is a misfortune incident to republican government, though in a less degree than to other governments, that those who administer it may forget their obligations to their constituents, and prove unfaithful to their important trust. In this point of view, a senate, as a second branch of the legislative assembly, distinct from, and dividing the power with, a first, must be in all cases a salutary check on the government. It doubles the security to the people, by requiring the concurrence of two distinct bodies in schemes of usurpation or perfidy, where the ambition or corruption of one would otherwise be sufficient. This is a precaution founded on such clear principles, and now so well understood in the United States, that it would be more than superfluous to enlarge on it. I will barely remark, that as the improbability of sinister combinations will be in proportion to the dissimilarity in the genius of the two bodies, it must be politic to distinguish them from each other by every circumstance which will consist with a due harmony in all proper measures, and with the genuine principles of republican government.

Secondly; the necessity of a senate is not less indicated by the propensity of all single and numerous assemblies to yield to the impulse of sudden and violent passions, and to be seduced by factious leaders into intemperate and pernicious resolutions. Examples on this subject might be cited without number; and from proceedings within the United States, as well as from the history of other nations. But a position that will not be contradicted, need not be proved. All that need be remarked is, that a body which is to correct this infirmity ought itself to be free from it, and consequently ought to be less numerous. It ought, moreover, to possess great firmness, and consequently ought to hold its authority by a tenure of considerable duration.

Thirdly; another defect to be supplied by a senate lies in a want of due acquaintance with the objects and principles of legislation. It is not possible that an assembly of men called for the most part from pursuits of a private nature, continued in appointment for a short time, and led by no permanent motive to devote the intervals of public occupation to a study of the laws, the affairs, and the comprehensive interests of their country, should, if left wholly to themselves, escape a variety of important errors in the exercise of their legislative trust. It may be affirmed, on the best grounds, that no small share of the present embarrassments of America is to be charged on the blunders of our governments; and that these have proceeded from the heads rather than the hearts of most of the authors of them. What indeed are all the repealing, explaining, and amending laws, which fill and disgrace our voluminous codes, but so many monuments of deficient wisdom; so many impeachments exhibited by each succeeding against each preceding session; so many admonitions to the people, of the value of those aids which may be expected from a well-constituted senate?

A good government implies two things: first, fidelity to the object of government, which is the happiness of the people; secondly, a knowledge of the means by which that object can be best attained. Some governments are deficient in both these qualities; most governments are deficient in the first. I scruple not to assert, that in American governments too little attention has been paid to the last. The federal Constitution avoids this error; and what merits particular notice, it provides for the last in a mode which increases the security for the first.

Fourthly; the mutability in the public councils arising from a rapid succession of new members, however qualified they may be, points out, in the strongest manner, the necessity of some stable institution in the government. Every new election in the States is found to change one half of the representatives. From this change of men must proceed a change of opinions; and from a change of opinions, a change of measures. But a continual change even of good measures is inconsistent with every rule of prudence and every prospect of success. The remark is verified in private life, and becomes more just, as well as more important, in national transactions.

To trace the mischievous effects of a mutable government would fill a volume. I will hint a few only, each of which will be perceived to be a source of innumerable others.

In the first place, it forfeits the respect and confidence of other nations, and all the advantages connected with national character. An individual who is observed to be inconstant to his plans, or perhaps to carry on his affairs without any plan at all, is marked at once, by all prudent people, as a speedy victim to his own unsteadiness and folly. His more friendly neighbors may pity him, but all will decline to connect their fortunes with his; and not a few will seize the opportunity of making their fortunes out of his. One nation is to another what one individual is to another; with this melancholy distinction perhaps, that the former, with fewer of the benevolent emotions than the latter, are under fewer restraints also from taking undue advantage from the indiscretions of each other. Every nation, consequently, whose affairs betray a want of wisdom and stability, may calculate on every loss which can be sustained from the more systematic policy of their wiser neighbors. But the best instruction on this subject is unhappily conveyed to America by the example of her own situation. She finds that she is held in no respect by her friends; that she is the derision of her enemies; and that she is a prey to every nation which has an interest in speculating on her fluctuating councils and embarrassed affairs.

The internal effects of a mutable policy are still more calamitous. It poisons the blessing of liberty itself. It will be of little avail to the people, that the laws are made by men of their own choice, if the laws be so voluminous that they cannot be read, or so incoherent that they cannot be understood; if they be repealed or revised before they are promulgated, or undergo such incessant changes that no man, who knows what the law is to-day, can guess what it will be to-morrow. Law is defined to be a rule of action; but how can that be a rule, which is little known, and less fixed?

Another effect of public instability is the unreasonable advantage it gives to the sagacious, the enterprising, and the moneyed few over the industrious and uniformed mass of the people. Every new regulation concerning commerce or revenue, or in any way affecting the value of the different species of property, presents a new harvest to those who watch the change, and can trace its consequences; a harvest, reared not by themselves, but by the toils and cares of the vast majority of their fellow-citizens. This is a state of things in which it may be said with some truth that laws are made for the FEW, not for the MANY.

In another point of view, great injury results from an unstable government. The want of confidence in the public councils damps every useful undertaking, the success and profit of which may depend on a continuance of existing arrangements. What prudent merchant will hazard his fortunes in any new branch of commerce when he knows not but that his plans may be rendered unlawful before they can be executed? What farmer or manufacturer will lay himself out for the encouragement given to any particular cultivation or establishment, when he can have no assurance that his preparatory labors and advances will not render him a victim to an inconstant government? In a word, no great improvement or laudable enterprise can go forward which requires the auspices of a steady system of national policy.

But the most deplorable effect of all is that diminution of attachment and reverence which steals into the hearts of the people, towards a political system which betrays so many marks of infirmity, and disappoints so many of their flattering hopes. No government, any more than an individual, will long be respected without being truly respectable; nor be truly respectable, without possessing a certain portion of order and stability.

PUBLIUS.
FEDERALIST No. 63
<u>The Senate Continued</u>
For the Independent Journal.
Alexander Hamilton or **James Madison**

To the People of the State of New York:

A FIFTH desideratum, illustrating the utility of a senate, is the want of a due sense of national character. Without a select and stable member of the government, the esteem of foreign powers will not only be forfeited by an unenlightened and variable policy, proceeding from the causes already mentioned, but the national councils will not possess that sensibility to the opinion of the world, which is perhaps not less necessary in order to merit, than it is to obtain, its respect and confidence.

An attention to the judgment of other nations is important to every government for two reasons: the one is, that, independently of the merits of any particular plan or measure, it is desirable, on various accounts, that it should appear to other nations as the offspring of a wise and honorable policy; the second is, that in doubtful cases, particularly where the national councils may be warped by some strong passion or momentary interest, the presumed or known opinion of the impartial world may be the best guide that can be followed. What has not America lost by her want of character with foreign nations; and how many errors and follies would she not have avoided, if the justice and propriety of her measures had, in every instance, been previously tried by the light in which they would probably appear to the unbiased part of mankind?

Yet however requisite a sense of national character may be, it is evident that it can never be sufficiently possessed by a numerous and changeable body. It can only be found in a number so small that a sensible degree of the praise and blame of public measures may be the portion of each individual; or in an assembly so durably invested with public trust, that the pride and consequence of its members may be sensibly incorporated with the reputation and prosperity of the community. The half-yearly representatives of Rhode Island would probably have been little affected in their deliberations on the iniquitous measures of that State, by arguments drawn from the light in which such measures would be viewed by foreign nations, or even by the sister States; whilst it can scarcely be doubted that if the concurrence of a select and stable body had been necessary, a regard to national character alone would have prevented the calamities under which that misguided people is now laboring.

I add, as a SIXTH defect the want, in some important cases, of a due responsibility in the government to the people, arising from that frequency of elections which in other cases produces this responsibility. This remark will, perhaps, appear not only new, but paradoxical. It must nevertheless be acknowledged, when explained, to be as undeniable as it is important.

Responsibility, in order to be reasonable, must be limited to objects within the power of the responsible party, and in order to be effectual, must relate to operations of that power, of which a ready and proper judgment can be formed by the constituents. The objects of government may be divided into two general classes: the one depending on measures which have singly an immediate and sensible operation; the other depending on a succession of well-chosen and well-connected measures, which have a gradual and perhaps unobserved operation. The importance of the latter description to the collective and permanent welfare of every country, needs no explanation. And yet it is evident that an assembly elected for so short a term as to be unable to provide more than one or two links in a chain of measures, on which the general welfare may essentially depend, ought not to be answerable for the final result, any more than a steward or tenant, engaged for one year, could be justly made to answer for places or improvements which could not be accomplished in less than half a dozen years. Nor is it possible for the people to estimate the SHARE of influence which their annual assemblies may respectively have on events resulting from the mixed transactions of several years. It is sufficiently difficult to preserve a personal responsibility in the members of a NUMEROUS body, for such acts of the body as have an immediate, detached, and palpable operation on its constituents.

The proper remedy for this defect must be an additional body in the legislative department, which, having sufficient permanency to provide for such objects as require a continued attention, and a train of measures, may be justly and effectually answerable for the attainment of those objects.

Thus far I have considered the circumstances which point out the necessity of a well-constructed Senate only as they relate to the representatives of the people. To a people as little blinded by prejudice or corrupted by flattery as those whom I address, I shall not scruple to add, that such an institution may be sometimes necessary as a defense to the people against their own temporary errors and delusions. As the cool and deliberate sense of the community ought, in all governments, and actually will, in all free governments, ultimately prevail over the views of its rulers; so there are particular moments in public affairs when the people, stimulated by some irregular passion, or some illicit advantage, or misled by the artful misrepresentations of interested men, may call for measures which they themselves will afterwards be the most ready to lament and condemn. In these critical moments, how salutary will be the interference of some temperate and respectable body of citizens, in order to check the misguided career, and to suspend the blow meditated by the people against themselves, until reason, justice, and truth can regain their authority over the public mind? What bitter anguish would not the people of Athens have often escaped if their government had contained so provident a safeguard against the tyranny of their own passions? Popular liberty might then have escaped the indelible reproach of decreeing to the same citizens the hemlock on one day and statues on the next.

It may be suggested, that a people spread over an extensive region cannot, like the crowded inhabitants of a small district, be subject to the infection of violent passions, or to the danger of combining in pursuit of unjust measures. I am far from denying that this is a distinction of peculiar importance. I have, on the contrary, endeavored in a former paper to show, that it is one of the principal recommendations of a confederated republic. At the same time, this advantage ought not to be considered as superseding the use of auxiliary precautions. It may even be remarked, that the same extended situation, which will exempt the people of America from some of the dangers incident to lesser republics, will expose them to the inconveniency of remaining for a longer time under the influence of those misrepresentations which the combined industry of interested men may succeed in distributing among them.

It adds no small weight to all these considerations, to recollect that history informs us of no long-lived republic which had not a senate. Sparta, Rome, and Carthage are, in fact, the only states to whom that character can be applied. In each of the two first there was a senate for life. The constitution of the senate in the last is less known. Circumstantial evidence makes it probable that it was not different in this particular from the two others. It is at least certain, that it had some quality or other which rendered it an anchor against popular fluctuations; and that a smaller council, drawn out of the senate, was appointed not only for life, but filled up vacancies itself. These examples, though as unfit for the imitation, as they are repugnant to the genius, of America, are, notwithstanding, when compared with the fugitive and turbulent existence of other ancient republics, very instructive proofs of the necessity of some institution that will blend stability with liberty. I am not unaware of the circumstances which distinguish the American from other popular governments, as well ancient as modern; and which render extreme circumspection necessary, in reasoning from the one case to the other. But after allowing due weight to this consideration, it may still be maintained, that there are many points of similitude which render these examples not unworthy of our attention. Many of the defects, as we have seen, which can only be supplied by a senatorial institution, are common to a numerous assembly frequently elected by the people, and to the people themselves. There are others peculiar to the former, which require the control of such an institution. The people can never wilfully betray their own interests; but they may possibly be betrayed by the representatives of the people; and the danger will be evidently greater where the whole legislative trust is lodged in the hands of one body of men, than where the concurrence of separate and dissimilar bodies is required in every public act.

The difference most relied on, between the American and other republics, consists in the principle of representation; which is the pivot on which the former move, and which is supposed to have been unknown to the latter, or at least to the ancient part of them. The use which has been made of this difference, in **reasonings contained in former papers, will have shown that I am** disposed neither to deny its existence nor to undervalue its importance. I feel the less restraint, therefore, in observing, that the position concerning the ignorance of the ancient governments on the subject of representation, is by no means precisely true in the latitude commonly given to it. Without entering into a disquisition which here would be misplaced, I will refer to a few known facts, in support of what I advance.

In the most pure democracies of Greece, many of the executive functions were performed, not by the people themselves, but by officers elected by the people, and REPRESENTING the people in their EXECUTIVE capacity.

Prior to the reform of Solon, Athens was governed by nine Archons, annually ELECTED BY THE PEOPLE AT LARGE. The degree of power delegated to them seems to be left in great obscurity. Subsequent to that period, we find an assembly, first of four, and afterwards of six hundred members, annually ELECTED BY THE PEOPLE; and PARTIALLY representing them in their LEGISLATIVE capacity, since they were not only associated with the people in the function of making laws, but had the exclusive right of originating legislative propositions to the people. The senate of Carthage, also, whatever might be its power, or the duration of its appointment, appears to have been ELECTIVE by the suffrages of the people. Similar instances might be traced in most, if not all the popular governments of antiquity.

Lastly, in Sparta we meet with the Ephori, and in Rome with the Tribunes; two bodies, small indeed in numbers, but annually ELECTED BY THE WHOLE BODY OF THE PEOPLE, and considered as the REPRESENTATIVES of the people, almost in their PLENIPOTENTIARY capacity. The Cosmi of Crete were also annually ELECTED BY THE PEOPLE, and have been considered by some authors as an institution analogous to those of Sparta and Rome, with this difference only, that in the election of that representative body the right of suffrage was communicated to a part only of the people.

From these facts, to which many others might be added, it is clear that the principle of representation was neither unknown to the ancients nor wholly overlooked in their political constitutions. The true distinction between these and the American governments, lies IN THE TOTAL EXCLUSION OF THE PEOPLE, IN THEIR COLLECTIVE CAPACITY, from any share in the LATTER, and not in the TOTAL EXCLUSION OF THE REPRESENTATIVES OF THE PEOPLE from the administration of the FORMER. The distinction, however, thus qualified, must be admitted to leave a most advantageous superiority in favor of the United States. But to insure to this advantage its full effect, we must be careful not to separate it from the other advantage, of an extensive territory. For it cannot be believed, that any form of representative government could have succeeded within the narrow limits occupied by the democracies of Greece.

In answer to all these arguments, suggested by reason, illustrated by examples, and enforced by our own experience, the jealous adversary of the Constitution will probably content himself with repeating, that a senate appointed not immediately by the people, and for the term of six years, must gradually acquire a dangerous pre-eminence in the government, and finally transform it into a tyrannical aristocracy.

To this general answer, the general reply ought to be sufficient, that liberty may be endangered by the abuses of liberty as well as by the abuses of power; that there are numerous instances of the former as well as of the latter; and that the former, rather than the latter, are apparently most to be apprehended by the United States. But a more particular reply may be given.

Before such a revolution can be effected, the Senate, it is to be observed, must in the first place corrupt itself; must next corrupt the State legislatures; must then corrupt the House of Representatives; and must finally corrupt the people at large. It is evident that the Senate must be first corrupted before it can attempt an establishment of tyranny. Without corrupting the State legislatures, it cannot prosecute the attempt, because the periodical change of members would otherwise regenerate the whole body. Without exerting the means of corruption with equal success on the House of Representatives, the opposition of that coequal branch of the government would inevitably defeat the attempt; and without corrupting the people themselves, a succession of new representatives would speedily restore all things to their pristine order. Is there any man who can seriously persuade himself that the proposed Senate can, by any possible means within the compass of human address, arrive at the object of a lawless ambition, through all these obstructions?

If reason condemns the suspicion, the same sentence is pronounced by experience. The constitution of Maryland furnishes the most apposite example. The Senate of that State is elected, as the federal Senate will be, indirectly by the people, and for a term less by one year only than the federal Senate. It is distinguished, also, by the remarkable prerogative of filling up its own vacancies within the term of its appointment, and, at the same time, is not under the control of any such rotation as is provided for the federal Senate. There are some other lesser distinctions, which would expose the former to colorable objections, that do not lie against the latter. If the federal Senate, therefore, really contained the danger which has been so loudly proclaimed, some symptoms at least of a like danger ought by this time to have been betrayed by the Senate of Maryland, but no such symptoms have appeared. On the contrary, the jealousies at first entertained by men of the same description with those who view with terror the correspondent part of the federal Constitution, have been gradually extinguished by the progress of the experiment; and the Maryland constitution is daily deriving, from the salutary operation of this part of it, a reputation in which it will probably not be rivalled by that of any State in the Union.

But if anything could silence the jealousies on this subject, it ought to be the British example. The Senate there instead of being elected for a term of six years, and of being unconfined to particular families or fortunes, is a hereditary assembly of opulent nobles. The House of Representatives, instead of being elected for two years, and by the whole body of the people, is elected for seven years, and, in very great proportion, by a very small proportion of the people. Here, unquestionably, ought to be seen in full display the aristocratic usurpations and tyranny which are at some future period to be exemplified in the United States. Unfortunately, however, for the anti-federal argument, the British history informs us that this hereditary assembly has not been able to defend itself against the continual encroachments of the House of Representatives; and that it no sooner lost the support of the monarch, than it was actually crushed by the weight of the popular branch.

As far as antiquity can instruct us on this subject, its examples support the reasoning which we have employed. In Sparta, the Ephori, the annual representatives of the people, were found an overmatch for the senate for life, continually gained on its authority and finally drew all power into their own hands. The Tribunes of Rome, who were the representatives of the people, prevailed, it is well known, in almost every contest with the senate for life, and in the end gained the most complete triumph over it. The fact is the more remarkable, as unanimity was required in every act of the Tribunes, even after their number was augmented to ten. It proves the irresistible force possessed by that branch of a free government, which has the people on its side. To these examples might be added that of Carthage, whose senate, according to the testimony of Polybius, instead of drawing all power into its vortex, had, at the commencement of the second Punic War, lost almost the whole of its original portion.

Besides the conclusive evidence resulting from this assemblage of facts, that the federal Senate will never be able to transform itself, by gradual usurpations, into an independent and aristocratic body, we are warranted in believing, that if such a revolution should ever happen from causes which the foresight of man cannot guard against, the House of Representatives, with the people on their side, will at all times be able to bring back the Constitution to its primitive form and principles. Against the force of the immediate representatives of the people, nothing will be able to maintain even the constitutional authority of the Senate, but such a display of enlightened policy, and attachment to the public good, as will divide with that branch of the legislature the affections and support of the entire body of the people themselves.

PUBLIUS.
FEDERALIST No. 64
<u>**The Powers of the Senate**</u>
From the New York Packet.
Friday, March 7, 1788.
John_Jay

To the People of the State of New York:

IT IS a just and not a new observation, that enemies to particular persons, and opponents to particular measures, seldom confine their censures to such things only in either as are worthy of blame. Unless on this principle, it is difficult to explain the motives of their conduct, who condemn the proposed Constitution in the aggregate, and treat with severity some of the most unexceptionable articles in it.

The second section gives power to the President, "BY AND WITH THE ADVICE AND CONSENT OF THE SENATE, TO MAKE TREATIES, PROVIDED TWO THIRDS OF THE SENATORS PRESENT CONCUR."

The power of making treaties is an important one, especially as it relates to war, peace, and commerce; and it should not be delegated but in such a mode, and with such precautions, as will afford the highest security that it will be exercised by men the best qualified for the purpose, and in the manner most conducive to the public good. The convention appears to have been attentive to both these points: they have directed the President to be chosen by select bodies of electors, to be deputed by the people for that express purpose; and they have committed the appointment of senators to the State legislatures. This mode has, in such cases, vastly the advantage of elections by the people in their collective capacity, where the activity of party zeal, taking the advantage of the supineness, the ignorance, and the hopes and fears of the unwary and interested, often places men in office by the votes of a small proportion of the electors.

As the select assemblies for choosing the President, as well as the State legislatures who appoint the senators, will in general be composed of the most enlightened and respectable citizens, there is reason to presume that their attention and their votes will be directed to those men only who have become the most distinguished by their abilities and virtue, and in whom the people perceive just grounds for confidence. The Constitution manifests very particular attention to this object. By excluding men under thirty-five from the first office, and those under thirty from the second, it confines the electors to men of whom the people have had time to form a judgment, and with respect to whom they will not be liable to be deceived by those brilliant appearances of genius and patriotism, which, like transient meteors, sometimes mislead as well as dazzle. If the observation be well founded, that wise kings will always be served by able ministers, it is fair to argue, that as an assembly of select electors possess, in a greater degree than kings, the means of extensive and accurate information relative to men and characters, so will their appointments bear at least equal marks of discretion and discernment. The inference which naturally results from these considerations is this, that the President and senators so chosen will always be of the number of those who best understand our national interests, whether considered in relation to the several States or to foreign nations, who are best able to promote those interests, and whose reputation for integrity inspires and merits confidence. With such men the power of making treaties may be safely lodged.

Although the absolute necessity of system, in the conduct of any business, is universally known and acknowledged, yet the high importance of it in national affairs has not yet become sufficiently impressed on the public mind. They who wish to commit the power under consideration to a popular assembly, composed of members constantly coming and going in quick succession, seem not to recollect that such a body must necessarily be inadequate to the attainment of those great objects, which require to be steadily contemplated in all their relations and circumstances, and which can only be approached and achieved by measures which not only talents, but also exact information, and often much time, are necessary to concert and to execute. It was wise, therefore, in the convention to provide, not only that the power of making treaties should be committed to able and honest men, but also that they should continue in place a sufficient time to become perfectly acquainted with our national concerns, and to form and introduce a a system for the management of them. The duration prescribed is such as will give them an opportunity of greatly extending their political information, and of rendering their accumulating experience more and more beneficial to their country. Nor has the convention discovered less prudence in providing for the frequent elections of senators in such a way as to obviate the inconvenience of periodically transferring those great affairs entirely to new men; for by leaving a considerable residue of the old ones in place, uniformity and order, as well as a constant succession of official information will be preserved.

There are a few who will not admit that the affairs of trade and navigation should be regulated by a system cautiously formed and steadily pursued; and that both our treaties and our laws should correspond with and be made to promote it. It is of much consequence that this correspondence and conformity be carefully maintained; and they who assent to the truth of this position will see and confess that it is well provided for by making concurrence of the Senate necessary both to treaties and to laws.

It seldom happens in the negotiation of treaties, of whatever nature, but that perfect SECRECY and immediate DESPATCH are sometimes requisite. These are cases where the most useful intelligence may be obtained, if the persons possessing it can be relieved from apprehensions of discovery. Those apprehensions will operate on those persons whether they are actuated by mercenary or friendly motives; and there doubtless are many of both descriptions, who would rely on the secrecy of the President, but who would not confide in that of the Senate, and still less in that of a large popular Assembly. The convention have done well, therefore, in so disposing of the power of making treaties, that although the President must, in forming them, act by the advice and consent of the Senate, yet he will be able to manage the business of intelligence in such a manner as prudence may suggest.

They who have turned their attention to the affairs of man, must have perceived that there are tides in them; tides very irregular in their duration, strength, and direction, and seldom found to run twice exactly in the same manner or measure. To discern and to profit by these tides in national affairs is the business of those who preside over them; and they who have had much experience on this head inform us, that there frequently are occasions when days, nay, even when hours, are precious. The loss of a battle, the death of a prince, the removal of a minister, or other circumstances intervening to change the present posture and aspect of affairs, may turn the most favorable tide into a course opposite to our wishes. As in the field, so in the cabinet, there are moments to be seized as they pass, and they who preside in either should be left in capacity to improve them. So often and so essentially have we heretofore suffered from the want of secrecy and dispatch, that the Constitution would have been inexcusably defective, if no attention had been paid to those objects. Those matters which in negotiations usually require the most secrecy and the most despatch, are those preparatory and auxiliary measures which are not otherwise important in a national view, than as they tend to facilitate the attainment of the objects of the negotiation. For these, the President will find no difficulty to provide; and should any circumstance occur which requires the advice and consent of the Senate, he may at any time convene them. Thus we see that the Constitution provides that our negotiations for treaties shall have every advantage which can be derived from talents, information, integrity, and deliberate investigations, on the one hand, and from secrecy and despatch on the other.

But to this plan, as to most others that have ever appeared, objections are contrived and urged.

Some are displeased with it, not on account of any errors or defects in it, but because, as the treaties, when made, are to have the force of laws, they should be made only by men invested with legislative authority. These gentlemen seem not to consider that the judgments of our courts, and the commissions constitutionally given by our governor, are as valid and as binding on all persons whom they concern, as the laws passed by our legislature. All constitutional acts of power, whether in the executive or in the judicial department, have as much legal validity and obligation as if they proceeded from the legislature; and therefore, whatever name be given to the power of making treaties, or however obligatory they may be when made, certain it is, that the people may, with much propriety, commit the power to a distinct body from the legislature, the executive, or the judicial. It surely does not follow, that because they have given the power of making laws to the legislature, that therefore they should likewise give them the power to do every other act of sovereignty by which the citizens are to be bound and affected.

Others, though content that treaties should be made in the mode proposed, are averse to their being the SUPREME laws of the land. They insist, and profess to believe, that treaties like acts of assembly should be repeatable at pleasure. This idea seems to be new and peculiar to this country, but new errors, as well as new truths, often appear. These gentlemen would do well to reflect that a treaty is only another name for a bargain, and that it would be impossible to find a nation who would make any bargain with us, which should be binding on them ABSOLUTELY, but on us only so long and so far as we may think proper to be bound by it. They who make laws may, without doubt, amend or repeal them; and it will not be disputed that they who make treaties may alter or cancel them; but still let us not forget that treaties are made, not by only one of the contracting parties, but by both; and consequently, that as the consent of both was essential to their formation at first, so must it ever afterwards be to alter or cancel them. The proposed Constitution, therefore, has not in the least extended the obligation of treaties. They are just as binding, and just as far beyond the lawful reach of legislative acts now, as they will be at any future period, or under any form of government.

However useful jealousy may be in republics, yet when like bile in the natural, it abounds too much in the body politic, the eyes of both become very liable to be deceived by the delusive appearances which that malady casts on surrounding objects. From this cause, probably, proceed the fears and apprehensions of some, that the President and Senate may make treaties without an equal eye to the interests of all the States. Others suspect that two thirds will oppress the remaining third, and ask whether those gentlemen are made sufficiently responsible for their conduct; whether, if they act corruptly, they can be punished; and if they make disadvantageous treaties, how are we to get rid of those treaties?

As all the States are equally represented in the Senate, and by men the most able and the most willing to promote the interests of their constituents, they will all have an equal degree of influence in that body, especially while they continue to be careful in appointing proper persons, and to insist on their punctual attendance. In proportion as the United States assume a national form and a national character, so will the good of the whole be more and more an object of attention, and the government must be a weak one indeed, if it should forget that the good of the whole can only be promoted by advancing the good of each of the parts or members which compose the whole. It will not be in the power of the President and Senate to make any treaties by which they and their families and estates will not be equally bound and affected with the rest of the community; and, having no private interests distinct from that of the nation, they will be under no temptations to neglect the latter.

As to corruption, the case is not supposable. He must either have been very unfortunate in his intercourse with the world, or possess a heart very susceptible of such impressions, who can think it probable that the President and two thirds of the Senate will ever be capable of such unworthy conduct. The idea is too gross and too invidious to be entertained. But in such a case, if it should ever happen, the treaty so obtained from us would, like all other fraudulent contracts, be null and void by the law of nations.

With respect to their responsibility, it is difficult to conceive how it could be increased. Every consideration that can influence the human mind, such as honor, oaths, reputations, conscience, the love of country, and family affections and attachments, afford security for their fidelity. In short, as the Constitution has taken the utmost care that they shall be men of talents and integrity, we have reason to be persuaded that the treaties they make will be as advantageous as, all circumstances considered, could be made; and so far as the fear of punishment and disgrace can operate, that motive to good behavior is amply afforded by the article on the subject of impeachments.

PUBLIUS.
FEDERALIST No. 65
The Powers of the Senate Continued
From the New York Packet.
Friday, March 7, 1788.
Alexander Hamilton

To the People of the State of New York:

THE remaining powers which the plan of the convention allots to the Senate, in a distinct capacity, are comprised in their participation with the executive in the appointment to offices, and in their judicial character as a court for the trial of impeachments. As in the business of appointments the executive will be the principal agent, the provisions relating to it will most properly be discussed in the examination of that department. We will, therefore, conclude this head with a view of the judicial character of the Senate.

A well-constituted court for the trial of impeachments is an object not more to be desired than difficult to be obtained in a government wholly elective. The subjects of its jurisdiction are those offenses which proceed from the misconduct of public men, or, in other words, from the abuse or violation of some public trust. They are of a nature which may with peculiar propriety be denominated POLITICAL, as they relate chiefly to injuries done immediately to the society itself. The prosecution of them, for this reason, will seldom fail to agitate the passions of the whole community, and to divide it into parties more or less friendly or inimical to the accused. In many cases it will connect itself with the pre-existing factions, and will enlist all their animosities, partialities, influence, and interest on one side or on the other; and in such cases there will always be the greatest danger that the decision will be regulated more by the comparative strength of parties, than by the real demonstrations of innocence or guilt.

The delicacy and magnitude of a trust which so deeply concerns the political reputation and existence of every man engaged in the administration of public affairs, speak for themselves. The difficulty of placing it rightly, in a government resting entirely on the basis of periodical elections, will as readily be perceived, when it is considered that the most conspicuous characters in it will, from that circumstance, be too often the leaders or the tools of the most cunning or the most numerous faction, and on this account, can hardly be expected to possess the requisite neutrality towards those whose conduct may be the subject of scrutiny.

The convention, it appears, thought the Senate the most fit depositary of this important trust. Those who can best discern the intrinsic difficulty of the thing, will be least hasty in condemning that opinion, and will be most inclined to allow due weight to the arguments which may be supposed to have produced it.

227

What, it may be asked, is the true spirit of the institution itself? Is it not designed as a method of NATIONAL INQUEST into the conduct of public men? If this be the design of it, who can so properly be the inquisitors for the nation as the representatives of the nation themselves? It is not disputed that the power of originating the inquiry, or, in other words, of preferring the impeachment, ought to be lodged in the hands of one branch of the legislative body. Will not the reasons which indicate the propriety of this arrangement strongly plead for an admission of the other branch of that body to a share of the inquiry? The model from which the idea of this institution has been borrowed, pointed out that course to the convention. In Great Britain it is the province of the House of Commons to prefer the impeachment, and of the House of Lords to decide upon it. Several of the State constitutions have followed the example. As well the latter, as the former, seem to have regarded the practice of impeachments as a bridle in the hands of the legislative body upon the executive servants of the government. Is not this the true light in which it ought to be regarded?

Where else than in the Senate could have been found a tribunal sufficiently dignified, or sufficiently independent? What other body would be likely to feel CONFIDENCE ENOUGH IN ITS OWN SITUATION, to preserve, unawed and uninfluenced, the necessary impartiality between an INDIVIDUAL accused, and the REPRESENTATIVES OF THE PEOPLE, HIS ACCUSERS?

Could the Supreme Court have been relied upon as answering this description? It is much to be doubted, whether the members of that tribunal would at all times be endowed with so eminent a portion of fortitude, as would be called for in the execution of so difficult a task; and it is still more to be doubted, whether they would possess the degree of credit and authority, which might, on certain occasions, be indispensable towards reconciling the people to a decision that should happen to clash with an accusation brought by their immediate representatives. A deficiency in the first, would be fatal to the accused; in the last, dangerous to the public tranquility. The hazard in both these respects, could only be avoided, if at all, by rendering that tribunal more numerous than would consist with a reasonable attention to economy. The necessity of a numerous court for the trial of impeachments, is equally dictated by the nature of the proceeding. This can never be tied down by such strict rules, either in the delineation of the offense by the prosecutors, or in the construction of it by the judges, as in common cases serve to limit the discretion of courts in favor of personal security. There will be no jury to stand between the judges who are to pronounce the sentence of the law, and the party who is to receive or suffer it. The awful discretion which a court of impeachments must necessarily have, to doom to honor or to infamy the most confidential and the most distinguished characters of the community, forbids the commitment of the trust to a small number of persons.

These considerations seem alone sufficient to authorize a conclusion, that the Supreme Court would have been an improper substitute for the Senate, as a court of impeachments. There remains a further consideration, which will not a little strengthen this conclusion. It is this: The punishment which may be the consequence of conviction upon impeachment, is not to terminate the chastisement of the offender. After having been sentenced to a perpetual ostracism from the esteem and confidence, and honors and emoluments of his country, he will still be liable to prosecution and punishment in the ordinary course of law. Would it be proper that the persons who had disposed of his fame, and his most valuable rights as a citizen in one trial, should, in another trial, for the same offense, be also the disposers of his life and his fortune? Would there not be the greatest reason to apprehend, that error, in the first sentence, would be the parent of error in the second sentence? That the strong bias of one decision would be apt to overrule the influence of any new lights which might be brought to vary the complexion of another decision? Those who know anything of human nature, will not hesitate to answer these questions in the affirmative; and will be at no loss to perceive, that by making the same persons judges in both cases, those who might happen to be the objects of prosecution would, in a great measure, be deprived of the double security intended them by a double trial. The loss of life and estate would often be virtually included in a sentence which, in its terms, imported nothing more than dismission from a present, and disqualification for a future, office. It may be said, that the intervention of a jury, in the second instance, would obviate the danger. But juries are frequently influenced by the opinions of judges. They are sometimes induced to find special verdicts, which refer the main question to the decision of the court. Who would be willing to stake his life and his estate upon the verdict of a jury acting under the auspices of judges who had predetermined his guilt?

Would it have been an improvement of the plan, to have united the Supreme Court with the Senate, in the formation of the court of impeachments? This union would certainly have been attended with several advantages; but would they not have been overbalanced by the signal disadvantage, already stated, arising from the agency of the same judges in the double prosecution to which the offender would be liable? To a certain extent, the benefits of that union will be obtained from making the chief justice of the Supreme Court the president of the court of impeachments, as is proposed to be done in the plan of the convention; while the inconveniences of an entire incorporation of the former into the latter will be substantially avoided. This was perhaps the prudent mean. I forbear to remark upon the additional pretext for clamor against the judiciary, which so considerable an augmentation of its authority would have afforded.

Would it have been desirable to have composed the court for the trial of impeachments, of persons wholly distinct from the other departments of the government? There are weighty arguments, as well against, as in favor of, such a plan. To some minds it will not appear a trivial objection, that it could tend to increase the complexity of the political machine, and to add a new spring to the government, the utility of which would at best be questionable. But an objection which will not be thought by any unworthy of attention, is this: a court formed upon such a plan, would either be attended with a heavy expense, or might in practice be subject to a variety of casualties and inconveniences. It must either consist of permanent officers, stationary at the seat of government, and of course entitled to fixed and regular stipends, or of certain officers of the State governments to be called upon whenever an impeachment was actually depending. It will not be easy to imagine any third mode materially different, which could rationally be proposed. As the court, for reasons already given, ought to be numerous, the first scheme will be reprobated by every man who can compare the extent of the public wants with the means of supplying them. The second will be espoused with caution by those who will seriously consider the difficulty of collecting men dispersed over the whole Union; the injury to the innocent, from the procrastinated determination of the charges which might be brought against them; the advantage to the guilty, from the opportunities which delay would afford to intrigue and corruption; and in some cases the detriment to the State, from the prolonged inaction of men whose firm and faithful execution of their duty might have exposed them to the persecution of an intemperate or designing majority in the House of Representatives. Though this latter supposition may seem harsh, and might not be likely often to be verified, yet it ought not to be forgotten that the demon of faction will, at certain seasons, extend his sceptre over all numerous bodies of men.

But though one or the other of the substitutes which have been examined, or some other that might be devised, should be thought preferable to the plan in this respect, reported by the convention, it will not follow that the Constitution ought for this reason to be rejected. If mankind were to resolve to agree in no institution of government, until every part of it had been adjusted to the most exact standard of perfection, society would soon become a general scene of anarchy, and the world a desert. Where is the standard of perfection to be found? Who will undertake to unite the discordant opinions of a whole commuity, in the same judgment of it; and to prevail upon one conceited projector to renounce his INFALLIBLE criterion for the FALLIBLE criterion of his more CONCEITED NEIGHBOR? To answer the purpose of the adversaries of the Constitution, they ought to prove, not merely that particular provisions in it are not the best which might have been imagined, but that the plan upon the whole is bad and pernicious.

PUBLIUS.
FEDERALIST No. 66
Objections to the Power of the Senate To Set as a Court for Impeachments Further Considered
From the New York Packet.
Tuesday, March 11, 1788.
Alexander Hamilton

To the People of the State of New York:

A REVIEW of the principal objections that have appeared against the proposed court for the trial of impeachments, will not improbably eradicate the remains of any unfavorable impressions which may still exist in regard to this matter.

The FIRST of these objections is, that the provision in question confounds legislative and judiciary authorities in the same body, in violation of that important and well established maxim which requires a separation between the different departments of power. The true meaning of this maxim has been discussed and ascertained in another place, and has been shown to be entirely compatible with a partial intermixture of those departments for special purposes, preserving them, in the main, distinct and unconnected. This partial intermixture is even, in some cases, not only proper but necessary to the mutual defense of the several members of the government against each other. An absolute or qualified negative in the executive upon the acts of the legislative body, is admitted, by the ablest adepts in political science, to be an indispensable barrier against the encroachments of the latter upon the former. And it may, perhaps, with no less reason be contended, that the powers relating to impeachments are, as before intimated, an essential check in the hands of that body upon the encroachments of the executive. The division of them between the two branches of the legislature, assigning to one the right of accusing, to the other the right of judging, avoids the inconvenience of making the same persons both accusers and judges; and guards against the danger of persecution, from the prevalency of a factious spirit in either of those branches. As the concurrence of two thirds of the Senate will be requisite to a condemnation, the security to innocence, from this additional circumstance, will be as complete as itself can desire.

It is curious to observe, with what vehemence this part of the plan is assailed, on the principle here taken notice of, by men who profess to admire, without exception, the constitution of this State; while that constitution makes the Senate, together with the chancellor and judges of the Supreme Court, not only a court of impeachments, but the highest judicatory in the State, in all causes, civil and criminal. The proportion, in point of numbers, of the chancellor and judges to the senators, is so inconsiderable, that the judiciary authority of New York, in the last resort, may, with truth, be said to reside in its Senate. If the plan of the convention be, in this respect, chargeable with a departure from the celebrated maxim which has been so often mentioned, and seems to be so little understood, how much more culpable must be the constitution of New York?[1]

A SECOND objection to the Senate, as a court of impeachments, is, that it contributes to an undue accumulation of power in that body, tending to give to the government a countenance too aristocratic. The Senate, it is observed, is to have concurrent authority with the Executive in the formation of treaties and in the appointment to offices: if, say the objectors, to these prerogatives is added that of deciding in all cases of impeachment, it will give a decided predominancy to senatorial influence. To an objection so little precise in itself, it is not easy to find a very precise answer. Where is the measure or criterion to which we can appeal, for determining what will give the Senate too much, too little, or barely the proper degree of influence? Will it not be more safe, as well as more simple, to dismiss such vague and uncertain calculations, to examine each power by itself, and to decide, on general principles, where it may be deposited with most advantage and least inconvenience?

If we take this course, it will lead to a more intelligible, if not to a more certain result. The disposition of the power of making treaties, which has obtained in the plan of the convention, will, then, if I mistake not, appear to be fully justified by the considerations stated in a former number, and by others which will occur under the next head of our inquiries. The expediency of the junction of the Senate with the Executive, in the power of appointing to offices, will, I trust, be placed in a light not less satisfactory, in the disquisitions under the same head. And I flatter myself the observations in my last paper must have gone no inconsiderable way towards proving that it was not easy, if practicable, to find a more fit receptacle for the power of determining impeachments, than that which has been chosen. If this be truly the case, the hypothetical dread of the too great weight of the Senate ought to be discarded from our reasonings.

But this hypothesis, such as it is, has already been refuted in the remarks applied to the duration in office prescribed for the senators. It was by them shown, as well on the credit of historical examples, as from the reason of the thing, that the most POPULAR branch of every government, partaking of the republican genius, by being generally the favorite of the people, will be as generally a full match, if not an overmatch, for every other member of the Government.

But independent of this most active and operative principle, to secure the equilibrium of the national House of Representatives, the plan of the convention has provided in its favor several important counterpoises to the additional authorities to be conferred upon the Senate. The exclusive privilege of originating money bills will belong to the House of Representatives. The same house will possess the sole right of instituting impeachments: is not this a complete counterbalance to that of determining them? The same house will be the umpire in all elections of the President, which do not unite the suffrages of a majority of the whole number of electors; a case which it cannot be doubted will sometimes, if not frequently, happen. The constant possibility of the thing must be a fruitful source of influence to that body. The more it is contemplated, the more important will appear this ultimate though contingent power, of deciding the competitions of the most illustrious citizens of the Union, for the first office in it. It would not perhaps be rash to predict, that as a mean of influence it will be found to outweigh all the peculiar attributes of the Senate.

A THIRD objection to the Senate as a court of impeachments, is drawn from the agency they are to have in the appointments to office. It is imagined that they would be too indulgent judges of the conduct of men, in whose official creation they had participated. The principle of this objection would condemn a practice, which is to be seen in all the State governments, if not in all the governments with which we are acquainted: I mean that of rendering those who hold offices during pleasure, dependent on the pleasure of those who appoint them. With equal plausibility might it be alleged in this case, that the favoritism of the latter would always be an asylum for the misbehavior of the former. But that practice, in contradiction to this principle, proceeds upon the presumption, that the responsibility of those who appoint, for the fitness and competency of the persons on whom they bestow their choice, and the interest they will have in the respectable and prosperous administration of affairs, will inspire a sufficient disposition to dismiss from a share in it all such who, by their conduct, shall have proved themselves unworthy of the confidence reposed in them. Though facts may not always correspond with this presumption, yet if it be, in the main, just, it must destroy the supposition that the Senate, who will merely sanction the choice of the Executive, should feel a bias, towards the objects of that choice, strong enough to blind them to the evidences of guilt so extraordinary, as to have induced the representatives of the nation to become its accusers.

If any further arguments were necessary to evince the improbability of such a bias, it might be found in the nature of the agency of the Senate in the business of appointments.

It will be the office of the President to NOMINATE, and, with the advice and consent of the Senate, to APPOINT. There will, of course, be no exertion of CHOICE on the part of the Senate. They may defeat one choice of the Executive, and oblige him to make another; but they cannot themselves CHOOSE, they can only ratify or reject the choice of the President. They might even entertain a preference to some other person, at the very moment they were assenting to the one proposed, because there might be no positive ground of opposition to him; and they could not be sure, if they withheld their assent, that the subsequent nomination would fall upon their own favorite, or upon any other person in their estimation more meritorious than the one rejected. Thus it could hardly happen, that the majority of the Senate would feel any other complacency towards the object of an appointment than such as the appearances of merit might inspire, and the proofs of the want of it destroy.

A FOURTH objection to the Senate in the capacity of a court of impeachments, is derived from its union with the Executive in the power of making treaties. This, it has been said, would constitute the senators their own judges, in every case of a corrupt or perfidious execution of that trust. After having combined with the Executive in betraying the interests of the nation in a ruinous treaty, what prospect, it is asked, would there be of their being made to suffer the punishment they would deserve, when they were themselves to decide upon the accusation brought against them for the treachery of which they have been guilty?

This objection has been circulated with more earnestness and with greater show of reason than any other which has appeared against this part of the plan; and yet I am deceived if it does not rest upon an erroneous foundation.

The security essentially intended by the Constitution against corruption and treachery in the formation of treaties, is to be sought for in the numbers and characters of those who are to make them. The JOINT AGENCY of the Chief Magistrate of the Union, and of two thirds of the members of a body selected by the collective wisdom of the legislatures of the several States, is designed to be the pledge for the fidelity of the national councils in this particular. The convention might with propriety have meditated the punishment of the Executive, for a deviation from the instructions of the Senate, or a want of integrity in the conduct of the negotiations committed to him; they might also have had in view the punishment of a few leading individuals in the Senate, who should have prostituted their influence in that body as the mercenary instruments of foreign corruption: but they could not, with more or with equal propriety, have contemplated the impeachment and punishment of two thirds of the Senate, consenting to an improper treaty, than of a majority of that or of the other branch of the national legislature, consenting to a pernicious or unconstitutional law, a principle which, I believe, has never been admitted into any government. How, in fact, could a majority in the House of Representatives impeach themselves? Not better, it is evident, than two thirds of the Senate might try themselves. And yet what reason is there, that a majority of the House of Representatives, sacrificing the interests of the society by an unjust and tyrannical act of legislation, should escape with impunity, more than two thirds of the Senate, sacrificing the same interests in an injurious treaty with a foreign power? The truth is, that in all such cases it is essential to the freedom and to the necessary independence of the deliberations of the body, that the members of it should be exempt from punishment for acts done in a collective capacity; and the security to the society must depend on the care which is taken to confide the trust to proper hands, to make it their interest to execute it with fidelity, and to make it as difficult as possible for them to combine in any interest opposite to that of the public good.

So far as might concern the misbehavior of the Executive in perverting the instructions or contravening the views of the Senate, we need not be apprehensive of the want of a disposition in that body to punish the abuse of their confidence or to vindicate their own authority. We may thus far count upon their pride, if not upon their virtue. And so far even as might concern the corruption of leading members, by whose arts and influence the majority may have been inveigled into measures odious to the community, if the proofs of that corruption should be satisfactory, the usual propensity of human nature will warrant us in concluding that there would be commonly no defect of inclination in the body to divert the public resentment from themselves by a ready sacrifice of the authors of their mismanagement and disgrace.

PUBLIUS.

1. In that of New Jersey, also, the final judiciary authority is in a branch of the legislature. In New Hampshire, Massachusetts, Pennsylvania, and South Carolina, one branch of the legislature is the court for the trial of impeachments.

A Comprehensive List of Federalist Papers Dealing with the Sovereignty of Each of the States

Federalist Index For State Sovereigns.

This information is provided to give the Citizens of the Union States the necessary background to inform their elected Senators should they discover that he believes he is representing the People of their Union State that he applied for the wrong job. The People of each Union State are Constitutionally already represented in the House of

Representatives of Congress. The other House, called the Senate, is Constitutionally for exclusive representation of the Union States and no other.

From the searching of the Federalist Papers for "Sovereign States" we get the following hits." The reading of these Papers will lend to the reader a better comprehension of the ideology of Dual Sovereignty analyzed in detail in Appendix B.

1. Federalist Papers: FEDERALIST No. 39

> They ought, with equal care, to have preserved the FEDERAL form, which regards the Union as a CONFEDERACY of *sovereign states*; instead of which, . . .

2. Federalist Papers: FEDERALIST No. 20

> The union is composed of seven coequal and *sovereign states*, and each state or province is a composition of equal and independent cities. . . .

3. Federalist Papers: FEDERALIST No. 16

> Even in those confederacies which have been composed of members smaller than many of our counties, the principle of legislation for *sovereign States*, . . .

4. Federalist Papers: FEDERALIST No. 62

> The appointment of them by the State legislatures; III. . . . and that among independent and *sovereign States*, bound together by a simple league, the parties, . . . www.foundingfathers.info/federalist papers/fed62.htm

5. Federalist Papers: FEDERALIST No. 18

The members retained the character of independent and *sovereign states*, and had equal votes in the federal council. This council had a general authority to . . . www.foundingfathers.info/federalistpapers/fed18.htm

6. Federalist Papers: FEDERALIST No. 69

The President of the United *States* would be liable to be impeached, ... But this arises naturally from the *sovereign* power which relates to treaties. . . .

7. Federalist Papers: FEDERALIST No. 17

There was a common head, chieftain, or *sovereign*, whose authority extended . . . and the great fiefs were erected into independent principalities or *States*. . . . www.foundingfathers.info/federalistpapers/fed17.htm

8. Federalist Papers: FEDERALIST No. 32

This must necessarily be exclusive; because if each *State* had power to . . . the *sovereign* power; and the rule that all authorities, of which the *States* are . . . www.foundingfathers.info/federalistpapers/fed32.htm

9. Federalist Papers: FEDERALIST No. 19

To the People of the *State* of New York: . . . had not abolished, gradually threw off the yoke and advanced to *sovereign* jurisdiction and independence. . . . www.foundingfathers.info/federalistpapers/fed19.htm

10. Federalist Papers: FEDERALIST No. 81

They confer no right of action, independent of the *sovereign* will. To what purpose would it be to authorize suits against *States* for the debts they owe? . . .

11. Federalist Papers: FEDERALIST No. 40

The *States* would never have appointed a convention with so much solemnity, . . . are left in the enjoyment of their *sovereign* and independent jurisdiction. . . . www.foundingfathers.info/federalistpapers/fed40.htm

12. Federalist Papers: FEDERALIST No. 75

They are not rules prescribed by the *sovereign* to the subject, but agreements . . . created and circumstanced as would be a President of the United *States*. . . . www.foundingfathers.info/federalistpapers/fed75.htm

13. Federalist Papers: FEDERALIST No. 45

The Alleged Danger From the Powers of the Union to the *State* Governments . . . and the sympathy in some instances between the general *sovereign* and the latter . . .

14. Federalist Papers: FEDERALIST No. 80

The *States*, by the plan of the convention, are prohibited from doing a variety of things . . . would not, if unredressed, be an aggression upon his *sovereign*, . . . www.foundingfathers.info/federalistpapers/fed80.htm

15.   Federalist Papers: FEDERALIST No. 9

"This form of government is a convention by which several smaller *STATES* agree to . . . certain exclusive and very important portions of *sovereign* power. . . .

16.   Federalist Papers: FEDERALIST No. 30

In the Ottoman or Turkish empire, the *sovereign*, though in other respects . . . feeble as it is intended to repose in the United *States*, an unlimited power of . . . www.foundingfathers.info/federalistpapers/fed30.htm

17,   Federalist Papers: FEDERALIST No. 6

Concerning Dangers from Dissensions Between the *States* . . . For if there ever was a *sovereign* who bid fair to realize the project of universal monarchy, . . . www.foundingfathers.info/federalistpapers/fed06.htm

18.   Federalist Papers: FEDERALIST No. 36

. . . passed into laws by the authority of the *sovereign* or legislature. . . . When the *States* know that the Union can apply itself without their agency, . . . www. foundingfathers.info/federalistpapers/fed36.htm

19.   Federalist Papers: FEDERALIST No. 15

While they admit that the government of the United *States* is destitute of energy, ... In addition to all this, there is, in the nature of *sovereign* power, . . . www.foundingfathers.info/federalistpapers/fed15.htm

20. Federalist Papers: FEDERALIST No. 73

It is there provided that "The President of the United *States* shall, ... A king of Great Britain, with all his train of *sovereign* attributes, . . .

21. Federalist Papers: FEDERALIST No. 4

. . . which affect only the mind of the *sovereign*, often lead him to engage in wars not . . . . The history of the *states* of Greece, and of other countries, . . .

Now you know how important Union State sovereignty is to the Constitutional structure of your country and the longevity of your own Liberty and Sovereignty.

Devolution of Power: Federal Territories

A Global Pro Bono Law Firm

Quick Guide

Prepared by
The Public International Law & Policy Group
December 2006

Executive Summary

The purpose of this memorandum is to provide an overview of comparative state practice with regard to territories that are administered directly by Federal Governments.

Federal territories, also called federal districts and union territories, are territories that the central government administers directly. Federal territories are typically established in areas of economic, geographic, historic, or administrative importance. Federal territories have been established in Malaysia, India, Australia, and the United States.

Comparative state practice illustrates that the central government typically devolves some authority to federal territories while retaining ultimate executive and legislative authority. Federal territories often have municipal

244 M. Kenneth Creamer

administrations, either elected by the population of the territory or appointed by the central government. Federal territories sometimes have legislative assemblies that have authority to pass legislation on limited matters. Typically, the legislature and executive branches of the central government retain the ultimate authority to amend or veto measures undertaken by the federal territories.

Statement of Purpose

The purpose of this memorandum is to provide an overview of comparative state practice with regard to territories that are ruled directly by the central government.

Introduction

Federal territories are territories within a federation that are ruled directly by the central government. Federal territories may also be referred to as federal districts, capital districts, or union territories. They are typically established to ensure that the central government can maintain direct control over cities of administrative, economic, or historical significance. Federal territories have been established in Malaysia, India, Australia, and the United States.

The administration of federal territories and their relationship to the central government varies according to geography, natural resources, population, and historic and cultural identities. In some cases, the central government administers the territory directly with very minimal local government. In others, the central government retains general administrative control over the territory, but devolves limited executive or legislative authority to a local government within the territory.

Federal Territory, Malaysia—N/A—Redacted

Union Territories, India—N/A—Redacted

Australian Capital Territory, Australia—N/A—Redacted

District of Columbia and Federal Territories, United States of America

The United States is comprised of 50 states, the District of Columbia, and several federal territories. The federal territories include Puerto Rico, American Samoa, Guam, and the U.S. Virgin Islands.[96] The District of Columbia and the federal territories are administered by the Federal Government.

Federal Territories

Not all federal territories have the same administrative structure or relationship to the U.S. Government. Most federal territories, including Puerto Rico, American Samoa, Guam, and the U.S. Virgin Islands, have some common features. Nearly all are administered by the Federal Government. A Governor is appointed or elected as the territory's executive, and most have a popularly elected legislative assembly or senate. Most also have a non-voting member in the House of Representatives that can participate in debate, sit on committees, and propose

---

[96]   The U.S. Federal territories also include several uninhabited islands, including Baker Island, Howland Island, Jarvis Island, Johnston Atoll, Kingman Reef, Navassa Island, and Wake Island. Nearly all of these islands were acquired for their value in mining guano. Many of these islands are located in the South Pacific Ocean and were used as naval and air bases during World War II. After the war, most of these islands were abandoned.

legislation. **The federal territories**[97] **have no representation in the Senate.**

While not all federal territories are alike, most have significant autonomy similar to states. The legislatures of federal territories are empowered to pass legislation on issues of local concern, such as the territorial budget and education.[98] Constitutional and Federal laws apply directly to the federal territories. Federal district courts have been established for Puerto Rico, the U.S. Virgin Islands, Guam, and the Northern Mariana Islands.

The District of Columbia

The District of Columbia houses the U.S. capital city, Washington. The city and the district are co-extensive and occupy less than 70 square miles (181 sq km). The land on which the capital sits was voluntarily ceded by the state of Maryland to provide a neutral cite for the capital.

The District of Columbia is administered directly by the Federal Government. Congress has legislative authority and general police power in the District.[99] Residents of the District of Columbia elect a non-voting representative to the Federal

---

[97]   The Federal territories are basically "Instrumentalities of the United States" and thus a taxable employer as defined at IRC section 3111 involved in the act of employment. See IRC Section 3121(h)(1) (This footnote not in original)

[98]   The Guam Public School System has, until recently, been funded by the U.S. Federal Government. Concerns over fiscal accountability have caused the U.S. Government to put a freeze on Federal funds. Madeline Bordallo, Delegate from Guam, *USDOE Discuss Status of Federal Education Funds*, June 29, 2006, *available at* http://www.house.gov/bordallo/Press_Releases/2006/pr062906-1.html.

[99]   *Block v. Hirsh*, 256 U.S. 135, 156 (1921).

legislature. A 1961 Amendment to the U.S. Constitution gave residents the right to vote for President.[100]

Congress has devolved municipal powers to the District of Columbia, including authority over the budget, education, streets, and sanitation. The District of Columbia is administered by an elected mayor and a 13-member city council, but Congress retains the right to review and overrule local laws. Like the federal territories, the District of Columbia is represented by a non-voting delegate in the House of Representatives that can participate in debate, sit on committees, and propose legislation.

Conclusion

The establishment of a federal territory is a method that states have used to ensure that the central government can retain direct authority over cities or small territories that have special administrative, economic, or historical significance. Typically, the central government devolves limited administrative or legislative authority to the territory, but retains final control authority to veto or amend legislation.

---

[100] Constitution of the United States, Amendment XXXIII, *available at* http://www.archives.gov/national-archives-experience/charters/constitution_amendments_11-27.html#23.

Famous Quotes by our Founders, The Champions Of Liberty

All, too, will bear in mind this sacred principle, that though the will of the majority is in all cases to prevail, that will, to be rightful, must be reasonable; that the minority possess their equal—rights, which equal laws must protect, and to violate which would be oppression.—**Thomas Jefferson**

Certainly one of the highest duties of the citizen is a scrupulous obedience to the laws of the nation. But it is not the highest duty.—**Thomas Jefferson**

Happiness is not being pained in body or troubled in mind. **Thomas Jefferson**

If ignorance is bliss, why aren't more people happy?—**Thomas Jefferson**

It is error alone which needs the support of government. Truth can stand by itself.—**Thomas Jefferson**

If a nation expects to be ignorant and free, in a state of civilization, it expects what never was and never will be.—**Thomas Jefferson**

Do not bite the bait of pleasure till you know there is no hook beneath it.—**Thomas Jefferson**

We are firmly convinced, and we act on that conviction, that with nations as with individuals, our interests soundly calculated will ever be found inseparable from our moral duties.—**Thomas Jefferson**

The will of the people is the only legitimate foundation of any government, and to protect its free expression should be our first object.—**Thomas Jefferson**

I have no fear but that the result of our experiment will be that men may be trusted to govern themselves without a master. Could the contrary of this be proved I should conclude either that there is no God, or that He is a malevolent Being.—**Thomas Jefferson**

With all the imperfections of our present government, it is without comparison the best existing, or that ever did exist.—**Thomas Jefferson**

Ignorance is preferable to error, and he is less remote from the truth who believes nothing than he who believes what is wrong.—**Thomas Jefferson**

If we can prevent the government from wasting the labors of the people under the pretense of taking care of them, they must become happy.—**Thomas Jefferson**

It is neither wealth nor splendor, but tranquility and occupation, that gives happiness.—**Thomas Jefferson**

We are not afraid to follow truth wherever it may lead, nor to tolerate any error so long as reason is left free to combat it.—**Thomas Jefferson**

No free man shall ever be debarred the use of arms. The strongest reason for the people to retain the right to keep and bear arms is, as a last resort, to protect themselves against tyranny in government.—**Thomas Jefferson**

The laws that forbid the carrying of arms are laws of such nature. They disarm only those who are neither inclined nor determined to commit crimes . . . such laws serve rather to encourage than to prevent homicides, for an unarmed man may be attacked with greater confidence than an armed man. ('Commonplace Book' 1775)—**Thomas Jefferson**

Truth is certainly a branch of morality and a very important one to society.—**Thomas Jefferson**

It is strangely absurd to suppose that a million of human beings, collected together, are not under the same moral laws which bind each of them separately.—**Thomas Jefferson**

Bonaparte was a lion in the field only. In civil life, a cold-blooded, calculating, unprincipled usurper, without a virtue; no statesman, knowing nothing of commerce, political economy, or civil government, and supplying ignorance by bold presumption.—**Thomas Jefferson**

Every citizen should be a soldier. This was the case with the Greeks and Romans, and must be that of every free state.—**Thomas Jefferson**

That government is best which governs least.—**Thomas Jefferson**

Were we directed from Washington when to sow and when to reap, we should soon want bread.—**Thomas Jefferson**

In every country and every age, the priest had been hostile to Liberty.—**Thomas Jefferson**

The ground of liberty is to be gained by inches, and we must be contented to secure what we can get from time to time and eternally press forward for what is yet to get. It takes time to persuade men to do even what is for their own good.—**Thomas Jefferson**

The god who gave us life, gave us liberty at the same time: the hand of force may destroy, but cannot disjoin them.—**Thomas Jefferson**

I would rather be exposed to the inconveniences attending too much liberty than to those attending too small a degree of it.—**Thomas Jefferson**

What country can preserve its liberties if its rulers are not warned from time to time that their people preserve the spirit of resistance?—**Thomas Jefferson**

Of liberty I would say that, in the whole plenitude of its extent, it is unobstructed action according to our will. But rightful liberty is unobstructed action according to our will within limits drawn around us by the equal rights of others. I do not add 'within the limits of the law,' because law is often but the tyrant's will, and always so when it violates the right of an individual.—**Thomas Jefferson**

The new Constitution has secured these [individual rights] in the Executive and Legislative departments; but not in the Judiciary. It should have established trials by the people themselves, that is to say, by jury.—**Thomas Jefferson**

The Judiciary of the United States is the subtle corps of sappers and miners constantly working under ground to undermine the foundations of our confederated fabric. (1820)—**Thomas Jefferson**

. . . the Federal Judiciary; an irresponsible body (for impeachment is scarcely a scarecrow), working like gravity by night and by day, gaining a little today and a little tomorrow, and advancing its noiseless step like a thief, over the field of jurisdiction, until all shall be usurped from the States, and the government of all be consolidated into one. When all government . . . in little as in great things, shall be drawn to Washington as the centre of all power, it will render powerless the checks provided of one government on another and will become as venal and oppressive as the government from which we separated. (1821)—**Thomas Jefferson**

The opinion which gives to the judges the right to decide what laws are constitutional and what not, not only for themselves in their own sphere of action, but for the legislative and executive also in their spheres, would make the judiciary a despotic branch.—**Thomas Jefferson**

Let this be the distinctive mark of an American that in cases of commotion, he enlists himself under no man's banner, inquires for no man's name, but repairs to the standard of the laws. Do this, and you need never fear anarchy or tyranny. Your government will be perpetual.—**Thomas Jefferson**

No man has a natural right to commit aggression on the equal rights of another, and this is all from which the laws ought to restrain him.—**Thomas Jefferson**

Laws are made for men of ordinary understanding and should, therefore, be construed by the ordinary rules of common sense. Their meaning is not to be sought for in metaphysical subtleties which may make anything mean everything or nothing at pleasure.—**Thomas Jefferson**

It is more dangerous that even a guilty person should be punished without the forms of law than that he should escape.—**Thomas Jefferson**

Enlighten the people generally, and tyranny and oppressions of body and mind will vanish like spirits at the dawn of day.—**Thomas Jefferson**

The legitimate powers of government extend to such acts only as are injurious to others. But it does me no injury for my neighbor to say there are twenty gods, or no God. It neither picks my pocket nor breaks my leg.—**Thomas Jefferson**

I am not a friend to a very energetic government. It is always oppressive.—**Thomas Jefferson**

But friendship is precious, not only in the shade, but in the sunshine of life; and thanks to a benevolent arrangement of things, the greater part of life is sunshine.—**Thomas Jefferson**

I hold it, that a little rebellion, now and then, is a good thing, and as necessary in the political world as storms in the physical.—**Thomas Jefferson**

It should be remembered as an axiom of eternal truth in politics, that whatever power in any government is independent, is absolute also; in theory only at first while the spirit of the people is up, but in practice as fast as that relaxes.—**Thomas Jefferson**

The man who fears no truth has nothing to fear from lies.—**Thomas Jefferson**

He who knows nothing is closer to the truth than he whose mind is filled with falsehoods and errors.—**Thomas Jefferson**

Difference of opinion leads to enquiry, and enquiry to truth.—**Thomas Jefferson**

The concentrating [of powers] in the same hands is precisely the definition of despotic government. It will be no alleviation that these powers will be exercised by a plurality of hands, and not by a single one.—**Thomas Jefferson**

Power is not alluring to pure minds.—**Thomas Jefferson**

In matters of power let no more be heard of the confidence in man but bind them down from mischief by the chains of the constitution.—**Thomas Jefferson**

The republican is the only form of government which is not eternally at open or secret war with the rights of mankind.—**Thomas Jefferson**

Thank you for your interest in the history of the greatest nation that has defended freedom for the entire world. There are so many people that feel a one world government is the savior of the human race. This government.-**Thomas Jefferson**

The spirit of resistance to government is so valuable on certain occasions that I wish it to be always kept alive. It will often be exercised when wrong, but better so than not to be exercised at all.—**Thomas Jefferson**

The loss of the battle of Waterloo was the salvation of France.—**Thomas Jefferson**

Merchants have no country. The mere spot they stand on does not constitute so strong an attachment as that from which they draw their gains.—**Thomas Jefferson**

The glow of one warm thought is to me worth more than money.—**Thomas Jefferson**

Never spend your money before you have it.—**Thomas Jefferson**

Nothing gives a person so much advantage over another as to remain always cool and unruffled under all circumstances.—**Thomas Jefferson**

My only fear is that I may live too long. This would be a subject of dread to me.—**Thomas Jefferson**

Shake off all the fears of servile prejudices, under which weak minds are serviley crouched. Fix reason firmly in her seat, and call on her tribunal for every fact, every opinion. Question with boldness even the existence of a God, because, if there be one, he must more approve of the homage of reason than that of blind faith.—**Thomas Jefferson**

With respect to our state and Federal Governments, I do not thing their relations correctly understood by foreigners. They generally suppose the former subordinate to the latter. But this is not the case. They are co-ordinate departments of one simple and integral whole. To the state governments are reserved all legislation administration, in affairs which concern their own citizens only; and to the Federal Government is given whatever concerns foreigners and citizens of other states; these functions alone being made federal. The one is the domestic, the other the foreign branch of the same government—neither having control over the other, but within its own department. *from Thomas Jefferson's letter to Major John Cartwright, of June 5th, 1824 (vol. 4, p. 396)*

Does the government fear us? Or do we fear the government? When the people fear the government, tyranny has found victory. The Federal Government is our servant, not our master!—**Thomas Jefferson**

When governments fear people, there is liberty. When the people fear the government, there is tyranny.—**Thomas Jefferson**

The happiest moments of my life have been the few which I have passed at home in the bosom of my family.—**Thomas Jefferson**

Life is of no value but as it brings us gratifications. Among the most valuable of these is rational society. It informs the mind, sweetens the temper, cheers our spirits, and promotes health.—**Thomas Jefferson**

Bodily decay is gloomy in prospect, but of all human contemplations the most abhorrent is body without mind.—**Thomas Jefferson**

Always take hold of things by the smooth handle.
-Thomas Jefferson

The sovereign invigorator of the body is exercise, and of all the exercises walking is the best.—**Thomas Jefferson**

What signify a few lives lost in a century or two? The tree of liberty must be refreshed from time to time with the blood of patriots and tyrants. It is its natural manure.—**Thomas Jefferson**

Liberty is the great parent of science and of virtue; and a nation will be great in both in proportion as it is free.—**Thomas Jefferson**

Timid men prefer the calm of despotism to the tempestuous sea of liberty.—**Thomas Jefferson**

The natural progress of things is for liberty to yield and government to gain ground.—**Thomas Jefferson**

And the day will come, when the mystical generation of Jesus, by the Supreme Being as His Father, in the womb of a virgin, will be classed with the fable of the generation of Minerva, in the brain of Jupiter.—**Thomas Jefferson**

Resistance to tyrants is obedience to God.—**Thomas Jefferson**

Question with boldness even the existence of a God; because, if there be one, he must more approve of the homage of reason, then that of blindfolded fear.—**Thomas Jefferson**

Peace and friendship with all mankind is our wisest policy, and I wish we may be permitted to pursue it.—**Thomas Jefferson**

Unlike those nations whose rulers use their country's resources to seek conquests, to carry on warring contests with one another, and consequently plunge their people into debt and devastation, free societies are organized for the happiness and prosperity of their people, and this is best pursued in a state of peace.—**Thomas Jefferson**

The spirit of monarchy is war and enlargement of domain: peace and moderation are the spirit of a republic. (copied into his Commonplace Book)—**Thomas Jefferson**

The central bank is an institution of the most deadly hostility existing against the Principles and form of our Constitution. I am an Enemy to all banks discounting bills or notes for anything but Coin. If the American People allow private banks to control the issuance of their currency, first by inflation and then by deflation, the banks and corporations that will grow up around them will deprive the People of all their Property until their Children will wake up homeless on the continent their Fathers conquered.—**Thomas Jefferson**

The true foundation of republican government is the equal right of every citizen in his person and property and in their management.—**Thomas Jefferson**

. . . judges should be withdrawn from the bench whose erroneous biases are leading us to dissolution. It may, indeed, injure them in fame or fortune; but it saves the Republic . . .—**Thomas Jefferson**

Banking establishments are more dangerous than standing armies.—**Thomas Jefferson**

Mankind are more disposed to suffer, while evils are sufferable, than to right themselves by abolishing the forms to which they are accustomed.—**Thomas Jefferson**

If we run into such debts as that we must be taxed in our meat and in our drink, in our necessaries and our comforts, in our labors and our amusements, for our callings and our creeds, as the people of England are, our people, like them, must come to labor sixteen hours in the twenty-four, and give the earnings of fifteen of these to the government for their debts and daily expenses; And the sixteen being insufficient to afford us bread, we must live, as they do now, on oatmeal and potatoes, have no time to think, no means of calling the mismanagers to account; But be glad to obtain subsistence by hiring ourselves to rivet their chains around the necks of our fellow sufferers; And this is the tendency of all human governments. A departure from principle in one instance becomes a precedent for a second, that second for a third, and so on 'til the bulk of society is reduced to mere automatons of misery, to have no sensibilities left but for sinning and suffering . . . and the forehorse of this frightful team is public debt. Taxation follows that, and in its train wretchedness and oppression.—**Thomas Jefferson**

The accounts of the United States ought to be, and may be made, as simple as those of a common farmer, and capable of being understood by common farmers.—**Thomas Jefferson**

Free government is founded in jealousy, and not in confidence; it is jealousy and not confidence, which prescribes limited constitutions, to bind down those whom we are obliged to trust with power.—**Thomas Jefferson**

Pride costs more than hunger, thirst and cold.—**Thomas Jefferson**

Honesty is the first chapter of the book of wisdom.—**Thomas Jefferson**

We confide in our strength, without boasting of it; we respect that of others, without fearing it.—**Thomas Jefferson**

I have never been able to conceive how any rational being could propose happiness to himself from the exercise of power over others.—**Thomas Jefferson**

Nothing . . . is unchangeable but the inherent and unalienable rights of man.—**Thomas Jefferson**

A Bill of Rights is what the people are entitled to against every government on earth, general or particular; and what no just government should refuse, or rest on inferences.—**Thomas Jefferson**

The Constitution of most of our states (and of the United States) assert that all power is inherent in the people; that they may exercise it by themselves; that it is their right and duty to be at all times armed and that they are entitled to freedom of person, freedom of religion, freedom of property, and freedom of press.—**Thomas Jefferson**

Take not from the mouth of labor the bread it has earned.—**Thomas Jefferson**

Our greatest happiness does not depend on the condition of life in which chance has placed us, but is always the result of a good conscience, good health, occupation and freedom in all just pursuits.—**Thomas Jefferson**

Leave all the afternoon for exercise and recreation, which are as necessary as reading. I will rather say more necessary because health is worth more than learning.—**Thomas Jefferson**

The art of life is the art of avoiding pain.—**Thomas Jefferson**

This should be a man's attitude: 'Few things will disturb him at all; nothing will disturb him much.'—**Thomas Jefferson**

Nothing can stop the man with the right mental attitude from achieving his goal; nothing on earth can help the man with the wrong mental attitude.—**Thomas Jefferson**

I'm a great believer in luck, and I find the harder I work the more I have of it.—**Thomas Jefferson**

I like the dreams of the future better than the history of the past.—**Thomas Jefferson**

Here was buried Thomas Jefferson, author of the Declaration of American Independence, of the statute of Virginia for religious freedom, and father of the University of Virginia.

Epitaph of Jefferson at Charlottesville, Virginia, written by himself, 1825

I have sworn upon the altar of God eternal hostility against every form of tyranny over the mind of man."—**Thomas Jefferson**

"The course of history shows that as a government grows, liberty decreases."—**Thomas Jefferson**

"Let your gun therefore be the constant companion of your walks."—**Thomas Jefferson**

"Single acts of tyranny may be ascribed to the accidental opinion of the day, but a series of oppressions, begun at a distinguished period, unalterable through every change of ministers, too plainly prove a deliberate, systematical plan of reducing us to slavery."—**Thomas Jefferson**

"False is the idea of utility that sacrifices a thousand real advantages for one imaginary or trifling inconvenience; that would take fire from man because it burns, and water because one may drown in it; that has no remedy for evils, except destruction. The laws that forbid the carrying of arms are laws of such a nature. They disarm those only who are neither inclined nor determined to commit crimes. Can it be supposed that those who have the courage to violate the most sacred laws of humanity, will respect the less important arbitrary ones . . . . and which, if strictly obeyed would put a end to personal liberty? . . . . Such laws make things worse for the assaulted and better for the assailants; They serve rather to encourage than to prevent homicides, for an unarmed man may be attacked with greater confidence than a armed man."—**Thomas Jefferson**

"Democracy is two wolves and a sheep deciding what's for Dinner. *Liberty* is a well-armed lamb contesting the vote." **Benjamin Franklin**

"To be prepared for war is one of the most effective ways of preserving peace."—**Pres. George Washington**

"Government is not reason: it is not eloquence; it is a force! Like fire it is a dangerous servant and a fearful master."—**Pres. George Washington**

"I disapprove of what you say, but I will defend to the death your right to say it."—**Voltaire**

"Experience has shown that even under the best forms (of government) those entrusted with power have, in time, and by slow operations, perverted it into tyranny."—**Thomas Jefferson**

"That the said constitution shall never be construed to authorize Congress to infringe just liberty of the press, or the rights of conscience or to prevent the people of the united states, who are peaceable Citizens, from keeping their own arms."—**Samuel Adams**

"If you love wealth greater than liberty, the tranquility of servitude greater than the animating contest for freedom, go home from us in peace. We seek not your counsel, nor your arms. Crouch down and lick the hand that feeds you; and may posterity forget that ye were our countrymen."—**Samuel Adams**

"Arms discourage and keep the invader and plunderer in awe and preserve order in the world as well as property. Horrid mischief would ensue when the law-abiding(are) deprived the use of them."—**Thomas Paine**

"These are the times that try men's souls. The summer soldier and the sunshine patriot will, in this crisis, shrink from the service of their country; but he that stands it now, deserves the love and thanks of man and woman. Tyranny, like hell, is not easily conquered; yet we have this consolation with us, that the harder the conflict, the more glorious the triumph."—**Thomas Paine**

"You need only reflect that one of the best ways to get yourself a reputation as a dangerous citizen these days is to go about repeating the very phrases which our founding fathers used in their struggle for independence."—**C.A. Beard**

"I heartily accept the motto, that the government is best which governs the least."—**Henry David Thoreau**

"They that give up liberty to obtain a little temporary safety deserve neither liberty nor safety."—**Benjamin Franklin**

"The very fame of our strength and readiness would be a means of discouraging our enemies; for 'tis a wise and true saying, that one sword often keeps another in the scabbard. The way to secure peace is to be prepared for war. They that are on their guard, and appear ready to receive their adversaries, are in much less danger of being attacked than the supine, secure and negligent."—**Benjamin Franklin**

"The constitution preserves the advantage of being armed which Americans possess over the people of almost every other nation . . . . Notwithstanding the military establishments in the several kingdoms of Europe, which are carried as far as the public resources will bear, the governments are afraid to trust their people with arms."—**James Madison**

"Before a standing army can rule, the people must be disarmed; as they are in almost every kingdom in Europe. The supreme power in America cannot enforce unjust laws by the sword, because the whole body of the people are armed and constitute a force superior to any band of regular troops that can be, in any pretense, raised in the United States."—**Noah Webster**

"If the representatives of the people betray their constituents, there is then no recourse left but in the exertion of the original right of self-defense which is paramount to all positive forms of government."—**Alexander Hamilton**

"The best we can hope for concerning the people at large is that they be properly armed."—**Alexander Hamilton**

"Why stand we here idle? Is life so dear, or peace so sweet, as to be purchased at the price of chains and slavery? Forbid it almighty God! I know not what course others may take; but as for me, give me liberty, or give me death!"—**Patrick Henry**

"If all Americans want is security, they can go to prison. They'll have enough to eat, a bed and a roof over their heads. But if an American wants to preserve his dignity and his equality as a human being, he must not bow his neck to any dictatorial government."—**Pres. Dwight Eisenhower**

I would remind you that extremism in the defense of liberty is no vice! And let me also remind you that moderation in the pursuit of justice is no virtue!"—**Barry Goldwater**

"There exists a law, not written down anywhere but inborn in our heart; a law that comes to us not by training or custom or reading but from nature itself, if our lives are endangered, any and every method of protecting ourselves is morally right."-**Roman Orator Cicero**

If tyranny and oppression come to this land, it will be in the guise of fighting a foreign enemy . . . The loss of Liberty at home is to be charged to the provisions against danger, real or imagined, front abroad . . ."—**James Madison**

NOTES